Inside Teacher Education

Inside Teacher Education

Challenging Prior Views of Teaching and Learning

Shawn Michael Bullock
University of Ontario, Institute of Technology, Canada

SENSE PUBLISHERS
ROTTERDAM/BOSTON/TAIPEI

A C.I.P. record for this book is available from the Library of Congress.

ISBN: 978-94-6091-401-0 (paperback)
ISBN: 978-94-6091-402-7 (hardback)
ISBN: 978-94-6091-403-4 (e-book)

Published by: Sense Publishers,
P.O. Box 21858,
3001 AW Rotterdam,
The Netherlands
https://www.sensepublishers.com

Printed on acid-free paper

All Rights Reserved © 2011 Sense Publishers

No part of this work may be reproduced, stored in a retrieval system, or transmitted in any form or by any means, electronic, mechanical, photocopying, microfilming, recording or otherwise, without written permission from the Publisher, with the exception of any material supplied specifically for the purpose of being entered and executed on a computer system, for exclusive use by the purchaser of the work.

DEDICATION

This book is dedicated to all the people in my life from whom I have had the honour of learning. From my former teachers and students, to my research participants and thesis committee, to my friends and family, thank you all for showing me the power of learning from experience.

TABLE OF CONTENTS

Acknowledgement ix

1. Becoming a Teacher 1
2. The Culture of Schools 11
3. The Development of Teachers' Professional Knowledge 21
4. Disrupting Initial Assumptions 39
5. Candidates in Crisis 61
6. Creating a Clear Signal against a Noisy Background 89
7. Consolidation and Looking Ahead 119
8. Disrupting the Apprenticeship of Observation 151

Appendix A 171

References 179

ACKNOWLEDGEMENT

Dr. Tom Russell and I have a professional friendship that began in his physics methods course in August 1997. I arrived to his class fresh from undergraduate experiences as a physics major, eager to learn how to be a teacher and excited to be at a Faculty of Education. I still remember the Predict-Observe-Explain activity that we did on the first day of class, although I could not possibly have known just how deeply my understanding of teaching and learning would change over the course of my preservice year, largely due to the learning experiences that Tom provided in our physics course. I also remember sending Tom an email on October 31, 1997, as a way of checking my developing understanding of the parallels between learning to teach (which I was doing) and learning physics (which I was trying to help my students to do on practicum). It was my first foray into theorizing teaching and learning, and Tom's response provided the right mixture of support and challenge.

What followed was a correspondence that went a long way to helping me navigate the tumultuous waters of my practicum experience. Each week, I sent him a summary of successes, challenges, and questions from my practicum placement. Without fail, he replied quickly and managed to help me through some dilemmas while challenging me to further develop my pedagogy. In the winter term, upon my return to Queen's for the on-campus portion of the B.Ed. program, Tom turned the tables and asked me to comment each week on the teaching journal that he kept for our methods class. It was a memorable early lesson in the power of collaborative self-study and the importance of critical friendship.

Tom mentored me through my early years as a physics teacher, my M.Ed., and my Ph.D. He has been generous with his time and has provided me with countless opportunities to develop as a scholar. It would be difficult to overestimate his influence on me as a teacher and an academic. Studying and working with Tom for the past 13 years has been a privilege. This book is, in many ways, a culmination of the thinking I have been doing about teaching and learning since we first met many years ago. I offer him my sincere thanks for his mentorship, for his friendship, and for helping me to become a more thoughtful teacher and researcher.

CHAPTER 1

BECOMING A TEACHER

Any plan to prepare teachers should include some teaching under the direction of an experienced practitioner ... Both students and professors have judged student teaching to be, without qualification, the best way to train teachers.

(Spalding, 1959, p. v)

How does one become a teacher? Some may argue that one is born to teach; indeed many of the teacher candidates that I have met over the years are quick to tell me that they have dreamed of becoming teachers ever since they were small children. A few candidates have even described moments in their childhood when they "played school" with friends, family, or perhaps stuffed toys. Other candidates have mentioned a critical moment later in life when they realized teaching is a career they would like to pursue. Perhaps they enjoy explaining their subject matter to others. Perhaps they had a meaningful experience as a camp counsellor that cemented an interest in working with young people. Perhaps, like me, they had an experience in secondary school as a teaching assistant for younger students, and decided that they would like to be the one at the front of the classroom.

In the province of Ontario, Canada, where I have been both a student and a secondary school teacher, one becomes a teacher by attending an 8-month pre-service program at a Faculty of Education. Upon graduation, a teacher candidate earns a Bachelor of Education (B.Ed.) degree and is recommended for professional certification to the Ontario College of Teachers. Over 80% of teacher candidates in Ontario attend consecutive education programs, which are taken after successful completion of an undergraduate degree (Crocker & Dibbon, 2008). The rest enrol in concurrent education programs when they enter university, completing a few education courses concurrently with their undergraduate degree. Most teacher candidates in concurrent programs complete their undergraduate degrees and then join candidates in a consecutive program to complete the B.Ed. degree. Thus graduates of a teacher education program in Ontario end up with two baccalaureate degrees at the end of 5 years of university study. Exceptions include those teachers who obtain teacher certification through one of two masters-level programs at the University of Toronto, and candidates who come from a career in the trades who receive a Diploma in Education and certified to teach in technology subjects.

The pathways to becoming a teacher in Ontario are relatively straightforward. Teacher education programs in Ontario, across Canada, and worldwide tend to include some mixture of course work and field experience. The implicit message is that there is theory to be learned in coursework that can be applied during the field experience in schools. There is considerable evidence in the education research literature that indicates teacher candidates tend to place a higher value on field experiences than on course work. Some teacher candidates, teachers, principals, and university professors question the content, validity, and utility of coursework in a preservice teacher education program. Although the pathway to teaching certification may be clear, the question of how one *learns* to become a teacher is considerably more ambiguous. What roles do coursework and field experience play in the process of becoming a teacher?

Calls for increased coherence in preservice programs are abundant in the teacher education literature (Darling-Hammond, 2006; Darling-Hammond & Bransford, 2005). In a presidential address to the American Educational Research Association, Cochran-Smith (2005, p. 14) advocated that the "new" teacher education be constructed both "as a policy problem and a political problem." Framing teacher education in this way may well help to change some of the structures of teacher education to more coherent program designs, but the humbling history of education reform indicates that changes in policy are unlikely to result in changes in the cultural routines associated with schools and, by extension, teacher education programs (Sarason, 2002). As a result, policy-level changes are unlikely to encourage teacher educators to reconceptualize how teacher candidates construct professional knowledge from teaching and learning experiences during a preservice teacher education program.

This book begins with the premise that learning to teach is a cultural, rather than a political or a policy-driven, problem. Most adults in North American society have been to school and hence have first-hand experiences of the routines of teaching and learning that occur in schools. Problematically, "teaching looks easy and is widely regarded as easy, the image of teaching as transmission and the perspective of technical rationality mask the many ways in which challenging and engaging teaching represents a highly disciplined view [of teaching and learning]" (Loughran & Russell, 2007, p. 217). In contrast to the dominant view of teaching as a relatively easy profession, Darling-Hammond (2006, pp. 34–35) argues:

> Teaching may be even more complex than law, medicine, or engineering. Rather than serving one client at a time, teachers work with groups of twenty-five to thirty at once, each with unique needs and proclivities. Teachers must balance these variables, along with a multitude of sometimes competing goals, and negotiate the demands of the content matter along with individual and group needs. They must draw on many kinds of knowledge – of learning and development, social contexts and culture, language and expression, curriculum and teaching – and integrate what they know to create engaging tasks and solve learning problems for a range of students who learn differently.

Darling-Hammond goes on to call attention to three problems in learning to teach (pp. 35–40):

1. *The Problem of the "Apprenticeship of Observation"*: Teacher candidates enter preservice programs after spending most of their lives as students in schools. They have well-developed ideas about the characteristics of good teaching, most of which are tacit and unexamined.
2. *The Problem of Enactment*: Teacher candidates often find it difficult to enact the propositional ideas that they have learned from their teacher education coursework during their practicum placements.

3. *The Problem of Complexity*: Teaching is a complicated act that requires teacher candidates to attend simultaneously to multiple, competing contextual factors in the relationships among students, subject matter, and themselves.

Russell (2008, p. 4) points out that the second and third problems can also be explained by a careful analysis of the implications of the problem of the apprenticeship of observation: "Most of what beginning teachers 'know' about teaching consists of images and patterns enacted before them by many different teachers through 12 years of schooling and into university. This knowledge is tacit; it has been conveyed to them unintentionally." It is not surprising that teacher candidates experience problems of enactment during their practicum placements, given that their tacit knowledge about how teaching *should* look, gained via their apprenticeships of observation, did not prepare them for the underlying complexities of the teaching profession. Their apprenticeships, noted Lortie (1975, p. 62), are obtained from a "specific vantage point": the vantage point of the student.

Taking the problem of the apprenticeship of observation as the overarching problem of learning to teach compels us to consider the degree to which learning experiences in teacher education programs help candidates to name and challenge their tacit, socialized assumptions about teaching and learning. To understand deeply the ways in which teacher candidates construct professional knowledge of teaching and learning, we must examine their prior assumptions in light of the cultural knowledge they construct during their preservice programs. We must also examine the taken-for-granted assumptions that seem to underlie many teacher education programs. Is the role of a teacher educator to synthesize research-based best practices for candidates to practise during field placements? Does the practicum experience challenge or reinforce a lifetime of socialized experiences in schools? Are methods courses destined to be seen by the majority of teacher candidates as little more than sites for collecting resources? Can powerful learning that challenges prior assumptions occur within a methods classroom? Where and how do candidates construct professional knowledge of teaching?

This book describes and interprets a study that assumes that many enduring questions of teacher education need to be considered through the lenses of the cultural assumptions, routines, and relationships between teachers and their students. As such, the study is ethnographic in its premise. It draws inspiration from two previous ethnographic accounts of learning to teach: Britzman's (1991/2003) *Practice Makes Practice* and Segall's (2002) *Disturbing Practice*. Britzman begins with the premise that "teaching is an interpretive relation" (p. 12) and ends with the conclusion that learning to teach is characterized by several existential crises that require candidates to construct an identity against three powerful cultural myths gained from a lifetime of schooling: everything depends upon the teacher, teachers are experts, and teachers are self-made (Britzman, pp. 224–232). These three cultural myths encourage many teacher candidates to set extraordinarily high expectations for their performances during practicum placements. Candidates tend to believe that they need to be in control of the classroom at all times, possess an exhaustive knowledge of their subject matter, and be able to instantly impress their host teachers with natural teaching abilities. It is this third belief, stemming from the cultural myth that teachers are self-made, that is particularly dangerous because it devalues "any meaningful attempt to make relevant teacher education, educational theory, and the social process of acknowledging the values and interests one brings to and constructs because of the educational encounter" (Britzman, p. 230).

While Britzman (1991/2003) focused on the field experience of learning to teach, in his ethnography Segall (2002) situated himself as a participant-observer in a social studies methods course at a large university in western Canada. Throughout his discussion Segall makes clear his "reading positions" (p. 8), which necessarily informs how he constructs and reports his research, including the fact he attended the same preservice program under consideration in his study. In particular, Segall "uses the lenses of critical pedagogy not only to examine preservice education but also to have prospective teachers use those very lenses to critically examine their own process of learning to teach" (p. 14). He concludes that teacher candidates are inherently restricted by "teacher education's inability to provide them 'otherwise' experiences that break with the traditional, the expected, the obvious, and the taken-for-granted" (p. 167). Thus Segall suggests that the effects of school socialization have implications not only for how teacher candidates learn to teach, but also for how teacher educators learn to teach teachers. After all, teacher educators have their own apprenticeships of observation with which to contend, including the reading positions they bring to faculties of education as a result of their own experiences as teacher candidates and school teachers.

This research shares with Britzman (1991/2003) and Segall (2002) the premises that cultural myths and routines exist that have an effect on how teacher candidates learn to teach. As Appendix A indicates, I used elements of Segall's research design to frame my study, although the focus is different from both Britzman and Segall. We share an interest in the process of learning to teach, but my research focuses on establishing warranted assertions (Dewey, 1938) for how teacher candidates construct professional knowledge from teaching and learning experiences that occur both in a methods course and during practicum placements. We also share a belief that teacher education needs to pay more explicit attention to the role of cultural expectations of teaching and learning in developing pedagogies of teacher education. As Segall (2002, p. 6) notes, "teacher education programs can no longer afford the 'luxury' of masquerading as an invisible, innocent context within which prospective teachers naturally build ideas, knowledge, and skills."

CONTEXT FOR THE STUDY

This book reports on a study conducted for my dissertation research. The study interviewed 5 teacher candidates and their teacher educator at various points during the two semester preservice teacher education (Bachelor of Education) program at Queen's University in Kingston, Ontario. In addition, I attended each meeting of the physics curriculum methods course taken by the participants in this study. This section of the chapter provides additional contextual details of the nature of the preservice teacher education program at Queen's University during the year in which the research was conducted. I have used a consistent terminology throughout this book to refer to particular features of a program. A university student enrolled in the preservice teacher education program is called a *teacher candidate*, the field experience in a *host school* setting is called a *practicum*, the teacher who supervises the teacher candidate during the practicum is called an *associate teacher*, and someone who teaches in the preservice teacher education program is called a *teacher educator*.

The preservice teacher education program at Queen's University began the day after Labour Day in September and ran until the end of April. The program alternated between on-campus coursework and blocks of practicum experiences in host schools. Teacher candidates were placed in cohort groups in host schools during the months of October (4 weeks), December (4 weeks), and February-March (5 weeks). The host schools were located as far west as Toronto, as far north as Ottawa, and as far east as the Québec border. One unique feature of the program was a 3-week placement in March in an alternative educational setting such as a museum, school board office, or international school. Successful candidates were awarded a Bachelor of Education (B.Ed.) during the spring convocation ceremony. There were two major streams in the program, one leading to certification as a Primary-Junior (Kindergarten to Grade 6) teacher, the other leading to certification as an Intermediate-Senior (Grade 7 to Grade 12) teacher. Teacher candidates in the Intermediate-Senior stream must take a curriculum methods course for each of two school subjects. The participants in this study had physics as one of their two subjects.

Curriculum methods courses in the intermediate-senior stream were scheduled for two 2 ½-hour classes per week. During the year this research was undertaken, the physics curriculum methods course had an enrolment of 19 teacher candidates (11 men and 8 women). The class met in a large room equipped with lab benches: Candidates spent most of their time sitting in small groups around circular tables arranged so that they could easily see one another, the front chalkboard, or the Smart Board on the side wall. Figures 1 and 2 help to convey a sense of the classroom environment:

Figure 1. The physics methods room as seen from the north wall.

CHAPTER 1

Figure 2. The physics methods room as seen from the east wall.

The photographs capture several of the elements that help to make this classroom a unique environment. For example, Figure 1 reveals that a number of brief statements about teaching and learning hang above the front blackboard. Both figures show ceiling tiles decorated by previous classes, a tradition that began in 1994. The names of former students help to convey a sense of shared ownership over this space. For example, the ceiling tile class of 1997–1998—the year in which I was a candidate in this same classroom—proudly displays our slogan "The Power of Experience" in the centre as our names and undergraduate university affiliations fan out toward the perimeter.

During the study, I was a participant-observer in the physics methods course offered as a part of the Queen's B.Ed. program taught by my supervisor Dr. Tom Russell. Although participant-observation is a familiar strategy for fieldwork, the nature of the participation "is a continuum that varies from complete immersion in the setting as full participant to complete separation from the setting as spectator, with a great deal of variation along the continuum between these two end points" (Patton, 2002, p. 265). I was present during each class throughout the year, but I had no official status in the course. The teacher candidates were aware of my purpose for attending every class and understood that I had no evaluative power over their grades. I often spoke to the teacher candidates before and after class in a social way, but these conversations were not part of the data collection. During each class, I sat at the back of the room and took notes on my laptop. I did not interact with the teacher candidates during class time, and I did not participate in class discussions or activities. Thus I tended toward the spectator end of the continuum described by Patton (2002), although I was not completely separated from the setting because I often spoke to Tom while the teacher candidates were engaged in a learning activity. Tom was both the teacher for the course and a participant in the research; our long history of critical friendship and collaborative self-study made it natural for us to have quick conversations as teaching and learning situations unfolded.

The selection of this particular environment was based on three factors. First, Tom is an experienced teacher educator with an extensive research program in both reflective practice and self-study. I expected that his participation in the research would yield rich data allowing me to describe and interpret the perspective of an experienced teacher educator as he enacts a pedagogy of teacher education. In addition, it seemed strange to investigate how teacher candidates construct professional knowledge from a physics methods course without considering the perspective and voice of the teacher educator. As Kane, Sandretto, and Heath (2002) argue, there is a paucity of literature that explores the relationship between teacher educators' beliefs about teaching and evidence of their actual teaching practice, noting that it is important "to make explicit the links between tertiary teachers' espoused theories and their teaching practice so that we can understand better how university academics learn to teach" (p. 242). Second, I believed that my prior experiences both as a teacher candidate and a teacher educator made me uniquely suited to attend to the pedagogy enacted in the physics methods course at Queen's University. In 1997–1998, I was a teacher candidate in the Queen's B.Ed. program and a student in Tom's physics methods course. In my first year of doctoral studies, I was appointed as a graduate teaching fellow for this same course while Tom was away on sabbatical leave. These prior learning and teaching experiences combined with my experience as a secondary school physics teacher provided me with powerful "reading positions" (Segall, 2002, p. 8) with which to describe and interpret Tom's evolving pedagogy of teacher education. Third, Tom and I have a 10-year history of critical friendship in which we have helped each other to frame and reframe our understandings of teaching and learning. Portions of this history have been published (Bullock, 2007; Russell & Bullock, 1999) and presented at academic conferences.

OUTLINE OF THE STUDY

This book poses three questions with the goal of exploring and interpreting the ways in which teacher candidates construct professional knowledge from teaching and learning experiences during a physics methods course and during practicum placements in host schools. The research questions that guide this study are:

1. How do teacher candidates construct professional knowledge from learning experiences in a methods course?
2. How do teacher candidates construct professional knowledge from teaching experiences during their practicum placements?
3. How do teacher educators construct their professional knowledge through collaborative self-study as they frame teaching as a discipline with teacher candidates in a physics methods course?

Data were collected from September to April of one year of the preservice teacher education program at Queen's University in Kingston, Ontario. The first two research questions were addressed primarily via focus-group and individual semi-structured interviews with five volunteer teacher candidates from the physics curriculum methods course at Queen's University. In addition, I attended the physics methods course as a participant-observer and kept detailed field notes of my

CHAPTER 1

perceptions of the teaching and learning that occurred during the course. These field notes often served as a catalyst for my ongoing conversations with Dr. Tom Russell, the teacher educator for the physics methods course and a participant in this research. Conversations between Tom and me form the basis for the collaborative self-study that addresses the third research question. Appendix A describes the design of the study, including its associated ethical dilemmas, and the methods of data analysis.

OUTLINE OF THE BOOK

The next two chapters present a synthesis of relevant literature. Chapter 2 begins with the argument that education is a cultural process that results in the transmission of dominant social patterns and ideas, making sustainable educational reform difficult. It concludes with a review of two influential sociological accounts of teaching, emphasizing the the importance of Lortie's (1975, p. 62) concept of the "apprenticeship of observation" to considerations of teaching and learning. Chapter 3 reviews relevant literature on how teachers construct professional knowledge. Although it is acknowledged that teachers can and do learn from propositions, the chapter argues the primary role experience plays in the construction of professional knowledge about teaching and learning. Schön's (1983) construct of knowing-in-action is framed as a highly productive way of thinking about the nature of teachers' professional knowledge.

Chapters 4 to 7 describe, analyze, and discuss the data collected for the study. Each chapter is devoted to a particular month of on-campus weeks during the preservice teacher education program at Queen's (September, November, January, and April). Sources of data include observations that I made as a participant-observer in each of during each of the during the on-campus block, a focus group interview with the five research participants, an individual follow-up interview with each participant, and regular face-to-face meetings and email correspondence with Tom Russell. Throughout the analysis, quotations and references are made to either my research journal or the six primary documents in each hermeneutic unit (Muhr, 2004) associated with a particular on-campus block. The naming conventions used to reference the data are consistent in each chapter. For example, The first primary document is the transcript of the first focus group (FG1); the remaining five primary documents are transcripts of the individual interviews for the participants (using the pseudonyms David, James, Irene, Max, and Paul). Specific references and quotations refer to the author, the interview number, and the quotation number within the hermeneutic unit. Thus a reference of (FG1, 85) refers to quotation 85 in the transcript of the first focus group. A reference of (David1, 5) refers to quotation 5 in the transcript of David's first interview. Finally, a reference of (Journal, September) refers to an entry made in my research journal in September of the year in which data was collected. I believe that there is significant value in allowing the reader to consider the comments made during the four focus groups (coded FG1, FG2, FG3, and FG4) compared to the individual interviews, since participants tended to share more personal thoughts in the individual setting. This distinction will become particularly evident in Chapter 6.

Chapter 4 discusses the ways in which teacher candidates' initial assumptions about teaching and learning were called into question by learning experiences in the physics methods course. These assumptions, rooted in their apprenticeships of observation, were disrupted by three types of experience during the month of September: a lesson study activity, interactions with their peers, and Tom's explicit focus on building a trusting environment in the physics class. Although there were no practicum experiences to report on, some of the participants expressed trepidation about their October practicum placements.

Chapter 5 names the ways in which the tensions experienced during the October practicum placement and during the November on-campus weeks caused teacher candidates to experience themselves as living contradictions. The candidates were frustrated by the fact that their enacted pedagogies on practicum did not match their expectations of themselves or their perceptions of the expectations placed on them by associate teachers and the Faculty of Education. Tom continued to focus on exploring the potential utility of active-learning pedagogies during the methods course, framing much of his lesson planning around a visit by Dr. Randy Knight of California Polytechnic State University.

Chapter 6 focuses on the challenges Tom faced in his efforts in January to develop a coherent signal against the noisy background of a teacher education program that was perceived as increasingly incoherent by participants in the study. He provided class time for candidates to engage in a self-directed learning activity, so candidates could have time to think more deeply about what they had learned from the course and to experience student-centred learning first-hand. The teacher candidates who participated in the research spent considerable time in their focus group interview discussing how and why Tom was using certain pedagogies in the methods course. Their experiences of themselves as living contradictions were magnified by the December practicum experience, to the point where two of the participants expressed a great deal of discomfort about the February practicum placement.

Chapter 7 interprets how the teacher candidates consolidated their learning while looking ahead to the future, as well as discussing the strategies that Tom used to bring the physics methods course to an appropriate conclusion. Few comments were made by candidates about their final practicum experiences in February and March. Tom found ways to touch on each major theme of the course, with a view to reminding candidates why the themes were important rather than trying to form propositions about teaching and learning. Four of the five participants theorized about the kinds of pedagogies they wished to enact in their future classrooms. All participants showed evidence of reframing their prior assumptions about teaching and learning as a result of experiences in the physics methods course.

Chapter 8 begins by revisiting the literature on teachers' professional knowledge, interpreting the data in light of both the narrative and reflection-in-action perspective of constructing knowledge from experience. Conclusions are then offered for each of the three research questions in the form of principles, rather than propositions, because principles are understood as contextually based and suggest future directions for productive lines of thinking. An interview conducted with Tom the year after data was collected for this study is analyzed to shed light on how Tom was encouraged to

CHAPTER 1

reframe his pedagogy after reading a thorough analysis of his teaching and how five candidates learned in his one year of his methods course. The question of how and why the candidates came to think about their professional knowledge in new ways is explored using the concept of the authority of experience. The book concludes that it is possible to disrupt and reframe teacher candidates' prior assumptions about teaching and learning, tacitly gained through their apprenticeships of observation, by providing learning experiences in a methods course that encourage candidates to analyze carefully how they think about teaching and learning.

CHAPTER 2

THE CULTURE OF SCHOOLS

It is not to disparage teacher training that we remark upon the fact that teachers still learn to teach by teaching. The teacher gets something from experience which is not included in his [sic] "professional" courses, an elusive something which it is difficult to put between the covers of a book or work up into a lecture.

(Waller, 1932/1961, p. 1)

Teaching is a part of our culture. Nearly every adult has been to school and consequently has a set of images and ideas about what teaching should look and feel like from a student's perspective (Lortie, 1975). As Knowles, Cole, and Presswood (1994, p. 121) noted, "schools, regardless of location, tend to look more similar than different." In this chapter I review relevant literature pertaining to the dominant culture of schools in North America and the associated problems of change and education reform. The chapter begins by developing the argument that education and education reform are cultural processes from both anthropological and sociological perspectives. The cultural routines associated with teaching and learning tend to be replicated by new teachers because of the unexamined yet powerful effects of the "apprenticeship of observation" (Lortie, 1975, p. 62). The chapter concludes by suggesting that prior assumptions about teaching and learning, created by cultural socialization through the education system, play a significant role in learning to teach.

EDUCATION AS A CULTURAL PROCESS

Over 40 years ago, Wolcott (1967, p. 86) stated, "education as a cultural process is the central concern of and link between anthropology and education." A few years later, Wax, Diamond, and Gearing (1971) charged anthropologists with failing to understand the equivalence of education with culture by arguing that culture, "socially transmitted or learned behaviour ... is education in every sense of the term" (p. 302). At first consideration, it seems reasonable to view education as a process rather than an event. But to what extent can the culture of schools and teacher education programs be examined using the methods and perspectives developed in anthropology and sociology, two disciplines dedicated to the study of cultural processes and interactions? Are education and culture "synonymous," as Wax et al. (p. 302) suggests? What insights might be gained from a consideration of the culture processes and "ceremonies" (Waller, 1932/1961, p. 103) that are prevalent in the North American schools and teacher education programs?

Cohen (1971, p. 19) asserted that culture is both a "way of shaping the mind" and a "self-perpetuating system." He makes a distinction, however, between socialization

CHAPTER 2

and education as cultural processes. Socialization, according to Cohen (1971), occurs primarily in the household as a result of interaction with parents and family members and is "geared toward the creation of attitudes, values, control of impulses, cognitive orientations, and the like, in the course of daily and routine activities" (p. 22). Education, by contrast, occurs primarily outside of the home and is concerned with "the inculcation of standardized and stereotyped knowledge, skills, values and attitudes by means of standardized and stereotyped procedures" (Cohen, 1971, p. 22). Both of these definitions imply that cultural processes are transmitted from one group to another as a result of social interactions.

In their review of social transmission theories and schooling, Bennett and LeCompte (1992) distinguish between *functional theory* and *reproduction theory*. Functional theory assumes that mass schooling exists for a particular function: to transmit the social and political expectations of a society. Bennett and LeCompte (1992 pp. 7–11) reviewed four purposes of schooling: intellectual (e.g., "to assist students in the acquisition of cognitive skills" (p. 7)), political (e.g., "to educate future citizens for appropriate participation in the given political order" (p. 8)), economic (e.g., "to prepare students for labour work roles" (p. 10), and social (e.g., "to serve as sites for the solution or amelioration of social problems" (p. 11)). Reproduction theory goes one step further and asserts that the transmission functions of schooling are far from benign, they "reproduce both the values and ideologies of the dominant social groups and the status rankings of the existing class structure" (p. 12). One might easily argue that teacher education programs, charged with the preparation of future teachers, might unwittingly function for teacher candidates in the same way that schools function for pupils.

Change in either the education system or teacher education programs is immensely difficult, in part because public schooling grew out of the ethos of the industrial revolution. Writing about the consequences of the industrial approach to education in Canada, Lockhart (1992, p. 107) stated:

> Public education in industrial societies is not simply a means for making formal knowledge publicly accessible; it is also an agent of political socialization, social valorization, cultural reproduction, and labour-force allocation, and as the latter became increasingly problematic, a warehouse for the containment of youthful unemployables. The nation's schools are thus facilitators and gatekeepers; providers and rationers; emancipators and custodians; critics and propagandists. That such a system produces both "winners and losers" (Anisef et al., 1982), and labels them accordingly, should surprise no-one who understands its fundamental dialectics.

In a sense, teacher education programs tend to attract the "winners" from the school system, those individuals that were successful enough in school to gain admission to an undergraduate university program. In places such as Ontario where teaching credentials are obtained in a second, post-baccalaureate program, there is a second level of selection. The process of education favours a preservation of the status quo because those who become teachers tend to be those who were successful as students. In general, Canada has a higher set of standards for admission to the teaching profession than many other countries, including the United States (Crocker & Dibbon, 2008).

Responsibility for the education system in Canada rests with the provinces and territories. Each ministry (in the case of the provinces) or department (in the case of the territories) sets a curriculum that teachers are expected to follow. Cohen (1971) argued that "one of the underlying premises of a system of education – whether it is conducted on an individual basis or in schools – is that teachers can be changed daily, or that the child can go from one teacher to another, without altering the content of what is being learned" (p. 39). This kind of thinking is behind many of the so-called standards-based education movements, particularly those that advocate a lockstep approach to teaching through large scale standardized testing. Wax and Wax (1971) criticized standards movements, the industrial approach to education, and the associated research in the following way:

> Researchers have been administering hundreds of tests to thousands of pupils and intellectual critics have devoted countless pages to the criticism of textbooks and other curricular materials. Yet, the bulk of their efforts contrasts markedly with its quality and its impact, because their vision has been constricted by an interlocking chain of assumptions: that schools are primarily and exclusively agencies of formal education (rather than being social institutions); that pupils are isolated individuals (rather than being social beings who participate in the life of peer societies, ethnic groups, and the like); that formal education is synonymous with education; and that the principal task of the teacher is to educate. Thus, instead of inquiring what sort of social processes are occurring in - and in relation to - the schools, researchers and critics have defined their problem as being one of discovering how to make the schools teach their individual pupils more, better, and faster. (p. 3)

The preceding characterization of education systems in North America and educational research may seem, at first, to be a rather dim view of the education system. Surely education, and particularly teacher education, is about more than standards and transmission of the status quo? Surely some of the many educational reform efforts that have occurred in last 40 years have disrupted such a model of education?

Many education reformers, particularly Sarason (1990; 1996; 2002), have argued that the education system as a whole in North America *has not fundamentally changed*. Sarason (2002, pp. 28–29) noted that reform efforts, regardless of whether or not they begin inside an education system (e.g., from teachers or principals) or as the result of external pressures on a system (e.g., from a university researcher's reform project or external consultants), share at least four assumptions:

1. Teachers who are participating in the change "understand the rationale for the change and what the change means for them" (p. 29) *before the change begins*.
2. The leader of the reform process has three clear sets of responsibilities: "to maintain open lines of communication with those who have ultimate and legal authority"; "to know well what those to whom responsibility is delegated are thinking, experiencing, and confronting"; and "to some degree provide personal knowledge of how teachers and parents feel about the dynamics of the implementation process" (p. 29).

CHAPTER 2

3. Conflicting opinions, when they inevitably arise, "can be resolved sensitively, fairly, and amicably" (p. 29).
4. The participants in the reform effort (teachers, principals, school board members, superintendants) will maintain their current roles and jobs throughout the reform process.

These assumptions are far from innocuous. The fact that teachers typically feel like they have not had a choice in the nature of reform efforts tends to make these assumptions even more problematic (Sarason, 2002). Kennedy (2005) notes that educational reformers have often failed to look at how realistic their expectations are, stating: "For the most part, the reform ideals also don't address the nitty-gritty problem of how to organize and manage learning in large groups ... and reformers tend not to think about the ways in which, in real schools, their ideals might conflict with each other" (p. 12). Teacher education programs, on the whole, have not faired much better despite some notable exceptions in the literature (e.g., Beck & Kosnik, 2006; Darling-Hammond, 2006; Kroll et al., 2008). One of the lessons from these success stories is that, for reform efforts to succeed, faculty members must play a part in planning and developing a coherent approach to reform while receiving ample support from administration during the process. As Cuban (2008, p. 188) observes: "Good intentions, simple answers, and hoped-for miracles don't make a dent in the real world of urban schools and classrooms, except to heighten disappointment."

Education and education reform are processes, both worthy of study and both affected deeply by cultural assumptions. One of the most significant features of education systems and schools, particularly with regard to reform, is that nearly every adult in North American society has first hand experience as a student in schools. Thus adults tend to have strong opinions about what schools should and should not do, regardless of whether or not they have had any involvement in school beyond their years as a pupil in the K-12 system. Their long experiences as students, without direct access to the thinking and reasoning of teachers and other school personnel, result in an "apprenticeship of observation" (Lortie, 1975, p. 62). Although not a true apprenticeship, because it does not hold the preparation of future teachers and school personnel as an explicit goal, the apprenticeship of observation goes a long way to ensuring that the dominant culture of teaching and learning remains relatively static.

THE CULTURE OF TEACHING AND LEARNING

In one of the first sociological studies of teaching, Waller (1932/1961) argued that schools play a significant role in the transmission of cultural norms, particularly because school culture is characterized by "complex rituals of personal relationships" (p. 103) between people who engage in a variety of rituals and ceremonies. One of the most familiar ceremonies requires students to sit and listen attentively as a teacher stands at the front of the room and talks about curricular content. Other familiar ceremonies include the social patterns evident in school clubs, assemblies, and athletic events. As Waller (1932/1961, p. 120) noted, "Ceremonies accumulate rapidly in the school, being easily devised and readily absorbed into the main current of tradition."

There is scant evidence that, over 75 years later, many of the traditions and ceremonies associated with schools have changed significantly. Teachers still, by and large, teach from the front of their classrooms and rely heavily on their abilities to talk about curricular content. Students still, by and large, spend a great deal of time copying notes from blackboards or projector screens. The ceremonies associated with teaching and learning are deeply embedded within our culture, in part, because many of the routines of school are tacit and unexamined (Lortie, 1975). "There is in these ceremonies and activities a serious meaning that fades out with routine description and analysis" (Waller, 1932/1961, p. 121). The culture of the school is highly resistant to change (Sarason, 1996).

Waller (1932/1961, pp. 6–7) outlined five reasons that schools should be studied from a socio-cultural perspective:

1. Schools have clearly defined populations.
2. Schools have a distinct political structure.
3. Schools contain a complicated network of social relationships.
4. Schools are characterized by a "we-feeling" (p. 7).
5. Schools have a unique culture.

The first point is clear; schools are designed to educate students within particular age ranges and employ teachers, principals, and support staff who fall within a certain age range and possess specific professional qualifications. The political structure of schools is one in which the teacher is dominant within the school walls (Waller), yet ultimately subordinate to school trustees and politicians, who are usually not members of the teaching profession. The resulting political reality of teaching is indeed complicated (Lortie, 1975). Teachers, students, and other members of the school form an intricate series of relationships that are based on a shared experience of the school. These relationships lead to a "we-feeling" that, according to Waller (p. 13), "is in part a spontaneous creation in the minds of those who identify themselves with the school and in part a carefully nurtured and sensitive growth." Taken together, these four characteristics result in a shared culture of the school.

This shared culture of teaching and learning has a profound impact on everyone who attends school. In North America, students spend thousands of hours in school absorbing and participating in a variety of cultural ceremonies. As a result, students are socialized into the teaching profession, regardless of whether they choose to become teachers:

> The comparative impact of initial socialization makes considerable difference in the overall life of an occupation. Where such socialization is potent, the predispositions of newcomers become less important through time; the selves of participants tend to merge with the values and norms built into the occupation. (Lortie, 1975, pp. 55–56)

Lortie named this initial socialization into the teaching profession the "apprenticeship of observation" (p. 61) and argued that students are subtly socialized into the teaching profession "as they move through a series of structured experiences and internalize the subculture" (p. 61) of the school. The effects of the initial socialization of students into the teaching profession are particularly powerful not only because of the amount of time they spend in schools, but also because their interactions with teachers have important consequences, including final grades.

One consequence of the apprenticeship of observation is that students learn how to behave like teachers without understanding why a teacher may act in particular ways. Lortie (1975, p. 62) noted:

> The motivation to engage in such role-taking is especially great when students have already decided to become teachers. But it is likely that taking the role of the teacher is general among students whatever their occupational intentions. It may be that the widespread idea that "anyone can teach" ... originated from this [socialization]; what child cannot, after all, do a reasonably accurate portrayal of a classroom teacher's actions?

Although it is easy to overlook the effects of K–12 schooling in considering how teachers learn to teach, Lortie argued that the effects of the apprenticeship of observation are particularly relevant because, compared to other professions, "teaching is relatively high on general schooling and somewhat low on specialized schooling" (p. 60).

Although the apprenticeship of observation provides most future teachers with a sense of the cultural routines and ceremonies associated with school, the effects of the apprenticeship are limited in at least four important ways (Lortie, 1975):

1. Students are "witnesses" to pedagogy rather than equal participants; thus they are not likely to "learn to see teaching in an ends-means frame" (p. 62).
2. Students learn about teaching in ways that are "intuitive and imitative rather than explicit and analytical" (p. 62).
3. "Students have no reliable basis for assessing the difficulty of demands of various teaching acts and thus may attribute teachers' actions to differences in personality or mood" (p. 63).
4. Students do not understand teaching as inherently problematic or complicated, thus they do not "perceive the teacher as someone making choices among teaching strategies," nor are students "likely to make useful linkages between teaching objectives and teaching actions" (p. 63).

All four limitations arise because the apprenticeship of observation is not a true apprenticeship, for teachers are not explicitly trying to teach students how to be teachers. Teachers try to teach a curriculum that may include both subject-matter content and cultural socialization skills, but they are unlikely to include any explicit lessons about pedagogy. *Thus the effects of the apprenticeship of observation are an unintentional yet powerful by-product of mass schooling.*

Sarason (1996) also called attention to the socializing effects of mass schooling. Although he wrote about the culture of school from his perspective as a psychologist and an educational reformer, there are unmistakable parallels between his ideas about the effects of school socialization and Lortie's (1975) concept of the apprenticeship

THE CULTURE OF SCHOOLS

of observation. Sarason believed that most people define school in a specific and narrow way:

> As observers of schools, we do not come to the task with blank minds. We come with images, expectations, and implicit and explicit attitudes. We come to the task after a long process of socialization and acculturation from which in countless ways, witting and unwitting, we have absorbed conceptions of and attitudes toward school settings. Far from being a random process, acculturation is directed to shaping a person's definition of reality, not only what it is but what it should be. (Sarason, 1996, p. 14)

Our experiences as students have a profound impact on how we understand the culture of the school. While Lortie argued that the effects of school socialization make it difficult to teach in ways other than how we were taught, Sarason focused his attention on the difficulties that school socialization present to educational reform.

There have been many attempts to reform the culture of schools; none have resulted in fundamentally different ways of thinking about teaching and learning (Sarason, 2002). The acculturating effects of the apprenticeship of observation contribute to a collective inability to acknowledge "the possibility that much of the difficulty [of school reform] is in the narrow perspective from which we view schools" (Sarason, 1996, p. 16). Many people use only their experiences as students and, perhaps, their perceptions of their children's experiences with school to justify "a sense of what counts as good teaching or bad teaching" (Kennedy, 2005, p. 1). A "sense" of good teaching is insufficient, however, because although most people can talk about "what teaching looks like," they have very little, if any, sense of the tacit, pedagogical decision-making processes in which teachers engage every day (Kennedy, p. 1).

One of the biggest consequences, then, of the apprenticeship of observation is that most people feel they know how to improve the quality of teaching and learning in schools. Unfortunately, many of these professional and lay critics are unaware that they are a part of the systems they critique (Sarason, 1996). Their apprenticeships of observation make them insiders, regardless of the current relationships they have with schools. It becomes important for anyone who examines the culture of schools to acknowledge the effects that their experiences as students have on their perceptions of the education system. Otherwise, they tend to become what Martin and Russell (2006, p. 186) called "lost in school," a condition that carries with it a set of socialized blinders that make it more difficult to critically analyze the teaching and learning occurring in schools.

Sarason (1996, p. 37) suggested three major barriers to understanding school culture. The first is that we tend to focus on individuals within schools, rather than on the structural characteristics of the culture of school. The second is that we fail to acknowledge that there is no such thing as a neutral school observer, by virtue of the fact that nearly every adult has attended school. Finally, despite an extraordinary amount of literature on educational change, we seem to know more about how *not* to reform schools than we do about how to encourage productive changes in school

CHAPTER 2

culture. This last point may be particularly contentious. Although one might argue that some of the cultural routines associated with school have changed dramatically since the advent of mass schooling, it is more likely that these changes are the result of broad societal shifts rather than of a focused mandate to make schools a productive place to learn (Sarason, 1996).

The deeply cultural problem of educational reform is particularly relevant to teacher education programs because teacher candidates are often tacitly or explicitly charged with the task of changing the prevailing culture of teaching and learning. The technical-rationalist assumption at the heart of many teacher education programs is that teacher candidates need only learn theories of best practice, which they can subsequently enact during practicum experiences (Schön, 1983). Although the concept of the apprenticeship of observation has been familiar in the literature for over 30 years, teacher educators seem to have paid little attention to its implications for teaching teachers. As Russell (2008, p. 2) argues, "while teacher educators might easily say that they are aware that teacher candidates already 'know' a great deal about teaching, they rarely go on to consider just what candidates do and do not know and how they know it." There is little evidence to indicate that teacher educators have explicitly reframed their pedagogy to challenge the effects of the apprenticeship of observation or that teacher education programs are designed to address the cultural problems of educational reform. Unfortunately, "efforts to challenge the norms that continue to govern and define teacher education as a site of inauthentic practice are consistently overpowered by status quo structures and perspectives" (Cole, 2003, p. 10).

Lortie (1975, p. 29) theorized that many teacher candidates have a positive attitude toward their experiences with school, so that they are "more likely to approve of existing arrangements [in schools] and … less motivated to press for change." Thus there is a "conservative bias" (Lortie, p. 29) in teacher education because many teacher candidates had successful, productive learning experiences within the existing system. Given the amount of time that children and adolescents spend immersed in the culture of school, it comes as no surprise that "some become so attached to it they are loath to leave" (Lortie, p. 29). The argument could easily be extended to many teacher educators, who in some ways represent the pinnacle of academic achievement in the traditional educational system. "The apprenticeship of observation is an ally of continuity rather than of change" (Lortie, p. 29).

Teacher education programs are typically divided into two major components: coursework that occurs at a faculty of education and practicum experiences that occur in host schools. Teacher candidates place a great deal of importance on the practicum (Ben-Peretz, 1995; Britzman, 1991/2003; Segall, 2002); it could be that teacher candidates primarily view the practicum as a space to prove they can actually teach a class (Lortie, 1975). The role of the practicum in how teacher candidates learn to teach has been historically problematic in teacher education (Vick, 2006), leading several researchers to call for a completely restructured approach to the practicum (LeCornu & Ewing, 2008; Zeichner, 2002). Many of the current problems associated with the practicum were articulated over 30 years ago:

> Because of its casualness and narrow scope, therefore, the usual practice teaching arrangement does not offset the unreflective nature of prior socialization; the

student teacher is not forced to compare, analyze, and select from diverse possibilities .... there is little indication that it is a powerful force away from traditionalism and individualism. (Lortie, 1975, p. 71)

Traditional wisdom maintains that the practicum experience is an essential part of any teacher education program. The technical-rationalist assumptions that underlie a theory-into-practice approach to teacher education reinforce the cultural myth that teacher candidates come to teacher education programs as blank slates, ready to be filled with theoretical knowledge before experiencing the practical world of the classroom. Such assumptions disregard the profound socialization into teaching all candidates receive by virtue of attending school. Their long apprenticeships of observation give candidates little choice other than to teach as they were taught (Sarason, 1996).

In many ways, those who do research on teaching and learning face similar challenges to teacher candidates learning to teach and reformers encouraging changes to our education system. All three groups tacitly and explicitly reinforce the cultural routines associated with schools because their prior socializations gained through a long apprenticeship of observation ensured that they never really left the school system. Whether one refers to these cultural routines as "ceremonies," "rituals" (Waller, 1932/1961, p. 103), "acculturation" (Sarason, 1996, p. 14) or "the grammar of schooling" (Tyack & Tobin, 1994, p. 453), the end result is clear: Any consideration of teaching, learning, or the school system must recognize the researcher's inherent insider perspective. Nuthall (2005, p. 896) makes a strong case for this idea in a retrospective article:

> Through nearly 45 years of research on teaching and learning in school classrooms, I have slowly become aware of how much of what we do in schools and what we believe about teaching and learning is a matter of cultural routines and myths. What is more, much of the research on teaching and learning in classrooms is itself caught up in the same rituals and myths and sustains rather than challenges these prevailing beliefs. The underlying theme, which the reader should keep constantly in mind, is that so long as we remain unaware of the extent to which our hidden culture determines how we practice, think about, and do research on teaching, attempts at reform are likely to be ineffective.

Those who would understand the process of learning to teach need to pay careful attention to the role of prior assumptions created by cultural socialization in the development of professional knowledge.

SUMMARY: THE CULTURE OF SCHOOLS

Calls for school reform are not new, nor are calls for reform of teacher education. The purpose of this consideration of the role that the culture of the school plays in how teacher candidates learn to teach is to encourage the reader to consider three issues of particular importance to this research:

1. Teaching is a cultural act and hence understanding how teachers learn to teach requires careful analysis of candidates' prior experiences as students in the culture

of the school and their experiences as new teachers in the cultures of their teacher education program, both at the university and in the host schools.
2. The culture of teaching and learning is replicated because of the tacit, unexamined effects of the apprenticeship of observation.
3. The way teachers teach is unlikely to change unless teacher educators help candidates to name and interpret how the effects of their apprenticeships of observation contribute to their default assumptions about teaching and learning.

Implicit in these considerations is the primary role of experience in the construction of professional knowledge about teaching and learning. Although teacher candidates can and do learn from propositional forms of knowledge, the role that experiences, particularly unexamined cultural experiences gained from the routines of schooling, play in the development of professional knowledge about teaching have often been undervalued in teacher education. This point is explored in greater detail in the following chapter that reviews relevant literature on how teachers learn to teach.

CHAPTER 3

THE DEVELOPMENT OF TEACHERS' PROFESSIONAL KNOWLEDGE

On the face of it, it looks relatively easy to depict teachers' knowledge as invented or acquired, and as acquired from others or from one's experiences, but this guide has shown otherwise. What is at first disarmingly simple turns out to be endlessly complex with many conceptions, many researchers, many viewpoints, and many epistemological and moral issues each vying for our attention .... There is a tension in the different views of what counts as professional knowledge and even of how to conceptualize knowledge.

(Munby, Russell, and Martin, 2001, p. 900)

This chapter develops the premise that, although teacher candidates can and do learn from propositional forms of knowledge, understanding the ways in which teacher candidates learn from experience offers a more productive way of thinking about learning to teach. In particular, the narrative inquiry perspective (Clandinin & Connelley, 1995) and the reflection-in-action perspective (Munby & Russell, 1990) are explored with a view to challenging the epistemological assumptions advocated by purely propositional views of learning to teach. Finally, the chapter concludes with a discussion of the importance of attending closely to the development of teachers' professional knowledge from teaching and learning experiences that occur during both coursework and practicum experiences.

TEACHERS' PROFESSIONAL KNOWLEDGE

Over the past 20 years, research on the development of teachers' professional knowledge has intensified in a number of different research programs, each with its own assumptions about teachers' professional knowledge and how it develops (Cochran-Smith & Lytle, 1999; Fenstermacher, 1994; Munby, Russell, & Martin, 2001). Although the construct of teachers' professional knowledge is readily accepted by members of the research community (Loughran, Mitchell, & Mitchell, 2003), epistemological debates on how teachers come to know continue to present day. This chapter considers research, primarily since 1990, on the broad topic of teachers' professional knowledge. In particular, I focus on issues and perspectives most relevant to the early development of professional knowledge by teacher candidates. The central tension in any consideration of teachers' professional knowledge is one of epistemology, particularly between the epistemologies of propositional knowledge (Shulman, 1987; Barnett & Hodson, 2001) and experiential knowledge (Clandinin & Connelly, 1995; Munby et al., 2001). I accept this tension as a useful perspective for organizing a review of literature on teachers' professional knowledge. In some

CHAPTER 3

cases, however, this review situates literature differently than other reviews with respect to the tension between propositional knowledge and experiential knowledge. The reasons for the differences reflect not only recent developments in certain research programs, but also the fact that, as Kagan (1992) pointed out, the synthesis of any body of literature is dependent on the experiences that the reader brings to various texts.

The purpose of this chapter is to describe and interpret two major theoretical perspectives of how teachers construct professional knowledge. Although some consideration is given to empirical studies, I focus on the epistemological underpinnings of each theoretical perspective. Implicit in the review is the assumption that teachers' professional knowledge is, like other forms of knowledge, constructed partly as a way to make sense of the cultural models shared by many in our society (Holland & Quinn, 1987). Although teacher candidates can and do learn from propositions, as evidenced by the fact that they are accepted into teacher education programs largely on the basis of marks obtained during heavily propositional undergraduate degree programs, I argue that a theoretical framework of the development of teachers' professional knowledge that is based solely on propositional forms of knowing is inadequate. Learning to teach is a more intricate process than allowed for by the constructs of the epistemology of propositional knowledge because such an epistemology fails to take into account the effects of either the apprenticeship of observation or the power of learning from teaching and learning experiences during a preservice teacher education program.

The review is divided into three sections. The first section explores the propositional views of teachers' professional knowledge, such as those offered by Shulman (1986, 1987), Grossman (1991, 1995), and Barnett and Hodson (2001). The second section challenges the epistemological underpinnings of propositional views by introducing Schön's (1983, 1987) conceptions of professional knowledge. The third section builds upon the second section by describing and interpreting two distinct views of how teachers' professional knowledge is constructed from experience: those of Clandinin and Connelley (1995, 1996) and Craig (1995, 2004), and those of Munby and Russell (1990, 1992b), Russell (1993, 2005), and Munby, Cunningham, and Lock (2000). Although I divide the research programs for purposes of analysis, the divisions should be considered heuristic groupings rather than discrete categories. As an example, a case might be made that elements of pedagogical content knowledge (Shulman, 1986) could be discussed under the lens of experiential rather than propositional knowledge. Here I group the research programs in a way that reflects their essential epistemological underpinnings.

It is difficult to articulate a precise definition of teachers' professional knowledge (Munby et al., 2001). For the purposes of this book, *teachers' professional knowledge is considered to encompass the knowledge, beliefs, and values that teachers possess and create in the course of their careers as educators in elementary and secondary schools*. Although van Manen (1991) makes a strong argument that professional knowledge of teaching is constructed outside of school contexts as well as within them, such a consideration is outside the scope of this review. Putnam and Borko (2000) advocate a situated perspective on cognition and learning that guides this review's conception of teachers' professional knowledge. Within this framework, teacher learning is considered to be a contextual, social process that occurs as a result of interactions among the individual, symbolic cognitive tools, and other people. Finally, the review is mindful of Borko and Putnam's (1996) earlier assumptions that:

1. Knowledge plays a "central role" in how teachers think, act, and learn (p. 673).
2. Learning, and hence learning to teach over the course of a career, is an "active constructive process" (p. 674).
3. Teachers interpret events based on prior beliefs, assumptions, and knowledge.

Teachers' professional knowledge as it develops and manifests itself in the school context during their careers seems best characterized as a form of situated cognition. The construct includes not only teachers' knowledge, but also their beliefs and values. Teachers' professional knowledge can be analyzed through the use of heuristic categories, which are articulated in several different research programs.

It is also important to frame the term *teachers' professional knowledge* within the context of this review. First, the word *professional* is itself a loaded term and carries for some the connotation of creating a professional knowledge base for teaching (Hiebert, Gallimore, & Stigler, 2002). The concept of a knowledge base for teaching is a contentious issue to which I return later in the chapter. Second, authors such as Shulman (1986, 1987) and Borko and Putnam (1996) append the word "beliefs" to form the construct "teachers' knowledge and beliefs." For the purposes of this book, I accept the premise that distinguishing between knowledge and belief is difficult and somewhat arbitrary (Calderhead, 1996; Fenstermacher, 1994). Thus I assume that teachers' beliefs are embedded within their professional knowledge. Third, it is important to consider the nature of the various groupings of teachers' knowledge that have been posited, such as subject-matter knowledge (Shulman, 1986, 1987), general pedagogical knowledge (Shulman, 1987), pedagogical content knowledge (Grossman, 1990, 1995), pedagogical context knowledge (Barnett & Hodson, 2001), personal practical knowledge (Clandinin & Connelly, 1995, 1996), and knowledge-in-action (Schön, 1983, 1987). Each of these groupings is ultimately heuristic in nature, and thus they should be regarded as frameworks for analysis rather than actual mental structures (Borko & Putnam, 1996). With these perspectives on cognition in mind, I turn to a consideration of those research programs advocating a propositional view of teachers' professional knowledge.

THE EPISTEMOLOGY OF PROPOSITIONAL KNOWLEDGE

Propositional knowledge, also called "paradigmatic knowledge" by Bruner (1986, p. 12), is the kind of theoretical knowledge generally assumed to be both created and taught by members of the academy. Cochran-Smith and Lytle (1999, p. 253) refer to this type of knowledge as "knowledge-for-practice" and suggest that propositional knowledge is predicated on the assumption that teaching can be improved by the transmission of research-based knowledge about teaching by university professors to teacher candidates. Learning to teach, then, is a process of applying knowledge learned in a university classroom to a practical situation, an assumption that has contributed to the use of the term *practice teaching* for practicum placements.

CHAPTER 3

Teachers, like doctors, architects, and engineers, are assumed to be consumers of an established knowledge base (Cochran-Smith & Lytle; Hiebert et al., 2002). Shulman (1987) argued that teachers can elevate their professional status through the construction of a knowledge base for teaching. The improvement of teaching, according to this line of reasoning, is a matter of skilled researchers finding the best possible knowledge to transmit both to teacher candidates and teachers. The concept of a knowledge base is strongly linked to various policy efforts aimed at reforming teacher education programs, including initiatives such as teacher testing and preservice licence examinations (Hiebert et al.).

This line of research was catalyzed by Shulman (1986), who argued that the division between content and pedagogy in the academy is a relatively new development in the history of higher education. As recently as the 19th century "the defining characteristic of pedagogical accomplishment was knowledge of content" (Shulman, 1986, p. 7). Shulman referred to content as "the missing paradigm" (p. 7) in teacher education and warned of the pitfalls of focusing on pedagogy at the expense of content. Fenstermacher (1994) believed that Shulman's focus on content reflects his conception of teacher education as normative; in other words, Shulman advocated that teacher educators must concern themselves with determining what teachers *should* know and be able to do.

Shulman's (1986) perspective had a significant impact on research programs concerned with teachers' professional knowledge. He felt that teachers should understand both the content of their subject-matter disciplines (the substantive knowledge) and the way the subject matter could be organized (the syntactic knowledge). Perhaps more importantly, however, Shulman introduced the concept of pedagogical content knowledge, which he defined as the kind of knowledge that "goes beyond knowledge of subject matter per se to the dimension of subject matter knowledge *for teaching* .... Pedagogical content knowledge also includes an understanding of what makes the learning of specific topics easy or difficult" (Shulman, p. 9). The process of learning to teach, according to Shulman, is a matter of acquiring pedagogical content knowledge such that teacher candidates have not only substantive and syntactic knowledge of their subject matter but also knowledge of common student misconceptions of subject matter.

Shulman (1987, p. 8) offered the following "categories of the knowledge base" for teacher knowledge:

1. Content knowledge
2. General pedagogical knowledge
3. Curriculum knowledge
4. Pedagogical content knowledge
5. Knowledge of learners and their characteristics
6. Knowledge of educational contexts
7. Knowledge of education ends, purposes, and values

Grossman (1990, 1995) credits Shulman's work in the late 1980s with helping to move research on teacher knowledge away from behaviourist approaches and toward cognitive approaches. General pedagogical knowledge, the "broad principles and strategies of classroom management and organization that appear to transcend subject matter" (Grossman, 1990, p. 8), initially received the most attention in the research literature. Grossman took Shulman's (1987, p. 8) assertion that pedagogical content knowledge "is of special interest because it identifies the distinctive bodies of knowledge for teaching" and focused on the posited four distinct components of pedagogical content knowledge (Grossman, 1990, pp. 8–9):

1. Knowledge of the goals for teaching a subject at various grade levels.
2. Knowledge of the conceptions and misconceptions students are likely to have about a subject at a given grade level.
3. Knowledge of the curriculum of a subject at various grade levels and the curricular materials available to enact the curriculum.
4. Knowledge of instructional strategies, metaphors, and images for teaching particular topics within a given subject.

These four components are not easily separated when teachers' classroom practice is considered. Grossman acknowledged the highly contextual nature of teachers' environments, but asserted that context is not a major source of teachers' pedagogical content knowledge.

The focus of Grossman's (1990) research was the development of pedagogical content knowledge. She identified four sources from which teachers develop pedagogical content knowledge: their experiences as students in elementary and secondary school (i.e., the apprenticeship of observation), their undergraduate degree programs, their methods courses in teacher education programs, and their experiences in the classroom. Although Grossman acknowledged the role of professional experience in developing pedagogical content knowledge, she clearly viewed propositional knowledge as a necessary precursor to experience: "Teaching experience provides the opportunity for prospective teachers to test the knowledge they have acquired from other sources in the crucible of the classroom" (p. 15). The comparison of a classroom environment to a piece of laboratory equipment is particularly revealing; the implication is that teachers are to experiment with the degree to which various propositions can be successfully enacted in the classroom.

In contrast to Grossman's (1990, 1995) work, Barnett and Hodson (2001) make the case that pedagogical content knowledge is inextricably linked, along with propositional academic knowledge, to the contextual environments in which teachers work. Barnett and Hodson (p. 436) define "pedagogical context knowledge" as an amalgam of internal and external sources of teachers' professional knowledge. In particular, pedagogical context knowledge is constructed on the premise that teachers move between the following internal and external sources of knowledge (Barnett & Hodson, pp. 437–438):

1. Academic and research knowledge, which includes knowledge of the substantive and syntactic structures of a discipline and knowledge about how students learn.
2. Pedagogical content knowledge, which includes the types of knowledge articulated in Grossman's (1990) description of pedagogical content knowledge.
3. Professional knowledge, which includes the knowledge of teaching acquired by "unconsciously reflected experience" (p. 438).
4. Classroom knowledge, which includes the situated knowledge that teachers have of their students and classroom contexts.

CHAPTER 3

Pedagogical context knowledge is founded in Barnett and Hodson's view that expert teachers "not only know more than novices, they have more accessible and usable knowledge because it is differently and better organized" (p. 440). To test their model of pedagogical context knowledge, the authors interviewed six exemplary science teachers about their views on particular curriculum units. The study concluded with the assertion that pedagogical context knowledge helps to reveal the intricacies of the knowledge that experienced teachers' access during their day-to-day teaching.

Loughran, Milroy, Berry, Gunstone, and Mulhall (2001) wished to document pedagogical content knowledge (PCK) by interviewing experienced, exemplary teachers. Initially, they concluded that:

> It is not quite so straightforward a process to recognise or articulate [pedagogical content knowledge] as we originally expected .... PCK may not be evident within the confines of one lesson or teaching experience .... Science teachers themselves do not use a language that includes (nor necessarily resembles) the construct of PCK, as much of their knowledge of practice is tacit. (p. 291)

Rather than studying pedagogical content knowledge solely by interviewing expert teachers, the researchers moved on to observe an array of factors that interact with teachers' pedagogical content knowledge. Loughran et al. coined the term "classroom windows" (p. 293) in order to critically examine a diverse array of teaching and learning situations that might reveal something about teachers' pedagogical content knowledge in addition to the interviews. In so doing, they realized that case studies of expert teachers were an insufficient way to explicate pedagogical content knowledge because cases "simply could not carry all that was necessary" (Loughran et al., p. 305) to understand the intricacies of the instances in which pedagogical content knowledge was used by teachers in classrooms. They surmised that "it is very difficult to offer an example [of pedagogical content knowledge] that is a neat concrete package .... [so] it became obvious ... why there was such a paucity of concrete examples of PCK in the literature" (p. 293).

Issues and Perspectives to Consider for Teacher Candidates

The epistemology of propositional knowledge is predicated on the assumption that teacher candidates are novice consumers, not expert producers, of knowledge (Cochran-Smith & Lytle, 1999). When Shulman (1986, 1987) offered a categorical account of teachers' knowledge, he opened the door for the creation of a knowledge base for teaching that would be transmitted to teacher candidates during a preservice program. A knowledge base for teaching, ironically, makes it possible to tell teacher candidates how they should teach without paying attention to how teacher candidates learn (Christensen, 1996).

A consideration of the structure of many teacher education programs reveals some of the difficulties inherent with a purely propositional approach to understanding how teacher candidates construct professional knowledge. Teacher education programs usually require teacher candidates to complete a certain amount of coursework before having a practicum experience. The assumption underpinning this design is that coursework can begin to transmit the knowledge base for teaching to teacher candidates. The practicum experience is then an opportunity for teacher candidates to practise applying the knowledge gained from both undergraduate course work (subject matter knowledge) and professional studies courses (pedagogical content knowledge). In addition, the practicum is an opportunity for teacher candidates (*novices*) to learn from their associate teachers (*experts*), who ostensibly have more pedagogical content knowledge than beginning teachers. In this line of reasoning, teacher educators teach pedagogical content knowledge during coursework, to be refined by teacher candidates under the guidance of an associate teacher in host schools.

Pedagogical content knowledge, the major construct in this school of thought, is an attempt to understand the intersection between academic knowledge and what Grimmett and MacKinnon (1992, p. 387) called "craft knowledge." Both Grossman (1995) and Loughran et al. (2001) admit to the difficulty of capturing teachers' pedagogical content knowledge. Grossman (1990) acknowledged the role of experience in developing pedagogical content knowledge, although she cautioned that learning from practice has pitfalls, given that one can "focus on 'what works' rather than overall goals for instruction" (p. 16). Loughran et al.'s recognition that pedagogical content knowledge is largely tacit and unexamined is of particular relevance to this theoretical framework. Although Grossman (1990) recognized the potential influence of the apprenticeship of observation on pedagogical content knowledge, she did not emphasize that the effects of the apprenticeship of observation tend to remain invisible to teachers. Thus experienced teachers may have more developed pedagogical content knowledge because they have assimilated more fully into the cultural routines of teaching and learning in schools. This assimilation occurs because the unnamed effects of the apprenticeship of observation are usually far more powerful than the effects of teacher education programs (Lortie, 1975; Zeichner & Tabachnick, 1981). The overriding assumption of this school of thought is that teacher candidates should be told theory before they have a practicum experience, where they can put theory into practice.

A recent review of science education literature reveals that research on pedagogical content knowledge remains challenging to this day (Berry, Loughran, & van Driel, 2008). Tangible examples that illustrate the development of pedagogical content knowledge remain elusive, a fact that has led some to question the value of pedagogical content knowledge as a construct. Berry et al. argue that pedagogical content knowledge remains a "seductive" (p. 1273) idea for researchers because it "was one way of opening up new possibilities for looking into, and better understanding the skills, knowledge and ability of expert teachers" (Berry et al., p. 1277). However, as Loughran et al. (2001) note, teachers typically lack the vocabulary to describe the development of their professional knowledge in a way that fits with the construct of pedagogical content knowledge, leading many teachers to dismiss the term as "jargon" (Berry et al., p. 1277).

In an interview conducted 20 years after his seminal paper that introduced the concept of pedagogical content knowledge, Shulman spoke of the genesis of PCK:

> The idea sort of grew slowly but the emphasis definitely was on this growing sense that emerged from our research that just knowing the content well was

CHAPTER 3

really important, just knowing general pedagogy was really important and yet when you added the two together, you didn't get the teacher. (Berry et al., 2008, p. 1274)

In proposing the idea of pedagogical content knowledge, Shulman and his research group were attempting to address "a gap in the field" (Berry et al., p. 1273) and provide a direction for future research. There was also, Shulman admits, a political imperative to define what teachers uniquely know about teaching their subjects to justify having subject-specific National Board exams for teaching. In his words, "we would not be able to establish the political integrity of teaching if we could not make the supportable claim that teachers knew how to do things that other people couldn't do" (Berry et al., p. 1275). Viewed in this light, pedagogical content knowledge seems more like a convenient label rather than a productive way to understand how teachers learn to teach.

It would be foolish to ignore some of the propositional ways that teachers learn, but the epistemology of propositional knowledge provides only a limited understanding of how teachers learn to teach. Pedagogical content knowledge has been an appealing construct for researchers in part because it names how difficult it is to understand the dynamic interplay between teachers' subject-matter knowledge and teachers' knowledge of pedagogy. At best, pedagogical content knowledge is a useful way to characterize the difference between expert teachers and novice teachers from a deficit perspective; expert teachers know more about how to teach subject-matter content than novices. Expert teachers have ostensibly more pedagogical content knowledge than novice teachers or teacher candidates, but the construct of pedagogical content knowledge and the epistemology of propositional knowledge tell us little about how expert teachers became experts. We are left with little understanding of how teacher candidates learn to teach.

CHALLENGING THE THEORY-INTO-PRACTICE ASSUMPTION

The idea that teacher candidates learn propositional theory in the academy, which they subsequently practise during practicum experiences, is a conceptualization of professional knowledge so firmly entrenched in our culture that Connelly and Clandinin (1995, pp. 8–9) have characterized it as a "sacred story" founded on a "rhetoric of conclusions." Connelly and Clandinin argue that the words *theory* and *practice* are inherently problematic for teachers, given that the general population conceptualizes theory as "the knowledge codified in books … [without] knowledge of the inquiry that gave rise to it" (p. 7). In this section, the sacred theory-practice story is challenged through consideration of the work of Schön (1983, 1987) and those who have considered the nature of teachers' professional knowledge in terms of the role of experience.

Schön (1983) reconceptualized the epistemology of professional knowledge (and hence teachers' professional knowledge) by critiquing what he referred to as the dominant assumptions of "technical rationality" (p. 21) inherent in professional schooling. Technical rationality assumes that "professional activity consists in instrumental problem solving made rigorous by the application of scientific theory and technique" (Schön, p. 21). Rather than thinking about professionalism as a matter of putting theory into practice, Schön introduces an epistemology of practice founded on the concepts of "knowing-in-action" and "reflecting-in-action" (p. 54), both of which recognize that much professional knowledge is tacit. Knowing-in-action, "the characteristic mode of ordinary practical knowledge" (Schön, p. 54), allows professionals to make decisions and carry out actions in the moment, without necessarily being able to articulate either their reasoning for taking such actions or how they learned to carry out such actions in the first place. Reflection-in-action refers to the kind of thinking professionals often do in the midst of making a decision or taking an action.

Schön (1983, p. 62) notes that "a practitioner's reflection-in-action may not be very rapid. It is bounded by the 'action-present,' the zone of time [possibly minutes, hours, or days] in which action can still make a difference to the situation." A professional confronts a situation, takes action, and must continually monitor the situation as it "'speaks back' to the practitioner, demanding more reflection and further action" (Furlong & Maynard, 1995, p. 47). This is reflection-in-action. The concept of "frame analysis" (Schön, p. 309) is a useful way to help professionals interpret and act upon problems when they occur, because it encourages professionals to consider multiple frames and to "attend to the ways in which they construct the reality in which they function" (Schön, p. 310). Frame analysis can help professionals consider multiple courses of action by naming a variety of frames and by possibly reframing the situation in a way that "gives central importance to his or her own role as a learner" (Schön, 1987, p. 92). This process is, by nature, experimental although not necessarily the result of conscious decision making (Furlong & Maynard). The professional "is *in* the situation that he or she seeks to understand" (Schön, 1983, p. 151).

Schön (1983) speaks of the inherent artistry of professional knowledge, frequently drawing comparisons between professionals and jazz musicians who "manifest a 'feel for' their material ... they feel where the music is going and adjust their playing accordingly" (p. 55). Just as jazz musicians improvise based on their understandings of musical situations at given moments, teachers improvise based on their understandings of unique situations within their classroom contexts. Although both jazz musicians and teachers bring prior propositional knowledge to bear on their understandings of situations, the more important issue is that both jazz musicians and teachers reflect as the situation is unfolding. As Munby et al. (2000, p. 195) note, "this concept emphasizes reflection that occurs *in the action* of teaching as a non-logical process rather than reflection that occurs in conjunction with associated control or subsequent thinking." The artistry of professional knowledge, then, is inherent both in how teachers reflect-in-action and how they frame and reframe unique and challenging situations.

The central message of Schön's argument is that the construction of professional knowledge (knowing-in-action) is not a matter of implementing propositions or putting theory into practice. Munby and Russell (1990, p. 116) state that "knowing-in-action is acquired through an interaction with experience that is non-logical and often sudden and unexpected." Teachers' professional knowledge, revealed through

CHAPTER 3

the lenses of knowing-in-action and reflection-in-action, is fundamentally grounded in professional experiences. There are, however, different ways of using Schön's ideas to understand how teachers construct professional knowledge from experience. Clandinin and Connelly (1995), for example, accept the idea of knowing-in-action while emphasizing the creation of shared narratives over the construct of reflection-in-action. Munby and Russell focus on describing and interpreting instances of reflection-in-action through the use of metaphor. The next section of this chapter examines these differences in detail.

THE EPISTEMOLOGY OF EXPERIENTIAL KNOWLEDGE

There are two main strands of research that emphasize the epistemology of experiential knowledge over the epistemology of propositional knowledge. The first strand, represented by Clandinin and Connelly (1995), posited a landscape of professional knowledge that is navigated through the creation of multiple narratives. The second strand reveals a group of researchers, such as Munby and Russell (1990, 1992b), primarily concerned with how reflection-in-action leads to knowing-in-action. This group of researchers "consider it far more of a task [than researchers in the narrative tradition] to tease out precisely what knowledge is involved in action and how this knowledge is altered in subsequent action" (Fenstermacher, 1994, p. 13). Fenstermacher argued that narrative constructs are "difficult to unpack with precision" (p. 11) and that narratives alone do not warrant claims about teachers' professional knowledge. Both groups of researchers, however, believe that the epistemology of experiential knowledge deserves far greater attention in any consideration of how teachers' professional knowledge develops.

Connelly and Clandinin (1995) use two metaphors in their discussion of teachers' professional knowledge: the metaphor of the landscape to describe how teachers construct and organize their knowledge and the metaphor of a funnel to discuss how policies are poured into the landscape from school boards, governments, and universities. Connelly and Clandinin (p. 4) state:

> The professional knowledge landscape that teachers inhabit creates epistemological dilemmas that we understand in terms of secret, sacred, and cover stories. The metaphor of the professional knowledge landscape provides a way to contextualize research-based understandings of teachers' personal practical knowledge.

The notions of secret, sacred, and cover stories are particularly important to the narrative tradition of describing and interpreting teachers' professional knowledge. Sacred stories are sacred in the sense that most people are unwilling to question their status and power in our culture. Secret stories are the stories of teachers in classrooms that are largely invisible to the public eye; they remain secret because teachers tend to guard closely the stories of their classroom experiences. Cover stories are the stories that teachers tell outside of their classrooms, particularly those that help them to deal with the values imposed upon them by policymakers and stakeholders via the funnel (Connelly & Clandinin, pp. 4–5).

THE DEVELOPMENT OF TEACHERS' PROFESSIONAL KNOWLEDGE

There is nothing in a teachers' professional knowledge landscape that is value-neutral. Teachers' professional knowledge and values are interwoven and inseparable. Teaching, characterized as a narrative experience within a vast landscape with its own history, is a process in which one constructs "personal practical knowledge" (Connelly & Clandinin, 1995, p. 4). Craig (1995) explored how this personal practical knowledge is created within the professional knowledge contexts of schools. These professional knowledge contexts are critically important to the development of new teachers' personal practical knowledge and are often safe spaces in which teachers can share their secret stories of classroom practice, which often results in the formation of important professional relationships among teachers (Craig, 2004).

Craig (2004) goes to great lengths to explicate the differences between the casual meetings of teachers in hallways and staffrooms and the meetings of teachers that allow for the creation of professional knowledge communities. These communities often serve as "a transitional narrative space—a bridging space [between the public and the private]—in which adjustments in relationships on teachers' landscapes can—and do—occur" (Craig, p. 421). Thus Craig advocates a shift away from the dominant transmission model of inservice teacher education. Instead, she suggests that teachers' professional knowledge involves a process of construction that can occur only if teachers feel safe in their contexts—contexts that are unlikely outside of a professional knowledge community founded on mutual trust. In professional knowledge communities, teachers "tentatively explore how they are making sense of situations, explain their own actions and excavate their stories in concert with others" (Olson & Craig, 2005, p. 178). These exploratory conversations provide opportunities for teachers to become conscious of the tensions between their cover stories and their secret stories, and thus more accurately map their professional knowledge landscapes (Olson & Craig).

There are, however, some epistemological problems with a narrative inquiry into teachers' professional knowledge. The constructs associated with narrative inquiry are "difficult concept[s] to unpack with precision" (Fenstermacher, 1994, p. 11). It is important to specify whether knowledge claims are made on an epistemic basis or a categorical basis, because

> [If] a researcher argues that teachers produce knowledge in the course of acting on experience, he or she could be saying merely that teachers generate ideas, conceptions, images or perspectives when performing as teachers (the grouping sense of knowledge) *or that teachers are justified in performing as they do for reasons or evidence they are able to provide* (the epistemic status sense of knowledge) [italics added]. (Fenstermacher, 1994, p. 31)

The narrative tradition can often function more in the grouping sense rather than the epistemic status sense of knowledge. In telling stories, teachers may not necessarily be able to provide evidence for *why* they constructed their narratives in a particular way. For this reason, the narrative tradition lacks a warrant for knowledge claims—what Fenstermacher (p. 34) calls "epistemic import." Clandinin and Connelly (1996) refute this characterization of their work by suggesting that Fenstermacher's argument does not take into account the contextual factors of teachers' professional

CHAPTER 3

knowledge. Furthermore, Clandinin and Connelly (1996, p. 28) state that "teachers know, and it is clear that they know what they know."

Loughran (2008) provoked a similar challenge to the narrative tradition by encouraging teacher educators to move beyond personal narratives in order to differentiate between telling stories of practice and naming knowledge derived from practice. He acknowledges that "a good story can be a very powerful way of sharing practice (and perhaps) influencing the practice of others" (p. 219). At the same time, however, Loughran (2008, p. 219) cautions that "a story can carry important messages and information about teaching without specifically focussing on the *why* [italics added] of teaching." Thus stories do not *necessarily* articulate the underlying assumptions and tensions associated with practice. In constructing a narrative, teachers need not articulate the reasoning behind any knowledge claims that they make.

Although it is clear that stories are important to the development of professional knowledge about teaching and learning, an argument can be made that stories are but one stage of the process of constructing knowledge about teaching. Teachers find considerable value in sharing stories with one another, and these stories can serve as a catalyst for critical analysis of practice. Loughran (2008, p. 219) acknowledges that the "why of teaching" may be buried in the story itself. To assume, however, that knowledge of practice is automatically created through the construction of narratives is potentially dangerous. Stories have embedded within them the assumptions and power differentials that tend to result in replication of cultural phenomena, such as the routines associated with the apprenticeship of observation.

The work of Munby and Russell (1990, 1992b) pays careful attention to establishing warrants for claims about teachers' professional knowledge (Fenstermacher, 1994). In particular, Munby and Russell (1990) suggest that the metaphors used by teachers to talk about teaching provide valuable evidence of how teachers think. Munby and Russell (1990, pp. 117–120) describe two case studies in which teachers use metaphors to talk about an aspect of their practice. The initial metaphors that the teachers use provide clues as to how they frame their professional understanding of their teaching. One teacher uses metaphorical language to describe her classroom as open and student-centred, often using the word "share" (Munby & Russell, 1990, p. 118). The other teacher uses metaphorical language to describe his understanding of the scientific method in relation to teaching elementary school science.

In the first case, the teacher reframes her professional understanding during a post-observation interview while reading over the transcript of the previous interview. The teacher realized that she was not providing her students with much choice in her classroom; as a result, she changed her metaphorical language, including "more attention to individual children and less use of the sharing metaphor" (Munby & Russell, 1990, p. 118). In the second case, the teacher's metaphorical understanding of science as a product rather than a process closely resembles his understanding of pedagogy. He did not reflect-in-action but found reflection-on-action a useful way to process daily events. Munby and Russell (p. 120) state that "reflection-on-action is evidently a powerful way for him to learn, just as he believes it to be the way in which we learn by scientific process." In both cases, changes in the teachers' metaphorical language reveal the reframing that occured as they reflect-in-action and reflect-on-action. Reflection-in-action helped the first teacher to see her classroom environment in a different way. Reflection-on-action, the more familiar of the two constructs, allowed the second teacher to attend to his reasons for his pedagogical decisions after they occurred. As Munby and Russell (p. 121) note, "careful attention to how one describes the world appears to give clues to how one constructs it." Most importantly, these metaphorical constructions serve as warrants for epistemic claims about teachers' professional knowledge and how teachers learn from experience because they are used almost unconsciously to describe situations, hence revealing more about tacit, unexamined knowledge than a narrative that is constructed for a specific purpose.

Munby et al. (2000) provide a useful interpretation of the epistemology of experiential knowledge. Teaching is not governed by a series of prescriptions for how to act in certain situations. Rather, teachers frame situations based on their understanding and reframe situations in response to experiences.

> Reframing is the process by which professional knowledge develops and it .... emphasizes reflection that occurs *in the action* of teaching as a non-logical process rather than reflection that occurs in conjunction with associated control or subsequent thinking .... Therefore, reflection-in-action leads to knowing-in-action via the process of reframing. (p. 195)

From this perspective, professional knowledge is generated by a teacher's ability to make his or her practice problematic, enact a new course of action based on a new frame of understanding, and then evaluate the new frame based on the results. Teachers' professional knowledge, then, is also based on how they reframe in response to experiences, not solely on how they enact propositions.

There are, however, barriers to creating professional knowledge via the process of reframing. Munby et al. (2000) investigated these barriers by observing and interviewing a new science teacher over a 4-month period. They discovered that providing an opportunity for a teacher to reflect on his or her practice does not necessarily lead to reframing of classroom situations. The teacher in the study "feels constrained by conventions condoned by the school institution .... by the demands imposed by the curriculum .... by her past experience, the expectations placed upon her at the school, and her interpretations of what works and what does not work in terms of her teaching" (Munby et al., pp. 204–205). Teachers work within the constraints of multiple internal and external contexts. These contexts can impede the process of framing and reframing, and in so doing impose "boundaries to the social scientific inquiries teachers might make of their teaching" (Munby et al., p. 208).

In addition to the contextual boundaries that can make it difficult for teachers to reframe their practice, there are other challenges to understanding Schön's constructs of learning from experience. One of the major obstacles to understanding how teachers learn from experience is the pervasive assumption that simply providing the experience is sufficient (Munby et al., 2001; Russell, 1993).

Russell (1993, p. 209) identifies a "ritual-practice problem in learning from experience" by considering that it is possible for those learning to teach to develop ritual rather than principled knowledge from experience. Ritual knowledge is constructed when a teacher does things without attending to the principles underlying actions. The culture of the school consists largely of ritualized, procedural knowledge, so it is often difficult to critically examine the principles underlying teaching practice, and hence the status quo remains firmly entrenched (Britzman, 1991/2003; Russell, 1993). In fact, many teachers are "*unaware of the ways in which principled understanding of their practice* could inform and support a career that offers significant opportunity to develop new practices" (Russell, p. 210). It becomes of critical importance, therefore, to engage in discussions with those learning to teach that encourage a principled, rather than a ritualized, understanding of teaching that goes beyond merely surviving the daily requirements of the classroom.

Both Clandinin and Connelly (1995, 1996) and Munby and Russell (1990, 1992b) believe in the primacy of experience in the construction of teachers' professional knowledge. Cochran-Smith and Lytle (1999) conceptualized this knowledge as "knowledge-in-practice....[where] the emphasis is on knowledge-in-action: what very competent teachers know as it is expressed or embedded *in* the artistry of practice, *in* teachers' reflections on practice, *in* teachers' practical inquiries, and/or *in* teachers' narrative accounts of practice" (p. 262). Although knowing-in-action is central to the epistemology of experiential knowledge, the role of reframing and reflection-in-action is conceptualized quite differently in the two research programs described in this section. For the narrative school of Clandinin and Connelly, knowing-in-action is concurrent with the construction of teachers' personal professional knowledge as secret stories of classroom life. The issue is whether these secret stories become uncovered in professional knowledge communities, because "the possibilities for reflective awakening and transformations are limited when one is alone" (Connelly & Clandinin, 1995, p. 13). The research program of Munby and Russell concludes that knowledge-in-action is constructed through reflection-in-action, reframing, and reflection-on-action. Knowledge-in-action is not automatically constructed as a result of experience; it occurs "through those interactions with experience that result in the often sudden and unanticipated ways in which we come to *see experience differently*" (Munby & Russell, 1992a, p. 3). By attending to the metaphors in teachers' rich descriptions of how they viewed experiences differently, researchers are able to learn more about teachers' tacit understandings and assumptions.

Issues and Perspectives to Consider for Teacher Candidates

The epistemology of experiential knowledge contends that teachers are actively involved in the creation of their own professional knowledge. Learning to teach requires opportunities for teacher candidates to "enhance, make explicit, and articulate the tacit knowledge embedded in experience" (Cochran-Smith & Lytle, 1999, pp. 262–263). Schön's (1983) criticism of the technical rationalism that dominates professional schools was a catalyst for researchers to think about a new construct for professional knowledge—knowing-in-action. Knowing-in-action directly contrasts with propositional knowledge because it reveals the importance of knowledge that professionals gain from personal experience. According to Munby and Russell (1994, p. 92), "there is a knowledge-in-action that cannot be fully expressed in propositions" which means that "learning from experience has its own epistemology." The implications of the epistemology of experiential knowledge for teacher education are profound, because the technical rationalist assumptions underlying most teacher education programs do not prepare candidates to learn from experience. Teacher education programs tend to be designed in ways that reinforces the sacred story of theory-into-practice by requiring teacher candidates to attend a significant number of classes to learn theory before they are permitted to have a practicum experience. This sacred story is so firmly entrenched that it is common for people to refer to practicum experiences as *practice teaching*, a term "founded on arrogance so deeply rooted that ... [it implies] all our students need to do to develop professional knowledge is to practice what teacher educators have preached" (Munby et al., 2001, p. 897).

Although knowledge-in-action can arise from practicum experiences, teacher candidates often do not "master learning from experience during preservice programs in a way that gives them direct access to the nature of the *authority of experience* [italics added]" (Munby & Russell, 1994, p. 92). The experience alone is not sufficient because it does not automatically encourage teacher candidates to articulate how and why they know what they know. Russell (1983, p. 30) outlined two common kinds of authority in schools: the *authority of knowledge*, which comes from the ability to make warranted claims about knowledge, and the *authority of position*, which is ostensibly given to someone who has the authority of knowledge. Although the theoretical framework underlying schools contends that the authority of knowledge precedes the authority of position, "a teacher's position in authority makes it *possible* to present knowledge claims *without* reasons" (Russell, p. 30). The apprenticeship of observation tends to emphasize the authority of position over other forms of authority as school routines become deeply ingrained. Munby and Russell (1994) also considered the implications of the authority of experience for experienced teachers teaching at faculties of education:

> Their knowledge-in-action gives them [teacher educators] the authority of experience. But the circumstances of telling their students about teaching unavoidably commits them to the authority of being in charge, and their students are automatically placed under authority. The authority of experience gets transformed into the authority that says, *I know because I have been there, and so you should listen*. The authority of experience simply does not transfer [to teacher candidates] because it resides in having that experience. This coincides with Schön's view that knowledge-in-action cannot be transformed into propositions. (pp. 92–93)

The gap between the authority of experience of a teacher educator and the authority of experience of a teacher candidate sheds some light on the reason that the search for pedagogical content knowledge has been so challenging. *Teacher educators cannot tell candidates how to teach because the authority of experience cannot be transmitted as a set of propositions.*

The epistemology of experiential knowledge requires careful consideration of how teacher candidates learn from the authority of their own teaching and learning experiences. It is also important to disrupt the sacred story by acknowledging that the learning experiences that occur during coursework in a teacher education program can be valuable for helping teacher candidates learn how to learn from the authority of their own experiences. There are at least two ways in which the authority of experience can be explored more fully in teacher education programs. The authority of experience might initially be expressed in the form of a secret story, until a teacher candidate feels comfortable enough to tell his or her story in a professional knowledge community. Teacher education classrooms may provide such a safe environment. Constructing a narrative, however, does not necessarily establish a warrant for knowledge claims based on the authority of experience. If narratives do not include *why* teacher candidates acted or felt certain ways, then they remain at the level of a story that, while useful to relate to other teachers, does not reveal a lot about the candidates' tacit professional knowledge.

The authority of experience seems more likely to be established through the metaphors teacher candidates use in their descriptions of teaching and learning situations. Changes in language may imply a change in the metaphors with which they understand teaching and learning situations that arise during the preservice year (Munby & Russell, 1990; 1992b). In particular, teacher candidates should have opportunities to critique their assumptions about teaching because, as Munby et al. (2001, p. 887) note, "good teaching tends to reinforce the view that teaching is effortless because the knowledge and experience surrounding it are invisible to those taught." The authority of experience must be explicitly named and interpreted with teacher candidates in order to both challenge practices ritualized by the culture of school and help candidates develop warranted claims about the development of their professional knowledge.

THE CULTURE OF SCHOOL AND ITS IMPLICATIONS FOR UNDERSTANDING THE DEVELOPMENT OF TEACHERS' PROFESSIONAL KNOWLEDGE

The powerful cultural ideas about teaching that result from the apprenticeship of observation have important implications for any consideration of how teachers construct their professional knowledge. The socializing effects of attending school result in tacit yet deeply rooted prior assumptions about how students learn, assumptions that must be addressed in teacher education programs. This chapter has considered the epistemologies of teachers' propositional knowledge and experiential knowledge, with a view to underscoring the relevance of warranted knowledge derived from the authority of experience, rather than the more familiar authorities of knowledge or position.

Three conclusions that are relevant to this research can be drawn from this review. First, teachers' professional knowledge can be conceptualized in a number of heuristic groupings that reflect underlying assumptions about what teachers know and how they learn. Each of the heuristic groupings discussed in this review speak to the situated nature of teachers' cognition. Teachers construct their professional knowledge based on a number of factors including propositional knowledge, their prior experiences as students, their interactions with other teachers and teacher educators, their practicum experiences, and their personal professional landscapes.

Teachers' professional knowledge is frequently tacit; even expert teachers are often unable to state how they know what they know about teaching and learning.

Second, Shulman's (1986) assertion that teacher education programs need to pay close attention to the role of subject-matter knowledge in the development of teachers' professional knowledge has sparked a considerable amount of research, particularly on the construct of pedagogical content knowledge. Although experienced teachers seem to have more pedagogical content knowledge than new teachers, describing and interpreting the pedagogical content knowledge of experienced teachers is not a straightforward task. There is very little research that establishes what pedagogical content knowledge is. A part of the reason for this gap in the literature may be that the construct of pedagogical content knowledge was created partially as a political move to claim that teachers have unique knowledge of how to teach their subject matter. Such claims played an important role in the development of National Board certification exams in the United States. Although expert teachers may indeed have pedagogical content knowledge, this particular heuristic grouping may function as a convenient label for researchers rather than as a productive way of understanding how teachers construct professional knowledge. Teacher candidates can and do learn from propositions, particularly about their subject matter, but the effects of the apprenticeship of observation are deeply socialized and hence unlikely to change as a result of sharing propositional knowledge alone.

Third, Schön's (1983, 1987) conception of the epistemology of professional knowledge was expressed in two major lines of research developed by Clandinin and Connelly (1995) and by Munby and Russell (1990, 1992b). Both research programs interpret how teachers construct knowledge-in-action by examining the authority of experience, although they differ in focus. The narrative perspective (Clandinin & Connelly) focuses on creating safe spaces for the sharing of teachers' secret stories, whereas the reflection-in-action perspective (Munby & Russell) attends closely to teachers' use of language to reveal how they frame and reframe their practice. Although construction of narratives has value for teachers, particularly as they navigate the competing demands of the contexts in which they teach, narratives alone do not necessarily have epistemic import. Evidence of reframing, particularly by attending to teachers' use of metaphorical language, provides a warrant with which to make epistemic claims about teachers' professional knowledge.

It is productive to consider teacher education programs in light of these competing heuristic groupings of teachers' professional knowledge. Although it has been many years since Schön's initial challenge to technical rationalism, there continue to be calls for a *new* teacher education because the old teacher education model, largely founded on propositional assumptions about how teachers come to know, is considered inadequate by many policymakers, teacher educators, and teacher candidates (Cochran-Smith, 2005; Darling-Hammond, 2000). To be clear, I am not advocating a complete rejection of propositional epistemologies of how teachers create their professional knowledge. Teachers need to be able to teach the subject matter that they learned in their undergraduate degree programs. Some teacher candidates may even find propositions offered by teacher educators, associate teachers, or their peers of some value. Knowledge-in-action, however, does not come from propositional knowledge, nor can it be transmitted from one person to another. Teacher education programs need to pay explicit attention to the role of experience in learning to teach. As Munby et al. (2001, p. 900) observe, "although the field of teachers' knowledge is too large for mundane consideration, the evidence is that we in teacher education still proceed as if it were simple." Professional knowledge of teaching is hard-earned because it requires teacher candidates to reframe their understanding of teaching and learning gained from the apprenticeship of observation within the context of the propositional knowledge typically offered in preservice classroom and practicum experiences. Simply having an experience is not enough. Classroom and practicum experiences that are unexamined do little more than reinforce existing patterns of teaching in schools. As Lortie (1975) noted, teacher candidates may simply regard the practicum as a way to prove to themselves that they can enact familiar teaching behaviours, many of which could have been reasons for their entrance into the profession. The apprenticeship of observation is not a stimulus for change.

    This book examines how teacher candidates construct professional knowledge from teaching and learning experiences that occur during both coursework and practicum experiences. Throughout the research, I frame the process of learning to teach as one fraught with tension, especially between familiar cultural routines codified in the apprenticeship of observation and the new experiences that teacher candidates acquire during their preservice education program. In the next 4 chapters we turn to the heart of the matter; an in-depth analysis of how 5 teacher candidates learned to teach in a preservice teacher education program.

CHAPTER 4

DISRUPTING INITIAL ASSUMPTIONS

Coming in here [to the Faculty of Education] I still didn't know the answer, but I thought, "I can do that." I've tutored and I've taught groups in that way, sort of repeating a textbook in a better way, but if you can do it in a way when you are talking to them. I thought coming here would be sort of polishing that ability ... and we haven't been. So I guess that's how physics class formed my questions.

(David, FG1, 14)

The first day of classes at a Faculty of Education is, in many respects, similar to the first day of school in any other educational environment. There is a palpable energy in the building as a new school year promises new opportunities for all involved. Teacher candidates rush through unfamiliar corridors to find their classes and meet their professors for the first time. In anticipation of a new beginning, many professors sleep just a little bit more fitfully the night before, particularly those who used to be elementary or secondary school teachers and have experienced some anxiety before school begins for many years. Candidates who knew each other prior to the beginning their preservice program, perhaps through a common undergraduate degree, experience a moment of jubilation when they catch a familiar face in the hallway or in a classroom. Just like any other educational environment, there are both "ceremonies" (Waller 1932/1961, p. 103) and a "grammar" (Tyack & Tobin, p. 453) to be learned at a Faculty of Education. Unlike the ceremonies of the K-12 system, which tend to be largely about establishing routines and control over the student population, the ceremonies of a Faculty of Education have much more to do with an unspoken question among teacher candidates: *Beyond a practicum placement, what is it that one does during a teacher preparation program?*

Teacher candidates come to a preservice program with both a lifetime of experiences observing teachers teach, and a set of assumptions about what good teaching should look like. Many candidates likely have favourite teachers who they wish to emulate, at least in part, during their teaching careers. It is little wonder, then, that candidates expect to learn "what works" during a teacher education program. They tend to adopt, at least tacitly, the viewpoint of the technical rationalists that assumes theory can be learned in one place and practiced in another. Thus an initial ceremony for many teacher candidates requires an appeal to education professors to find out how to make a positive impression on their first practicum experience. Typically (and naturally), candidates' concerns gravitate toward learning how to effectively "manage" a classroom. In other words, candidates wish to learn how to replicate the ceremonies that effectively controlled them when they were students.

Candidates' prior assumptions about what should happen during a preservice program pose a significant challenge for a teacher educator. If one rejects the premise

CHAPTER 4

that teacher education is more than a set of propositions that can be simply transferred to practice, then it is important to create experiences early in the program that disrupt candidates' prior assumptions about teaching and learning. This chapter outlines some of the ways that candidates who participated in this research experiences such disruptions.

The first section of this chapter describes the major events that occurred during the physics course in this block of classes. The data obtained from the focus group and individual interviews are then analyzed to provide insight into how teacher candidates constructed professional knowledge from learning experiences in the physics course. The comments made by teacher candidates as they looked ahead to their first practicum placements are then presented to indicate some of their initial thinking about how they expect to learn from practicum experiences. The next section provides the perspective and voice of the teacher educator as I analyze the discussions Tom and I engaged in during the September block. Finally, the chapter concludes with a summary of the professional knowledge constructed and co-constructed by the teacher candidates and the teacher educators who participated in this study.

CONTEXTUAL FEATURES OF THE PHYSICS METHODS COURSE

The physics curriculum methods course began with a special 90-minute class in the first week of September with 19 teacher candidates enrolled. The course went on to meet on eight more occasions during this block of classes. Regular class times were from 15:00–17:20 on Mondays and 12:00–14:50 on Thursdays, beginning the second week of September and concluding in the first week of October. Tom Russell was the teacher of the course and I attended each class as a participant-observer.

Tom began the class with a Predict-Observe-Explain (POE) activity designed to build community and encourage teacher candidates to feel comfortable engaging in exploratory, open-ended discussion about teaching and learning physics. After an additional POE activity on the second day, Tom quickly outlined the requirements for a Lesson Study activity that became the major focus for this block of classes. Teacher candidates were asked to plan lessons in groups of four with each person teaching one lesson planned by the group. All candidates were required to plan lessons based on the electromagnetism units in grade 11 and 12 physics from the Ontario curriculum. Two unique lessons were presented by each group during the first round of presentations; the second round of presentations were revised versions of the same two lessons, repeated by the remaining two members of each group. Thus each group had the opportunity to revise its two lessons based on feedback from their peers and from Tom. Asking each teacher candidate to present part of a physics lesson required that approximately three-quarters of the class time in September be devoted to presenting and critiquing those lessons. Candidates were also given some class time to plan their lessons in groups. Tom devoted most of the final class to discussing and processing the effects of the Lesson Study activity.

LEARNING EXPERIENCES IN THE PHYSICS CLASS: TEACHER CANDIDATES

The data provided by the participants during the focus group interview and the individual follow-up interviews were analyzed with a view to understanding how teacher candidates construct knowledge from learning experiences during a physics methods course. Four themes are discussed in this section: Prior Assumptions, Lesson Study, Learning from Peers, and Learning from Tom. Although each theme focuses on learning that occurs as a result of the methods course, there are many instances where the candidates invoke comparisons between past experiences as learners in other situations and their learning experiences in the B.Ed. program.

Prior Assumptions

Participants discussed their prior assumptions about teaching, how they learned physics, and what they expected from the Faculty of Education. Candidates acknowledged that they "were the ones who were successful in the [school] system" (FG1, 6). Their idea of good teaching focused on the transfer of information from a textbook to students in an entertaining way: "If you repeat the textbook, but do it really well, it can be effective" (FG1, 10). As Irene remarked: "I know the material and I've seen teachers all my life" (Irene1, 18). Max summarized the candidates' prior assumptions about teaching when he said: "I'll teach what's in the textbook, I'll get the classroom involved some of the time and hopefully they shouldn't need to read it" (FG1, 16). James agreed that traditional notions of teaching-as-telling dominated his thoughts before he came into to the program, stating: "I thought coming into this program that there was really only one way to teach: you get up and you talk to your students" (FG1, 3).

Assumptions about the "one way" to teach followed naturally from the candidates' prior assumptions about how they learned physics. David (FG1, 24) articulated the differences he saw between two ways of teaching high school physics:

> There were basically two approaches from high school teachers. Even if they were teaching from the textbook, there were some that stressed understanding concepts, and from that understanding the rules to equations ... then there are others [who provide] the equations which prove the physical phenomenon [first], which I think is the other way around. There are two different approaches for expressing different aspects, and I definitely prefer the former, the first.

The other participants agreed with how David framed the kind of teaching typically found in high schools. James extended the argument to include university physics by relating a story about his first-year professor who wrote the formula for Newton's Second Law on the board and said: "It was the only thing we [students in the physics class] needed to know because everything else could be derived from it" (FG1, 28). Candidates felt that physics teachers "stand and present the material and explain how things work and work through problems on the board" (David1, 5). Candidates assumed that physics teachers tell students about physics and that their only pedagogical decision concerns whether to explain the concept before giving the equations or to provide the equations and then explain the concept.

Candidates' prior conceptions about how they learned physics were closely linked to their ideas about how physics is taught. In acknowledging that they represent the people who were successful at learning physics in a traditional way, some candidates described tensions between the teaching methods they were familiar with from their experiences as students and the new teaching methods being espoused at the Faculty of Education. As Paul said: "Thinking back to my favourite physics teacher, he just wrote stuff on the board and now, being here, I question why I liked it so much. He wrote so much on the board. I loved it" (FG1, 19). Candidates believed that their abilities to learn from the traditional approach to teaching physics was innate, as shown by statements such as "I am just lucky ... because I learn that way" (FG1, 12); "When I was in high school, I was academic" (Irene1, 6); and "I've been lucky in that even with math and physics I've been able to pick it up kind of quickly initially" (Paul1, 19). Their success in physics class, then, was attributed to their rare ability to tune in to the transmission model of teaching that dominates high school and university classrooms.

The expectations and assumptions that the teacher candidates had for the Faculty of Education followed naturally from their prior assumptions about teaching and learning physics. David thought that B.Ed. coursework would focus on "polishing that [traditional] teaching ability" (FG1, 14). Candidates were "pleasantly surprised" (FG1, 51) by some elements of the program, particularly those classes that encouraged approaches to teaching that were not transmission-based. Paul "came to teachers' college [sic] with the expectation that [he] would be taught traditionally ... [it took] 2 or 3 weeks to really believe that they were going to do it differently in a lot of the courses" (Paul1, 3). Irene highlighted a shift in her expectations of the B.Ed. program, stating that at the beginning of September she wanted "someone to tell [her] how to improve ... [but] now it's all about finding your own beliefs on what to teach and how to do it" (FG1, 88).

The prior assumptions that teacher candidates held at the beginning of this study serve as a lens that reveals the effects of their apprenticeships of observation (Lortie, 1975). Teacher candidates acknowledged that they were successful at learning physics in school, attributing that success to a personal ability to relate conceptual ideas to mathematical formulae. They enjoyed physics lectures and problem-solving. Even when faced with a teacher who was unable to explain the material, candidates agreed that they "could pick up a [physics] textbook and pass the class" (FG1, 15). Coming into the program, candidates felt they were going to learn how to enact traditional pedagogies in a more efficient manner, presumably so physics would be more palatable to a wider range of students. This paradox is interesting: candidates saw themselves as the exceptions in physics class, yet they still felt that they could reach more people if they just taught traditionally in a more effective manner. They came into the program wanting to teach as they were taught, and they expected to learn how to teach well in traditional ways. The apprenticeship of observation shapes teacher candidates' prior assumptions about teaching and learning as well as their expectations of a Faculty of Education.

Lesson Study

Teacher candidates offered comments both on what they learned from the process of creating and enacting a physics lesson and on what they learned from interacting with their peers during the lesson study process. They unanimously felt that lesson study was a worthwhile way to spend the September block of time, because instead of "being lectured on how to teach per se, we're getting up there and practising our teaching" (James1, 3). Paul felt that it was "good to see what it takes to plan out half an hour" (Paul1, 12). Irene felt that lesson study encouraged her to "see through the eyes of a student again" (Irene1, 5) because so much time was devoted to watching her peers teach.

Most of the candidates felt that it was extraordinarily difficult to plan lessons as a group, for a number of reasons. Max offered that his group "wasn't really much of a model for group planning ... [because] none of us could meet together .... It was all individual for our lesson planning in our group" (Max1, 3). Irene's group "kind of worked together at the start ... [but] then each person prepared their own lesson pretty thoroughly" (Irene1, 4). Paul suggested that his group found it difficult to plan together because they had "four pretty different personalities" (Paul1, 15). David named a tension in his group between his willingness to plan a lesson based on using active-learning pedagogies and the group's desire to plan a more traditional lesson. He said: "You have to give concessions and accommodate, which I felt, at the time, might have taken away from what the real goal of the assignment was" (David1, 15). David felt that lesson study provided him with the opportunity to enact the active-learning pedagogies outlined by Knight (2004), so "it was frustrating [for him] to try to come up with a [traditional] lesson plan ... when [he] really wanted to just go that [active-learning] route, throw it out there, take a chance" (David1, 13). The other members of his group were more inclined toward "the old-style route," leading David to conclude that the other members of his group had not "bought into this [active-learning approach] yet" (David1, 13). David presented in the second round of lessons, enacting a lesson that "was more of what [he] wanted to do as opposed to what the group came up with" (David1, 13). In contrast to the other four participants in the study, James' comments indicated that he found planning lessons in a group helpful because "it was great to just talk to the other teacher candidates to see ideas they had and what they were doing" (James1, 8).

The structure of the lesson study activity meant that everyone in the course spent a good deal of time observing peers teach physics lessons. Participants in the study said they saw a lot of traditional, teacher-centred, transmission-based teaching from their peers. Max offered one explanation for the similarities in his peers' lessons: "I haven't seen that many [lessons] that are way off to the side of what you've seen before. We all learn to teach from the same kind of teachers" (Max1, 1). Irene noted that her peers "use the overhead and the board and work through the material ... [in the same way her] teachers always did" (Irene1, 10). In contrast to Max, however, Irene felt that there was a "wide range of teaching styles" because "the mannerisms of the people who were up there teaching ... [resulted in] different ways of talking to the class" (Irene1, 10). For Irene, the differences in her peers' mannerisms were sufficient to warrant a claim that they were using different teaching styles.

CHAPTER 4

Paul was much more critical of the lessons taught by his peers, saying that he saw "no real extremes in terms of ideas about teaching" (Paul1, 16). He learned the most from watching what he thought were the poorer lessons taught by his peers:

> When I see something [in a lesson] going well, which actually doesn't happen that often anyway to be honest ... then watching it doesn't help me that much because it's one person doing it; it's their style, and they're teaching a bunch of university kids. But it's when I've seen something they've done that clearly is a terrible idea ... we're not even talking the whole lesson or anything, just their manner, the way that they talk to people. That's what's influenced me the most. (Paul1, 1)

Paul and David were also vocal about their disappointment with the lack of peer interaction during the lesson study process. Paul offered this interpretation: "I was kind of excited about what it [lesson study] could teach me. But I also saw that it would really require a lot of investment from everyone in the class" (Paul1, 4). David also thought that the success of lesson study depended on "how people reacted or embraced the process," adding that he "embraced it [lesson study] early" (David1, 20). Both Paul and David felt that the majority of their classmates did not embrace the lesson study process, which resulted in many awkward silences during their lessons:

> The point is, if I was in a class where I could actually stand in front of people and people were really interacting with me, and giving me really valuable feedback about what I'd done there, I think that would be great. But as it was, you know, people weren't really into talking to me. When I was at the front, there weren't really any questions, which could be my fault. There doesn't seem to be that investment in taking that seriously. (Paul1, 6).

David articulated a similar frustration:

> The interaction with the class isn't really there. We're presenting to the class and we're not really getting feedback. People weren't really reacting like a class might, but they weren't really participating, they were more sitting back and absorbing. (David1, 17)

Both Paul and David mentioned that they felt that they had done a good job with their lessons, despite their perception that the rest of the class had not embraced the process. Paul credited his group with helping him to plan a good lesson, saying "I think I did a pretty good job ... given good [group] lesson planning and then my general lack of unease asking people about my teaching." Paul said on numerous occasions that he wished he had received more feedback from his peers.

In contrast to Paul and David, James was happy with the feedback he received from the group:

> I think feedback is very important. For instance, actually in class, we get up and we present a lesson and we get feedback from the other students. And in my lesson, I used overheads instead of PowerPoint ... one of the reasons that I did that is because, not only do I feel comfortable using overheads, but also

I wanted to see what my fellow classmates thought about it. And some of them ... made suggestions about how to improve that. But most of them seemed to think it was a good method. (James1, 6)

James added that he learned from watching his peers teach, saying "there are a variety of ways to fill ... however long a lesson is" (James1, 26). Irene suggested that watching her peers helped her to realize that "when people do different types of lessons ... [she] thinks about what makes people learn best" (Irene1, 1). Max felt that everyone was "treating the material in the same way" (Max1, 4) and that the lesson study process unfolded "as expected" (Max1, 1).

Irene and David offered some poignant comments about why lesson study was a difficult learning process for the teacher candidates. Irene suggested that the requirement to plan lessons as a group added an additional level of complexity to the process, making it difficult to focus on how she was learning from lesson study:

I think I also learned it's hard to do lessons ... we're all supposed to talk about the learning effect and from what I read ... [Tom] put us in groups to improve their lessons ... but I think the people got together at first and then went their own ways. It's hard to work together. (Irene1, 3)

David believed that the particular format that was used for lesson study might have been too complicated for those who are just beginning to learn to teach:

Maybe it could be predicted that it would be difficult to embrace the process of creating lesson plans and then revising and revisiting what went well and what went wrong and then coming up with something better. It's difficult to achieve that when we're all still grappling with these [new] ideas ... I've been challenged to think about education ... so much so that I wasn't prepared for it. So all of this information is coming at you, and you're not just jumping through hoops, there is actually something of essence there. So we're grappling with all of this, and at the same time trying to follow this [lesson study] process.

Lesson study was a complicated pedagogy that made significant demands on the teacher candidates, both as learners and as teachers. Although teacher candidates universally agreed that lesson study was a useful, productive experience, there was also a sense that the process could have been a more powerful learning experience if there had been more peer interaction. Interestingly, the things that some candidates found frustrating about their peers were almost exactly the same kinds of learning habits that they identified in themselves, namely, a tendency to sit back and absorb a traditional Socratic lecture. Throughout the process, candidates perceived no real deviations from traditional teaching strategies; any differences between the lessons enacted by their peers were due to personality differences. The lessons that were taught in the physics course in September were firmly rooted in a traditional approach to teaching and learning physics: teacher-centred, with a focus on telling the right answers and sharing solutions to problems. Perhaps the real value of lesson study was to give teacher candidates an experience to learn from their inner default teaching moves that they have developed over many years of primary, secondary, and tertiary education. Again, we come to the importance of confronting the socializing effects of the apprenticeship of observation.

Learning from Peers

The teacher candidates who participated in the study indicated that they learned from their interactions with other teacher candidates, both within the context of the physics course and within the context of the entire program. Comments about how candidates learned from peers in the physics course centred on the interactions that were a result of the lesson study exercise, which was discussed in the previous theme. The overall perception that candidates had of their peers during lesson study varied considerably. In the first focus group interview, Paul asked:

> I think we've all had a positive experience [in the physics course] but do you get the sense that there are people in the class who are feeling a lot differently from us? Do you think that there are people who are going, "I can't believe we are doing ... this is such a waste of time." There is a weird atmosphere; I am not sure what it means. (FG1, 70)

David agreed, although he was quick to point out that he had not heard any specific comments. James had not heard any comments from his peers one way or the other. Max theorized that "there are some people [in the class] who don't take comments or suggestions [from lesson study] that well" (FG1, 71). Irene commented at length on Paul's questions to the focus group:

> I think that part of [the atmosphere] is that it is so different every day. I honestly think that I get something out of it because you see good ideas about what to do and what not to do and you see the different takes people have on teaching the same lesson. But even, it depends on the day, how much people are getting out of it. If you have a good day and everybody had something new or different to offer, you might feel like you are getting something better out of it. I personally never felt the time was wasted. But some days, maybe the lessons were all kind of dry and that feels a bit more negative, and you come out of that feeling tired. But I don't feel like I've gotten any bad vibes from anyone on the whole about the experience. Because we have four presentations a day, it is hard for them all to be ... I just mean that could be where people might get the negative ideas from. (FG1, 76)

Thus four of the five teacher candidates in the study sensed some tension associated with how they learned from and with their peers in the physics course. Candidates perceived that there were different degrees to which their peers engaged with the lesson study process, and this resulted in a classroom atmosphere that was occasionally off-putting for the participants.

Participants found many of their interactions with other teacher candidates in the program to be overwhelming. Paul commented on the intensity of interactions with other candidates:

> One thing that I've been shocked about in coming here is that everyone takes it *so* [italics added] seriously .... I am really not used to taking things so seriously.

When things get too serious I usually make a joke. It's been kind of overwhelming in that sense, which is kind of refreshing because I am genuinely concerned about quality of education and quality of teaching. (FG1, 96)

Everything's important. It's important to do this, it's important to do that. Even the teacher candidates, you get into your groups to do group projects and the teacher will give you something to do, and people will take it so seriously and really try to do what the teacher tells us to do .... There is just this attitude that *everything* [italics added] that comes at you in this program is something to just go with, something to take seriously. (FG1, 101)

David noticed a similar phenomenon in his interactions with candidates outside the physics course, mentioning that many of his peers "are just devastated" (FG1, 61) if the assignments they prepare for courses are not well received by their teacher educators. The intensity with which many candidates approached the program was, according to Irene, directly related to the fact that many of them approached the B.Ed. program as the fulfillment of a lifelong dream. She said: "I want to be a teacher, it's not a non-dream, but it's not like I spent my entire life dreaming of it ... [while other candidates] seem like they have" (FG1, 102).

Despite the intensity with which many candidates approached the program, participants in the study stated that many of their peers complained about the low quality of learning in the program. David disagreed with this negative sentiment, saying "I am getting a ton out of it. I'm paying attention, I'm finding things, I'm pushing, so I am getting something out of it" (FG1, 48). James argued that the quality of learning in the program is a direct result of "what you put into it" (FG1, 47). Irene said that some of her peers figured out early on that it was not as necessary to complete the weekly readings as it was during their undergraduate degrees. Again, despite some of the negative attitudes of her peers, Irene completed her weekly reading assignments, saying "If I do the reading, I feel like I've gotten a lot more out of it. Some people say it's not real learning, but it's just different learning" (FG1, 52).

Candidates were challenged to think in new ways by the diversity of background experiences that many of their peers brought to the B.Ed. program. As David said:

Walking around the halls you come across people who've had a lot of experience, who've had none, and everything in between. Some people who've lived with their subject, some who haven't, and everything in between. There are people, maybe I'm not quite in awe of them, but I think that they are going to be fantastic, and maybe I should work as hard as them to be as positive as them. (FG1, 38)

Max mentioned that the diverse backgrounds of his peers encouraged him to think about equity issues in new ways: "Maybe I'm different than other people, but [equity issues are] something I've never really had to think about .... other people are constantly thinking about it" (FG1, 39). Irene provided a similar, more general comment, saying that she learned by "having people to work with who are in a different place" (Irene1, 8).

CHAPTER 4

The other candidates in the physics class had a profound effect on how lesson study was experienced by the research participants. The perceived lack of interaction in lesson study, discussed in the previous theme, caused some of the participants to feel that the other candidates in the physics course were not as committed to the lesson study process as they might have been. More generally, interactions with other candidates outside of the physics course had an impact on how participants perceived their own learning. Many of the other candidates seemed to approach the B.Ed. program with an intensity born of a lifelong desire to teach, while at the same time complaining about the quality of their learning. Although research participants found the intensity of some of their peers somewhat intimidating, they were generally happy with the quality of learning in the program, feeling that it was up to the individual to make the most of the program experience. Finally, participants felt that the interactions with other candidates who had different background experiences were beneficial to the quality of their learning, often finding that such interactions could catalyze new ways of thinking about issues in education.

Learning from Tom

Teacher candidates clearly stated that they learned about teaching from the way they were taught by Tom during the physics course. They were, however, less clear about *how* Tom's pedagogical strategies affected their learning. For example, Irene offered Tom's use of the Predict-Observe-Explain (POE) teaching strategy as an example of what she learned:

> I'd never seen a POE before I came here .... When I saw the first one I didn't know how it would work [for me] because I didn't know if I'd be very good at leading a discussion like that, but seeing them was pretty inspiring. (FG1, 1)

It is telling that Irene focused on her personal response to POE, instead of how she might use POE as a teaching strategy during her upcoming practicum placement. When candidates were asked how they learned from the lesson study experience, their initial reaction was "I am getting E and M [electricity and magnetism] drilled into me" (FG1, 67). Paul commented that "it's interesting that our [initial] answer to your question is that we know E and M really well now" (FG1, 68). They naturally focused on the familiar physics content of Tom's pedagogical strategy, perhaps because they had not yet developed a sophisticated of a language for talking about teaching and learning. David elaborated on this possibility:

> The nature of what we're doing makes it hard to answer ... all in all, it's been a positive experience and I am getting something out of it ... I don't have the words to describe what I am getting out of it [the physics course]. It is more of a feel. I know that I have the sense that I am definitely benefiting from it. (FG1, 69)

Candidates were more inclined to describe a general, positive feeling about the effect that Tom's teaching strategies were having on their learning rather than name specific effects of those strategies.

Despite the difficulty the candidates had in naming learning effects, David was able to articulate a contrast between Tom's pedagogy and other learning experiences that he was having in the program:

> I've been completely sort of turned upside down by this course. Right from the get-go, starting from Tom's just changing things up and his style and even the class is so different from all of the others, or most of the others, anyways. Right off the bat two days of thinking ... Realizing how differently I and maybe others react to what he is doing. Thinking that maybe this is the way or a way to go in teaching physics. More of the hands-on involvement style as opposed to presenting the material. (David1, 3)

David went on to suggest that Tom's pedagogy results in a low-risk, positive, environment:

> Here we are in this [physics] class, that pressure isn't being put upon us, nothing is make or break, you can try what you want. We have our professor saying, this is maybe a way that you want to go, aim for these kinds of goals and objectives, but other than that, do what you want. We have huge flexibility, not ridiculous pressure ... we aren't getting something that is super-negative. (FG1, 62)

For David, Tom's pedagogy "really comes back to 'trust the learner'" (David1, 4). Max picked up a similar thread: "From the beginning Tom believed that we could all do this" (Max1, 8). Both David and Max felt that the trust that Tom gave the class inspired them to pay careful attention to physics class. David remarked that he "put [his] effort toward this class and got the [physics] assignment finished first ... because we've been given all these latitudes [such as flexible deadlines for assignments]" (David1, 36). Max felt that the trust that Tom placed in the candidates had an opposite effect to what one might expect; instead of becoming lazy about deadlines, candidates in the physics course were "motivated to do things .... everyone's involved pretty well" (Max1, 6).

Teacher candidates who participated in the study seemed to see Tom's class as a productive place to learn, although they found it difficult to articulate what they learned from how Tom taught. There were a few easily named teaching strategies that got their attention, such as POEs and Lesson Study, but the trust that Tom placed in the class resonated much more powerfully with two of the five participants. The issue of trusting the learner stands out in particular because it suggests that they were treated somewhat differently in physics class than in the rest of the program.

Looking Ahead to the Practicum Experience

Although the teacher candidates had not yet had a practicum experience during the first round of data collection, they did talk about their expectations and hopes for the upcoming October practicum period. The comments that these five teacher candidates made can be summarized by two themes: a desire to succeed and trepidation about the impact they might have on students' learning. Often, candidates spoke of these themes at the same time:

> If I can get through the first practicum without completely messing up someone's knowledge ... if I can get the content right and I can keep some sort of decorum in the classroom, then I'm good to go .... Then, try and pique some interests and try and get some kids really interested in what we're doing at the time. Anything over and above that ... well, you call that a bonus for your first time around. (FG1, 77)

Both David and Irene spoke about the importance they placed on not "messing up anyone's knowledge" (FG1, 77; 83), as though enacting a particular pedagogy could have lasting detrimental effects on their students' abilities to construct knowledge. Max had a similar worry, "I've always been bad at slowing down for what pace I should be going at to make sure everyone gets everything by the time I move on" (FG1, 95).

Most of the comments about the upcoming practicum were quite positive. James said that he wanted to "take everything in and use it as a major learning experience" and "try different things in the classroom" (James1, 27). Irene looked forward to teaching physics because she felt there were "hands-on things readily available to show students" (Irene1, 21). Max noted that it would be important to try new things on practicum, although he suggested that lesson study showed him that "it's really hard to avoid teaching like you've been taught" (Max1, 5). Paul looked forward to "figuring out what high school is like" (FG1, 131) because his own high school experiences seemed distant. Overall, the teacher candidates were excited to begin their practicum experiences.

When thinking ahead to the practicum, Paul and David took a slightly different position than the other teacher candidates. Although they were both excited to begin their school placements, both expressed some reservation about how their relationships with students and associate teachers would unfold. Paul wanted "a reminder that [teaching] is something [that he] is good at" (FG1, 97), in part to counteract the "seriousness" (FG1, 95) that he observed in the other teacher candidates, an observation that seemed related to his sense of self-efficacy as a teacher. He was also concerned about "being the teacher all of a sudden," especially the "weird balance" between being approachable as a teacher and "being an authority figure" (FG1, 83). David was more concerned about developing a productive relationship with his associate teacher, because he had "been convinced" (FG1, 87) of the benefits of non-traditional pedagogy:

> Maybe the thing that is continuously going up against me is that maybe it isn't done that way in the field, in schools, especially if we have a teacher who is very "old-school" ... since I think I've really bought into a certain way of thinking here so far, a set of principles .... My worry is, "Am I going to be able to practice what I've been taught?" How will that be received by the teacher or teachers at the school? Are they going to be open to that [new way of teaching] or are we going to be required to conform? (FG1, 120)

David's biggest concern about the practicum was a fear that he would not be able to enact student-centred pedagogies, a non-traditional approach to teaching and learning that he had taken very much to heart. At the end of the focus group interview, David went so far as to suggest that he was "more ready to go and start [his] own class at the beginning of the year than [he was] to go and work with someone else's class," (FG1, 127) adding, "I am more scared about going in halfway through a class and working with kids who are used to a teacher than I would be right at the beginning" (FG1, 129).

The teacher candidates who participated in this study were both hopeful for and anxious about their upcoming practica. They looked forward to opportunities to try to teach according to their various pedagogical visions, but at the same time they were concerned about "messing up" students' understanding of curricular content. There was a general sense that the practicum was something that needed to happen; candidates were thirsting for their first experiences in host schools. David perceived the potential for a gap between the kind of teaching he would like to enact and the kind of teaching he expected to find, as well as the kind of teaching his associate teachers would allow. Although he bought into the active-learning ideas from the physics methods course, he sensed that most classrooms do not typically involve active learning.

LEARNING EXPERIENCES IN THE PHYSICS CLASS: TEACHER EDUCATORS

From the perspective of the teacher educators, the month of September can be represented by one overarching theme: learning from lesson study. The lesson study pedagogy represented a significant departure from the ways in which Tom had previously started his physics curriculum class. As mentioned earlier, lesson study took up approximately three-quarters of the class time in September. More significantly, this was the first time that Tom included lesson study as a part of his pedagogy of teacher education. Having been a part of three different September start-ups of the physics curriculum class, including one as a teacher candidate, I was uniquely positioned to help Tom interpret this new pedagogy.

The data interpreted in this section are presented chronologically using quotations and observations from my research journal. Data in my journal include my notes during each physics class and the notes I kept during conversations that Tom and I had over the month. The quotations listed in this section are based on transcriptions that I created as part of an observation journal and hence are cited using (Journal, September).

Setting the Stage for Lesson Study

Tom began the year by using Predict-Observe-Explain (POE) pedagogy as a way to create a low-risk environment and a commitment to exploring concepts rather than seeking answers. On the first day of class, he used most of the time to lead two POE sequences designed to encourage candidates to talk about the parallels between learning physics and learning to teach physics. He also drew the candidates

into dialogue about the effects of the POEs on their learning by asking several questions:
- What did you notice about what it was like to be learning using the POE approach?
- What features of your learning did you notice by virtue of my using POE to teach you?
- Did anyone feel embarrassed during the POE?
- What tends to make people feel embarrassed in a classroom setting?

(Journal, September)

By focusing on teaching strategies and learning effects rather than on the correct answer, Tom tried to set the stage for the risks that would be required by lesson study. He drew attention to the fact that the POE activities yielded a variety of predictions and explanations, despite the fact that everyone in the class had significant post-secondary study of physics. Implicit in the discussion was the notion that obtaining the right answer was less important than attending to the process of teaching and learning.

After beginning the second class with another POE, Tom introduced the concept of lesson study. Candidates were organized into groups of four and asked to prepare two 20-minute lessons, each to be taught twice to allow for improvements before the second presentation. Each group was asked to base its lessons on a different part of the electricity and magnetism units in the Ontario curriculum. Tom emphasized the atmosphere of trust created by doing POEs, saying:

> One of the things that is going to be really important is that everyone is going to feel a little uncomfortable when they present 20 minutes at the front .... We are going to be good students because we are going to be listening to the learning effects that the teaching has on us. We are never going to criticize one another in terms of "Do x instead of y." We are going to develop a team atmosphere, saying things like "Maybe if you did it this way, you might have this kind of learning effect." (Journal, September)

In the interest of making the risk of doing lesson study transparent, Tom reminded the candidates that the pedagogy was also new to him. He described his reasoning in these words:

> I am pretty sure that this is a different tack from your other curriculum course. Some of you might feel like you're missing out. I've been in this building too many years to be offended if an associate teacher asks you to forget everything you learned here in September. Everything you are told here is likely to go down the drain on the first day [of practicum] in October. Focusing on how teaching is affecting learning is far more useful than 6000 tips on how to teach physics. (Journal, September)

By explicitly describing the reasons for engaging in lesson study, Tom showed how a teacher educator can explicitly model his or her practice and create links between enacted pedagogies and theoretical literature.

Our discussion immediately following the second class helped us to identify some of the broad issues that we noticed after introducing lesson study. Tom commented:

> The issues around how I went into the lesson study were partly due to doing it for the first time. I wasn't unhappy with the way it came out. I actually felt an enormous amount of relief when I asked what they were making of things ... and I got the comment that something different was going to happen in this class. (Journal, September)

Perhaps it is not surprising that, as teacher, Tom's first comments about lesson study focused on how he set up the process and his initial reading of the candidates' reactions. Tom also mentioned that he was pleased that he changed the focus of the next class into planning time for lesson study. I had also picked up on the importance of giving the candidates additional time for lesson study:

> I think that giving more time for lesson study underscored your message of "We'll figure it out together as we go." I don't know what specifically made you make the decision, but there was certainly a palpable sense of relief—not that they didn't think they could do it, but just to have that time to sit with their group again. It was good that you had the opportunity to show that you are flexible by changing plans on the spot .... It came across as "I am listening to what you are saying and here is what we are going to do instead." (Journal, September)

Our post-class discussion allowed us to begin to understand how Tom continued to build trust in his classroom. A simple gesture such as allotting time in the next class for candidates to continue planning their lessons helped to underscore the supportive environment that he was trying to develop.

Beginning Lesson-study Presentations

Teacher candidates began presenting their lessons during the fourth class. At the outset, Tom asked the candidates to be mindful of the powerful tendency in teacher education to tell teachers about better ways to teach. This was intended to encourage candidates to think about pedagogy in terms of teaching strategies and learning effects, rather than in terms of best practices. During the first presentation, I recorded the following notes:

> The candidates were very polite and paid rapt attention to their peer who was brave enough to go first. One of the interesting things was that I could have predicted how the lesson would proceed. The candidate fell back on all the default practices of what he has seen teachers do time and time again. I could also have predicted the kind of assessment he would receive from an associate or a faculty liaison: voice control, pacing, timing, moving on quickly after the right answer was elicited. There was a demonstration so that it felt like a science class. (Journal, September)

At the conclusion of the first lesson, Tom called the candidates' attention to the influence of the apprenticeship of observation by asking "Where did he learn to do

CHAPTER 4

what he just did? Has he learned to teach that way in 10 days of classes?" (Journal, September). The candidates were then asked to record observations about the lesson on whiteboards in their small groups. When the whiteboards were displayed at the front of the class, Tom and Shawn both noted the striking similarity between the kinds of comments that candidates made about their peer's teaching and the kinds of comments they were likely to receive from associate teachers. Returning to the ideas that he introduced at the beginning of the class, Tom stated, "A lot of this reads like 'do X instead of Y.' What I am struggling with is that we haven't named the learning effects .... Can we get better, individually and collectively, at naming the learning effect?" (Journal, September). Tom challenged the candidates to attend to this issue when they made comments about the remaining lessons.

Difficulty Identifying Learning Effects

The link between teaching strategies and learning effects was a difficult concept for teacher candidates to understand and articulate. After the second presentation, the candidates continued to make comments in the language of best practices. When Tom commented on how the comments still were not focused on learning effects, several teacher candidates argued that there was merely a semantic difference between a comment such as "do X instead of Y" and a comment such as "the teaching strategy affected my learning in X ways." As Tom encouraged the candidates to talk more about teaching strategies and learning effects, I was thinking about learning effects from my position at the back of the classroom. I noted:

> The semantic differences matter because [phrasing things in terms of learning effects] might serve as a reminder that people are affected by things in different ways. If pedagogy is a unified whole, is it a fair question to ask for the learning effects to be teased out from the teaching strategies, or is it more appropriate to ask for phrases with conjunctions? Saying "The learning effect was A because the teacher did B" is different from saying "The teacher should do X because Y." Is the suggestion being made to conform to a perceived best practice, or is the suggestion being made to address a particular feature of the learning? (Journal, September)

I continued to think about the differences during the third candidate's lesson. Tom ended the class by asking candidates to anonymously record something that they learned about teaching and learning on an index card on their way out.

We explored the issue of learning effects in our discussion after class. We both felt that there was a qualitative difference in the kinds of comments the candidates made after they were asked to attend to the effects that particular teaching strategies had on their own learning. The anonymous comments that the candidates wrote revealed that many resisted the concept of a learning effect and felt that comments pertaining to trying specific teaching strategies were more valuable. We agreed that it was important to be patient with the candidates' focus on trying to tell one another how to teach, rather than talking about how they were learning. Their preference to talk about teaching rather than learning seemed to us to be one important element of the socializing effects of the apprenticeship of observation.

Before the sixth class, several candidates raised concerns about the lesson study process. Specifically, some candidates seemed upset with a perceived lack of participation from their peers. Often, the candidate teaching the lesson would ask for some sort of input from the audience and no one would respond. Candidates were asked to change their seating arrangement at the beginning of class, in the hope that sitting with different people would encourage more discussion and participation. The end of the sixth class was the halfway point in the exercise, as each group had presented its lessons once. Tom called attention to the fact that "it can feel like pulling teeth up here [in the role of teacher]" (Journal, September) and encouraged candidates to pay attention to those situations.

During the post-observation discussion, Tom and I discussed the difficulties that some candidates articulated with the process of lesson study. I felt that the silent majority in the class was slipping into a default student mode and that perhaps candidates were discouraged by some of the reactions from their peers, given the amount of time that they put into planning their lessons. I also noted that candidates, like many teachers, might have a tendency to say that there is a problem with the students, rather than with the lesson itself. Tom took a slightly different angle and brought the focus of the discussion back to the level of risk required by these short lesson-study presentations:

> They are revealing a lot about themselves in this class that they are not revealing in other classes. There may be some reaction here that it is too much, too quickly. I realize that I am getting to see sides of them that I never would have otherwise, but I think that in the long run, there is a payoff. (Journal, September)

Making Suggestions after Some Initial Teaching Experiences

Later that evening, Tom sent an email to the class to draw attention to many of the issues that had been raised. He included the following suggestions for candidates to consider when revising their lessons:
– We are not looking for perfection, just an improved approach that has reasons!
– Work whenever possible to move beyond "traditional" approaches (whatever that means—familiar, comfortable) to a plan that helps "students" be more active, more challenged, and more engaged in the lesson.
– Focus on a Concept—and name your concept somewhere in your plan.
– Just a thought—don't be afraid to stop at any point in the lesson, step out of your teacher role, and ask the class how they feel about particular aspects of what you are doing.
– Also, don't be afraid to call on people by name if you don't get responses—very few people have tried that so far, but that's always an option so it might be good to explore now.

By framing the email as a series of suggestions, Tom tried to encourage candidates to think about the concerns we articulated during our post-observation discussions. The email was powerful because until that class Tom had made few comments about the candidates' teaching. It seems particularly important that the comments focused on suggestions for improving the process, rather than on specific teaching strategies. He wanted to encourage candidates to think about how to improve the quality of their interactions with the class, and he thought that the ways in which the lessons changed would be an important marker for thinking about what candidates learned from the experience.

We both noticed significant differences during the second round of lessons. The most obvious difference was that candidates were trying to enact slightly riskier pedagogy, including a few demonstrations and POEs. There was more of an effort to engage the class in discussion, and Tom was more vocal about drawing candidates' attention to details such as font size on the overhead and the importance of admitting when one is lost in the middle of a derivation. At the same time, however, Tom was quick to comment that people will initially teach as they were taught, not as they were told to teach. At the end of the seventh class, Tom reiterated that he was using lesson study in the hope "that there will be connections between experiences and preconceptions in this class and what happens when you come back" (Journal, September).

One of the most significant challenges of enacting lesson study pedagogy was working out how to conclude the experience in a meaningful way that flowed naturally into the first practicum. After the final two lessons during the ninth and final class before practicum, Tom distributed a sheet of paper entitled "The Big Picture after 4 Weeks in Physics Class." Candidates were asked to try to describe some of their new perspectives on teaching and learning from (a) planning lessons in a group, (b) watching others teach, (c) presenting their own lessons, and (d) working with equipment for teaching electromagnetism. After 15 minutes of writing, Tom led a discussion based on the writing task.

Teacher candidates reported that, although they planned in groups, ultimately the way in which a particular lesson was enacted depended on the person at the front of the room. They also felt that planning a lesson as a group was quite time-consuming. Tom commented that he was particularly impressed with the fact that the groups got together on their own time to plan, without any prompting to do so. The candidates agreed that watching one another teach was a good way to learn different ways to think about physics content and how to present that content. A few candidates stated that they watched their peers with an interest in finding ideas on how to teach particularly challenging topics. The class seemed to unanimously agree that there was no reason for concepts in electromagnetism to be presented as dryly as they often are at the high school level.

The richest portion of the discussion centred on what candidates learned about their teaching as a result of lesson study. The general consensus was that knowing physics is not the same as knowing how to teach physics. We suspect that this realization was underscored by the feeling created in the class by the few candidates who tried to improvise their first lesson. Tom took the opportunity at the end of class to emphasize the link between providing experiences in teaching via lesson study and providing experiences in physics via POEs:

> I have always been fond of the idea of letting students have some experience with the stuff before you teach them the theory, and then let them go back

and ask them how things are different now. We don't give them much of a sense of the before-and-after; perhaps that is part of the reason kids walk away without a good conceptual understanding of physics. There is an incredible sense in science teaching of tell first, explore later. (Journal, October)

Ending the semester with a reminder that teaching is built on a culture of telling was an important way to bring the lesson study experiences full circle. Tom began the term by providing a POE experience that was unlike what students typically encounter on the first day of class. He ended the term by naming the experience of lesson study as a way of pushing the notion of "explore first, explain later" (Journal, October).

CONSTRUCTING PROFESSIONAL KNOWLEDGE FROM TEACHING AND LEARNING EXPERIENCES

Teacher candidates coming from physics backgrounds naturally began their conversations about teaching and learning with familiar rhetoric about learning physics. The idea that teaching-is-telling immediately came to their minds. The cultural routines of teaching internalized via the apprenticeship of observation, both at the secondary and tertiary levels of education, are particularly powerful as these effects seemed to be the bedrock on which candidates grounded their assumptions about teaching and learning. Candidates said that their prior conceptions of teaching physics were essentially limited to transmission models of education. Teaching physics was initially framed as a tension between explaining physics concepts and demonstrating mathematical equations through problem solving. The big pedagogical question for candidates was one of order: Should concepts be taught before formulas or after?

The effects of the apprenticeship of observation influenced not only candidates' assumptions about teaching and learning, but also their assumptions about what can and should be learned at the Faculty of Education. Essentially, candidates expected that a teacher education program would tell them the most effective ways to enact transmission-based pedagogies, while also providing plenty of opportunities to practise the same teaching moves they had witnessed former physics teachers and professors make time and time again. The teaching practice that teacher candidates had been exposed to over their entire lives is the same practice that helped them become successful students. It is precisely the same kind of teaching practice that, coming into the preservice program, they expected to be exposed to from professors at a faculty of education. The long apprenticeship of observation generated many prior assumptions that candidates had about teaching and learning.

During September, the effects of the apprenticeship of observation on teacher candidates were seen to be disrupted in three ways. The first and arguably most important disruption came in the form of the lesson study pedagogy. Here teacher candidates were encouraged to interpret their prior assumptions about teaching while confronting those inner teachers we all have inside us, created over many years of observing other people teach. Perhaps it was the tacit nature of the apprenticeship of observation that made it so difficult for candidates to plan lessons in groups; they were at once discovering their default teaching moves and trying to negotiate how to plan lessons with peers who were making similar discoveries about their own ideas about teaching. David and Paul found it particularly difficult to plan their lessons in a group because they were trying to interpret their default teaching moves and the needs of their groups, while also coming to terms with their self-imposed expectations to enact new pedagogies based on ideas that had resonated with them during the physics class. Strong dissonance occurred for these two candidates in particular, as evidenced by their repeated use of adjectives such as *frustrated* and *disappointed*.

The teacher candidates who participated in the study noticed the tendency of their classmates to plan and enact lessons based on traditional, transmission-oriented approaches to teaching and learning. Again, this tendency was of particular concern for David and Paul, both of whom indicated that they were disturbed by the lesson study experience. Both saw the potential for lesson study to push their thinking about teaching and learning in new directions; both felt that the experience fell short of its potential. In particular, David and Paul were frustrated by a perceived lack of willingness in the class to engage in discussions about the quality of teaching and learning during lesson study.

Peer interactions also had the potential to disrupt the effects of the apprenticeship of observation. Four of the five participants noted that there was some level of tension among people in the physics class during the lesson study process. Irene commented that the entire process felt exhausting, that there were good and bad days, and that any perceived tension was probably a result of feeling overloaded by lesson study. Thus the tension between candidates in the physics class may have reduced the possibility that peer feedback could disturb the effects of the apprenticeship of observation. In contrast, teacher candidates consistently reported that their interactions with other teacher candidates in the program, outside of physics class, encouraged them to reconsider many of their prior assumptions about teaching and learning. The diversity of perspectives offered by other teacher candidates in the program was a significant factor in disrupting participants' prior assumptions.

Finally, the pedagogy that Tom used throughout the month of September seemed to disrupt some of the effects of candidates' apprenticeships of observation. Although the participants were largely unable to name particular features of his pedagogy that had specific effects on their learning, they did speak of a different *feeling* in Tom's class. Tom's classroom was perceived as a low-risk environment that was grounded in his trust of the candidates. In particular, David was impressed by the degree of trust placed in candidates as shown by his enthusiasm for Tom's flexibility about due dates for assignments. A focus on *trusting the learner*, to borrow a phrase from David, represented a disruption of candidates' apprenticeship of observation. It is interesting that feeling trusted seemed to represent such a radical departure from candidates' previous experiences of school.

Lesson study was an explicit attempt to disrupt the effects of the apprenticeship of observation. From the perspective of a teacher educator, the pedagogy was viewed as a mixed success. Although Tom was able to create an environment in which candidates felt trusted and respected, lesson study may have been too complicated for teacher candidates at this early stage in their careers. Despite Tom's explicit modelling of how to talk about the effects particular teaching strategies had on learning, candidates were mostly unable to differentiate between teaching strategies and learning effects. This critical realization helped Tom and I understand the extent to which we had underestimated the effects of the apprenticeship of observation. The difficulty that candidates had talking about learning effects was a direct result of a lifetime of observing and learning to mimic teachers' behaviours. In hindsight, it was unrealistic to expect candidates to be able to do anything other than offer corrective advice about how to behave more like a teacher. It is unlikely that candidates' past educational experiences provided them with significant opportunities to systematically explore the effects of particular pedagogies on their own learning. Although candidates had witnessed thousands of hours of teaching, they had not had opportunities to explore the means-ends relationship between teaching strategies and learning effects. Instead, as Ethell and McMeniman (2000, p. 98) suggested, "they had been left to guess" about the pedagogical intentions of expert practitioners. Rare is the teacher who makes learning about learning the primary focus of a day's lesson.

In summary, September was a month of disruption. The degree and nature of the disruption of the apprenticeship of observation was varied but present across all five participants. They spoke of the ways in which their prior assumptions were challenged by Tom's pedagogy, including but not limited to lesson study and interactions with their peers. Two participants showed evidence of experiencing particularly strong dissonance between their prior assumptions about teaching and learning and their visions of the kind of teachers they wished to become. The traditional language that candidates use to discuss issues of teaching and learning began to move away from metaphors for telling about physics and toward metaphors associated with active learning. The teacher educators' perspective was also disrupted by the events of September. Although the effects of the apprenticeship of observation had been recognized in the past, the lesson study pedagogy provided fresh insight into the critically powerful role that prior experiences play in teacher candidates' development. The apprenticeship of observation creates an inner, default teacher in each of us as it also shapes and limits the language we use to talk about teaching.

CHAPTER 5

CANDIDATES IN CRISIS

I came back and a lot of my classes pretended we weren't just away on practicum. Like we came back and ... [it was] "Let's continue on doing whatever we were doing before ... so I don't really bring any of my practicum experience into this class at all." It's almost like they [teacher educators] are trying to treat it [the program] as four months of in-school and then four months of practicum, but just arranged it [alternating and separately]. (Max2, 20)

One of the most common findings in research on teacher education is that candidates place a high value on the practicum; some use the amount of time spent on practicum as a barometer of the quality of their learning in a teacher education program. Teacher candidates come to a program expecting to have a productive learning experience in school with a supportive associate teacher that will help them navigate the early days of their teaching careers. Many candidates are particularly conscious of the role that their practicum evaluations play in their ability to secure a job interview. For this reason, teacher candidates can feel an enormous pressure to impress the staff at their host schools, particularly if their practicum occurs in a school board where they would like to secure a teaching position.

The previous chapter indicated that participants in this study had both a strong desire to succeed during their placement and a fear of making mistakes that would have a negative impact on the quality of their students' learning. Such feelings are natural, but may also set the stage for teacher candidates to experience a significant amount of tension throughout their practicum as they constantly try to strike a balance between focusing on their development as new teachers, on pleasing their associate teacher, and on the quality of their students' learning. It is not surprising that, at the end of a month-long practicum block, teacher candidates typically feel tired and a bit burned out even if they are enjoying their practicum experience.

Anyone who has taught in a Faculty of Education has experienced the remarkable change in the building's atmosphere when candidates go on field experience, making hallways and classrooms seem underused. It might seem obvious to state that teacher educators do not go through the practicum placement experience with teacher candidates. It is less obvious, however, to draw attention to what can happen if teacher educators are not mindful of this fact. Even faculty liaisons, who are responsible for visiting teacher candidates during practicum placements, spend relatively little time with candidates in schools. What happens, then, if teacher educators pick up their courses where they left off when candidates return, as though the month in schools did not happen? During a practicum placement, teacher candidates have almost undoubtedly gone through a significant set of experiences that have affected them both cognitively and emotionally. Candidates have different learning needs as the result of their first practicum placement. How can teacher educators respond to and value these needs? In particular, how can teacher educators respond to teacher candidates experiencing a significant crisis of confidence?

The opening section of this chapter describes the major events that occurred during the physics course in this block of classes. The data obtained from the focus group and individual interviews are then analyzed for insights into how teacher candidates were constructing professional knowledge from learning experiences in the physics course. Selected narratives of the candidates' practicum experiences are then presented in order to reveal many of the tensions associated with constructing professional knowledge during the practicum. The next section provides the perspective and voice of the teacher educator as I analyze the discussions Tom and I engaged in during the November block. The chapter concludes with a summary of the professional knowledge constructed and co-constructed by the teacher candidates and the teacher educators who participated in this study.

CONTEXTUAL FEATURES OF THE PHYSICS METHODS COURSE

The physics curriculum course reconvened on the first Monday in November and met for an additional five classes, concluding on the third Thursday in November. Tom began this block of classes by giving candidates time to talk in small groups about their practicum experiences. The database for the Project for Enhancing Effective Learning (PEEL) (Baird & Northfield, 1992) was presented to candidates as a source of active-learning pedagogies during the second class. The second week of the November block focused on preparing for and processing a visit from Professor Randy Knight of California Polytechnic State University. His book *Five Easy Lessons* was one of the required course texts, and Tom had arranged an interactive presentation by Knight during the second week of classes. After Knight's visit, Tom devoted a class to exploring characteristics of simple DC circuits and to introducing the concept of a Think-Aloud. The final class concluded with a presentation by a local associate teacher of physics who incorporates many active-learning pedagogies in his classroom.

LEARNING EXPERIENCES IN THE PHYSICS CLASS: TEACHER CANDIDATES

The data provided by the participants during the focus group interview and the individual follow-up interviews were analyzed with a view to understanding how teacher candidates construct knowledge from learning experiences during a physics methods course. Four themes are considered in this section: Learning from the Program, Learning from Peers, Learning from Tom, and Theorizing Teaching and Learning. The first theme focuses on how teacher candidates learned from the structure of the program, with a particular emphasis on the transitions from Queen's to host schools and back to Queen's again. The second two themes focus on learning that occurs as a result of the physics methods course. Finally, the last theme explores the theories about teaching and learning that participants constructed as a result of their experiences.

Learning from the Program

Teacher candidates who participated in this study indicated two major ways in which the overall program contributed to their learning. First, the rhythm of the initial months of the program provided different kinds of teaching and learning experiences, on-campus and in host schools, for the candidates to consider. Second, the expectations and assumptions that teacher candidates had for their learning in the program appeared to be significantly different during the month of November. This section interprets both aspects of how candidates learned from the program.

The rhythm of the program, namely, one month at the Faculty in September followed by 4 weeks of practicum followed by a return to campus for 3 weeks, forced candidates to attend to the effects that two very different types of learning experiences had on their professional development. When faced with the prospect of returning to campus in November, James (FG2, 98) stated that he "was a little annoyed because [he was] just getting into how to teach and [he] wanted to continue on with the material." Max felt the same way, saying that the transition to campus "interrupted [me] just as [I was] getting into the class" (Max2, 19) and that he had "started figuring out the flow of everything" (FG2, 100). Irene commented on the "weird" shift from practicum back to the Faculty:

> The transition was weird because I went from trying to be professional and being on time every day back to being a little more relaxed, which is probably bad because I'm always late, but, you know, in the weird sense, [being at the Faculty] is kind of relaxing. (Irene2, 24)

David felt that the transition from practicum to Faculty was a welcome change:

> By the end of that fourth week [of practicum], it was kind of like hanging on by my teeth, in terms of the workload was that close to getting me. I was a hair shy of getting behind, un-recoverably getting behind .... I was looking forward to some sleep. A couple of weeks where I could get to the gym. Revisit and talk to other people about how their placements have gone. I guess that was my initial thought; I thought that I wanted to see how things were going for other people. (David2, 13)

Despite initial misgivings about returning to the Faculty, both James and Max admitted in their individual interviews that the interruption to the practicum provided an opportunity to think about their learning on practicum. James said, "the three weeks here [at the Faculty] actually give you a chance to think" (James2, 22) while Max said that by the end of October he felt he "could definitely use a break" (Max2, 18).

The break provided by the on-campus weeks was a productive use of time for some of the candidates because "it forced us to stop and think about what we did" (Irene2, 24). James found that the on-campus weeks provided time to "get some good advice on … what we're going to need to do when the time comes to start looking for jobs" (James2, 22). During the focus group, Irene made a comment that seemed to resonate with the group: "On a basic level, this [first] week is the break week and next week is catching up and the third week is when everything is due"

(FG2, 97). By the end of the three weeks, Paul was ready to go back to his host school because he was frustrated with the assignments he had to do on-campus:

> I think I'm kind of ready to start doing things again that I care about. If I have something due for class [on practicum] the next day, it'll be something that I want to do well and that I'm eager to get done, you know? As opposed to this assignment [for Queen's] that's ... I'm not really sure why I'm supposed to be writing a five-page essay about a poorly written article, about a very specific subject. In that sense, I think I'm looking forward to having work that's my own work and work that I care about. (Paul2, 10)

Paul's obvious frustration with the kinds of things he was being asked to do in the program underscored his changing expectations of the program. Increasingly, the participants in the study were recognizing some dissatisfaction with the teacher education program as a whole. As David noted in the second focus group, "I've seen people put their heads down here, just to tune out ... Now we understand why high school students do it" (FG2, 73).

Paul and David expressed the greatest dissatisfaction with the program as a whole at this point in the year. Although their needs as learners had changed as a result of the practicum, some of the elements of the teacher education program had not changed significantly in response to those changing needs. David noted that "this time around is just worse and worse in terms of classes that seem to be too open, or too restrictive, or too much information to digest, or not interesting at all ... Finally we're getting into a bit of that busy work that everyone talks about in a program like this" (David2, 21). Paul also commented on a general lack of intellectual engagement with the program, a feeling he did not experience in September:

> My frustrations with the classes right now have to do with a lot of talk of very little content sometimes ... [classes are] different from September .... It's either kind of a lecture that doesn't really have much interest or else it's a kind of group discussion where I'm just forced to sit and listen to everyone else's opinions on things. (Paul2, 50)

Both Paul and David expressed a desire to return to the practicum, the portion of the program that candidates tend to perceive as more relevant and productive.

Now that they had some distance from their early learning experiences in the program, candidates began to talk about the effects that experiences in September had on their learning and how practicum experiences shaped their revised expectations of the program. Although he had a positive outlook, James reported a disconnect between early experiences in the program and the practicum: "I thought September was good. All the theory they taught us was really good. When I got out on my practicum I realized that it's easier said than done" (James2, 24). Paul's perception of September ties in well to the overarching theme of disturbing prior assumptions, discussed in the previous chapter:

> September, I think, it just sort of was trying to shake you up a bit and get you thinking about what you would like to be doing and how you feel about teaching and having some people that could sort of nudge towards certain kinds of philosophies of teaching. (Paul2, 46)

I think there was already a lot of stuff [in September] and I think just sort of having it there, even just sort of in the back of your mind while you were teaching, was still kind of helpful ... just at least hearing it and getting to thinking about it and then sort of planting the seeds. (Paul2, 49)

Max also felt that September was a positive but idealistic learning experience: "Once you've figured out the basic ideas of teaching, you'll want to incorporate all of these things [learned at Queen's] in your teaching" (FG2, 43). Irene agreed with the idea that September put theory in the back of her mind during practicum: "The information was there and it maybe wasn't sinking in as much as it could but after going on practicum and then coming back and hearing some of it again, it really began to sink in much better" (Irene2, 25). David had a somewhat less enthusiastic opinion, stating that the "first week of school [in September] was surprisingly informative, helpful, and interesting" (David2, 18) and then positing that "maybe it was because the expectations [for teacher education] were so low that anything above that was a positive experience" (David2, 20).

The teacher candidates who participated in the research indicated that, although they felt that the program was a productive place for them to learn in September, the on-campus weeks in November generally fell short of their practicum-driven expectations. The candidates felt that the requirement to return to campus in November pulled them from their practicum placements just as they were becoming more familiar with their host schools, although most admitted that the slower pace offered by the Faculty was a welcome change. The major benefit offered by the three on-campus weeks in November was the time provided to think about the practicum experiences, outside the environment of the host school. The learning priorities for candidates were different than in September, when they were content to have their ideas about teaching and learning challenged. The practicum experiences changed their expectations for the program; aspects of the program that did not meet their expectation of helping them make sense of the practicum experience were criticized.

Learning from Peers

The participating teacher candidates continued to be influenced by their peers in the program. Again, the ways in which they learned from interactions with peers in the physics classroom differed from the ways in which they learned from peers in the program as a whole. This theme explores the ways in which participants learned from interactions with other teacher candidates in three different environments: their host schools, the physics course, and the program as a whole.

In the Queen's teacher education program, teacher candidates are assigned to host schools in cohorts ranging in size from about 4 to 20. They are asked to meet as a group once a week during their practica to discuss issues that arise during the week and topics that are suggested by their faculty liaison. The candidates who participated in the study had a mixed reaction to the learning opportunities afforded by these weekly meetings. On the one hand, the weekly meetings had the potential to serve as in-school support groups. As Irene said, "just to have a familiar face that first week and then be able to talk to someone, I found it helpful" (FG2, 115). David agreed: "It was

CHAPTER 5

nice, on day one, walking in the school to spend time with a couple of people I knew" (FG2, 114). James had the most positive view of the weekly meetings: "I found the weekly discussions were good for little teaching tips, learning what teacher candidates did in the class, the activities they did, the methods they used" (FG2, 104). Although there was general agreement about the potential utility of weekly meetings, the consensus was that they were of little value after the first few weeks of practicum: "It added to my workload, every week I had to talk to these people for 3 hours" (FG2, 157). James also noted that the meetings "almost felt like a bit of a competition" (James2, 18), as candidates in his host school would often share stories about the successes they were having in class. David seemed to sum up the thoughts of the group when he stated that, in terms of working through the situations that arose on the practicum, "I just need to do it on my own" (David2, 101).

According to two of the participants in the study, the general tone of candidates in the preservice program was more negative in November than it was in September. James mentioned that he "heard a lot of negative comments" (James2, 27) during the month of November, particularly around the assignments that candidates had to complete. He was quick to add, however, that he "didn't feel that way" (James2, 27) about the program. James appreciated the opportunity that classes provided to "hear what other students had to say … it was nice to hear that some of them had the same concerns" (James2, 5). David was critical of the effects that other teacher candidates had on his learning. In particular, he was upset by the general negative tone among teacher candidates:

> You come back here and it's negativity, negativity, negativity, and it just sucks the desire to teach right out of you …. It's always something that we're all complaining about. I've done my share, you know, but I'd like to think that I look at both sides and if I do complain about something, then I've gone to the professor to express my concern. (David2, 17)

David attributed the increase in complaints from teacher candidates to the recent practicum experience, saying that "now we have 700 experts [the other teacher candidates] in the field of teaching, everyone knows absolutely how things should be done" (David2, 14). He believed that candidates got into a habit of critique due to their relationships with their associate teachers: "You can't talk to anyone about their practicum without some sort of comment about what their associate does wrong" (FG2, 102). According to David, then, teacher candidates became far more critical of the quality of teaching in the program because the month on practicum had given them a warrant to criticize other teachers, in terms of what teacher educators were doing wrong in their teaching.

Although Max stated that "the whole physics class is really friendly … so it makes for a more open discussion" (Max2, 11), Paul was the only candidate who spoke at length about how interactions with his peers in the physics course affected his learning:

> I think that I am kind of frustrated by the people in the class [because] I don't think they're very willing to help [Tom] towards that [student-centred learning] … it's also making it a little harder to see what he's trying to do … but

> I really don't think it's his fault. I think that there's just sort of an attitude that I'm not all that fond of in the class. (Paul2, 12)

Paul was of the opinion that Tom was working toward a "framework" (Paul2, 12) of teaching and learning in the physics class that focused on sharing intellectual control of the class with teacher candidates. He notes a problem with Tom's decision to try to share control of the physics course:

> I think that approach also requires a lot of interest and honesty from people in the class about what they don't know and about what they want to know. And for some reason I feel like it's just this sort of quiet independence idea that everyone has, [a characteristic] which I think probably has served them pretty well for most of undergrad, given [our] backgrounds [in physics]. (Paul2, 16)

Paul's frustration with the physics course was quite different from his frustration with the program as a whole. He found that Tom's classes provided worthwhile learning experiences, but that the quality of these learning experiences depended on the participation of the other candidates as a group. Thus Paul's frustration was not with how the class was being taught, but with what he perceived as a missed opportunity on the part of others in the class.

Learning from Tom

The teacher candidates who participated in the research unanimously felt that Tom's class was a productive place for them to learn, yet they described how they learned in different ways. Irene and James named specific teaching strategies that Tom used that had an effect on how they thought about teaching and learning. Irene stated that "the POEs are really changing my thinking" (Irene2, 4). James felt that Tom's message about the power of active-learning pedagogies remained consistent during November: "Having Randy Knight in and doing the POEs reassured me that doing these sorts of things ... is a good way to get students more involved in class" (James2, 9). The "Dirty Tricks" note-taking PEEL procedure (Baird & Northfield, 1992, p. 254) had a particularly strong effect on James:

> The one thing that really had an influence on me was that exercise that Tom did when he wrote notes on the board. The paragraph that he wrote, as you know, made no sense, and I didn't really realize it made no sense until I was almost finished copying it down. A lot of the other people in the class felt the same way. So it really made me think about when I give notes as a teacher: Are students really thinking about what they're writing down and is it the best way to spend my time, the 75 minutes I have in a classroom? Say, the 15 minutes I would spend writing notes I could spend doing something else so it would be more productive for them, in terms of their learning. (James2, 4)

The way that James articulated his learning was an important step forward, because it represented the type of thinking that Tom was trying to encourage during the lesson study. During the month of September, however, most teacher candidates had particular difficulty linking teaching strategies to learning effects.

CHAPTER 5

Max realized the importance of the relationships that Tom had worked hard to develop in the physics course. He named the effect that Tom's focus on relationships had on his learning:

> Right away, Tom got to know everyone. So I don't want to show up late for Tom's class because Tom knows me and he knows that I don't have any reason to not show up on time ….When you know the person, even if it's hard, you still put in that effort to make it there and stay awake and pay attention. In some other courses where you go and you don't even know the instructors' names, you don't really have that drive. (Max2, 10)

Tom's early effort to connect with teacher candidates played a key role in the amount of effort that Max put into the class. He also felt that the physics course was "structured differently than most things and [he] seemed to be getting more out of it than most other courses that are lectures" (Max2, 2). One other significant thing that Max learned to consider as a result of the physics course was "the idea of preconceptions that people tend to keep" (Max2, 5).

Of the participants, Paul spoke most often about his perceptions of how Tom was teaching the course and offered several ideas about why Tom might be trying to teach the class in particular ways. He also perceived tensions between the ways in which Tom was teaching and the ways in which other teacher candidates in the course were prepared to learn. He believed that some tensions were a result of the nature of the relationship that Tom's pedagogy demanded:

> Tom is considering the relationship he has with us and is probably carefully trying to have us understand that and what he hopes [to accomplish] from it: what he's doing, why he's doing it, and who he is …. I feel like most people in the class aren't really buying it. It's not that they don't trust him or like him or anything …. I could be really wrong, but that's what it seems like; they're not taking him up on it. (Paul2, 25)

Paul's perception of the relationship between Tom and the majority of the candidates in the physics course was a source of frustration for him, as indicated in the previous theme. He still trusted that Tom knew what he was doing: "I feel like Tom, even when he asks us how we feel about everything and he just gets complete silence, I think he still probably has some sense of where things are going" (Paul2, 27). Although Paul was quite sure of the pedagogical importance of the relationship between Tom and the rest of the physics class and of the direction that Tom was leading the class, he was less sure of what that productive direction was:

> Tom doesn't do this sort of like, "Here's the focus today, and we're going to do this and this, and then by the end you're going to have x figured out." He just sort of keeps tossing stuff out …. I feel like [class is] this really sort of complicated thing … I think Tom actually has a lot more figured out than even it probably seems. But I feel more like I'm sort of slowly kind of getting a sense of his idea of teaching and not even in a way that I'm really able to express yet, I don't think. But certainly his ideas of classroom dynamics, although I don't think he's being very successful with that because I'm getting a

little frustrated with our class being too quiet, but I can see what he's trying to do and what he's hoping for, I think. And I think I can see some value in that .... I feel like we just keep getting more and more tastes of it and slightly different ways of looking at it in different kinds of activities that follow that sort of framework. But he never seems to want to conclude anything. He never seems to want to say, "So there you go. That's this." (Paul2, 11)

Paul's comments imply a belief that more co-operation from the other members of the class would help Tom to teach more effectively and thereby help the teacher candidates to take more from the class. Paul's beliefs seemed grounded in a deep trust in Tom's skills as a teacher; he believes that he can learn from what and how Tom teaches. Despite his frustrations, Paul is optimistic at this point in the year: "I think Tom's class is sort of a work-in-progress idea" (Paul2, 45).

Theorizing Teaching and Learning

For the first time, the teacher candidates who participated in the research used the interviews to theorize about the nature of teaching and learning beyond their prior assumptions. They talked about the nature of teaching and learning, both in their host schools and at the Faculty. Candidates' comments about the nature of learning fell into two broad categories: comments about how students in their host schools learn curricular content and comments about how teacher candidates learn to teach.

Max realized that students did not necessarily learn well from traditional ways of teaching: "Five guys at the front will be paying attention, writing notes, and thinking about what you're saying, and then the others would sort of copy down the notes and not really pay attention" (Max2, 4). For this reason, Max's goal for the next practicum was to "try not to teach in lecture mode" (Max2, 1). Paul also noted the effects that lecture-based teaching had on students' learning. Citing his frustrations with the tendency of some teacher educators to lecture, Paul stated: "It made me want to take it more seriously, in that math class when that one kid never wants to sit down and work on his homework. I'm starting to think that maybe I should let him walk around more" (Paul2, 6). Paul also noticed that traditional teaching strategies could produce "an active resistance to learning" (FG2, 29) because students had been so conditioned to trying to find the right answers to questions posed by the teacher. Irene had the same realization as Paul:

It seems like students learn pretty quickly [what is expected of them]. They get set in their ways, I guess .... My physics classes [that I taught on practicum] were really kind of lectures, you know, with questions and all but not very interactive. Originally, that was expected [by students] .... When I tried to teach differently and it's more involved, they just kind of look at me blankly and ask, "Is this on the test?" ... I guess it's just pretty impressive how ingrained that kind of mentality is. (Irene2, 8)

Irene, Paul, and Max all realized the shortcomings of the traditional, transmission-oriented approach to teaching that is so culturally familiar because of the apprenticeship of observation. At the same time, however, Irene and Paul noted a resistance

CHAPTER 5

from their students when they tried to enact pedagogies they saw as radical departures from traditional teaching.

Many of the teacher candidates theorized about the effect that a positive teacher-student relationship had on students' learning. Max made the following connection:

> I noticed the students who I could talk to or would come for extra help or would just come and say hi after the class were normally the ones who would pay attention during class or try and get something out of the lecture ... Just the fact that they were interested made them also want to pay attention and get to know me .... Maybe if I went that extra bit to get the ones who weren't paying attention to get to know me, they would perhaps start paying attention in class if they knew me. (Max2, 8)

Here Max implicitly drew a parallel between the effect that Tom's focus on relationships in the physics class had on his own learning and the effects that his relationship with students on practicum had on their desire to learn. James commented on a tension he felt about developing a relationship with his class: "I think it's really important to have a good relationship with your students, but at the same time you don't want to be friendly with them because you're really not there to be a friend, you're there to teach them" (James2, 13). Irene also experienced some difficulty developing relationships with students that were conducive to learning:

> I found on my practicum I had trouble getting to know students. So I had seating plans and I knew them, but not well enough that I felt comfortable shouting out names and name dropping and when they knew the answer because I might not be able to ask the other guy in the front row because I didn't know his name exactly. I feel guilty about that but it's something I'm going to change in December because I think they feel more involved if they actually think their teacher knows them and then cares about how they're doing. Even in terms of marking they might think "Oh, she doesn't know me ..." I'm trying to keep track of that kind of thing. (Irene2, 14)

Like Max and James, Irene set a goal to improve her relationships with her students during the December practicum, not because she was concerned about being liked, but because she theorized that a stronger teacher-student relationship would mean a more productive learning experience for her students.

David and James theorized about how teacher candidates learned to teach. David pointed out the effects of the apprenticeship of observation on teacher candidates' tendency to worry about grades: "We've got these candidates who've been programmed since the day they entered school. Don't forget that most of them have never been out of school yet, they have been trained to get the grades as opposed to getting something out of it" (David2, 26). He also recalled an incident, during Randy Knight's presentation, when he learned about the value of working through a problem in a group:

> Knight had [us work on] these Interactive Lecture Demonstrations, which were thermodynamics-based. I couldn't just look at that question and get the answer right .... He said, "OK, in groups, let's talk about this. See what you

can come up with and make a prediction." It was funny, because an hour earlier [at the beginning of his presentation] I had looked at this and said to myself that there was no way I could recall any of this, I don't know what's going on .... The process working with the group, just vocalizing stuff and forcing you to communicate with other people. Just by talking it out, you ended up fumbling down the correct path to the right answer, which we ended up with. Left to myself, I probably wouldn't have done it and I would have waited for the answer. (David2, 6)

David's instinct to wait for the right answer, as opposed to working with other people, when faced with a challenging problem was disrupted by Knight's requirement to discuss a problem in groups. James also spoke of his experiences learning to work in groups: "I feel more comfortable in a group of two or three people ... you can talk casually, rather than in front of the whole class, and it's good when you hear other students' ideas because they might trigger something that you were thinking about" (James2, 11). It is noteworthy that, although teacher candidates had been told about the value of learning in groups early on in the Faculty, they remained unconvinced of the power of learning in groups until they had a significant opportunity to work through a difficult physics problem with two or three of their peers.

Teacher candidates made more comments theorizing the nature of teaching than they did theorizing the nature of learning. Many of their comments about teaching described their visions of the kinds of teachers they wanted to be. Candidates often set goals for the kinds of teaching strategies they wanted to use during their December practica, in order to bring their visions of the kinds of teachers they wanted to be more closely in line with the kinds of teacher they thought they were. Max found it difficult to attend simultaneously to both the content of his lesson and the students he was teaching:

I guess I pay so much attention to what I am teaching, I stop paying attention to the class. So I basically turn into a completely different person when I start teaching. Stop talking. Get the class organized, start the lesson, teach all boring. I'll stop, look back, and be like, "I haven't paid attention to anything else for 5 minutes." And then you look out, and think, "Oh no, what's going on now?" It takes so much of my attention still to get up there and write the lesson down and make sure I am doing everything I want correctly. But I really need to do both at the same time. (FG2, 84)

James had a similar experience to Max: "I was so focused on *my* learning, how *I* was teaching, I forgot to focus on how all the kids were learning" (FG2, 85). James also noted the importance of working co-operatively with other teachers and teacher candidates because "you can just give each other teaching ideas if you're part of a team" (James2, 12). James was particularly interested in exploring teaching strategies that encouraged students to take a more active role in their own learning as opposed to "doing worksheets and going through the motions" (James2, 8).

Irene lamented the challenges of incorporating active-learning pedagogies into her teaching: "I want to try more, but I don't really know what I can do .... It's felt like all of my lessons have been, 'Here's the concept, now let's do the math so that

CHAPTER 5

you know it.'" She felt trapped by her tendency to fall back on familiar, default methods of teaching. Similarly, Paul stated that he wanted "to focus on the core of understanding math with these kids ... to get them to think about understanding what they are doing." Both Irene and Paul were concerned about becoming mired in the rote elements of problem solving, stating they wanted to help students to understand the conceptual foundations of mathematics.

In addition to setting specific goals for themselves during the next practicum, teacher candidates theorized about the nature of teaching in general. Paul, David, and James all discussed the importance of relationships in teaching. On a pragmatic level, James felt that "telling a personal story while you are teaching a lesson" (FG2, 38) could help students relate to their teachers, and hence become more interested in the material. David agreed, citing his practice of greeting students at the door and chatting about video games (FG2, 39) before class began as a way to form relationships with his students. David mentioned that he learned the importance of establishing relationships with students from observing the ways in which teacher educators interacted with teacher candidates in his classes:

> I found that teachers who establish an environment of trust, they're given a break compared to individuals who haven't.... [If] you start down the wrong path you're never going to get off it. It's important to start things the right way, or start out the way that you want the class to go ... establish the class environment that you want for the semester and model it. (David2, 8)

Paul went one step further:

> Working towards the relationship is pretty integral. It's not just sort of like a helpful thing, like "This will go better if you like me" or "You'll listen to my lectures more if you think I'm a fun person." But more that that relationship is actually a specific part of the teaching, and that if that relationship's not working, then there's some kind of failure there on someone's part. (Paul2, 29)

Significantly, both David and Paul articulated the importance of establishing a positive, productive relationship between teachers and students. Teacher candidates learned about the importance of relationship by considering their own relationships with their teacher educators and the impact of those relationships on their learning.

Teacher candidates used the term *the basics* to name traditional, teacher-centred approaches to teaching and learning. They admitted that they were more comfortable falling back on the basics in their own teaching; some went so far as to suggest that a mastery of the basics was a necessary prerequisite to using a more active, student-centred approach in their classrooms. Max characterized the practicum as follows: "You're learning the basics ... [about] how you really want to be a teacher" (Max2, 16). Irene was concerned about her tendency to try to "get down the basics first" because she was concerned about "things becoming so ingrained"; she did not "want to get used to teaching the way everybody did" at her high school when she was a student (Irene2, 17). During the focus group, Irene commented that teacher candidates "have this conception ... they have to teach in this general way that people always do" (FG2, 45) because they "assume that normal teaching is easy,

72

and we have to do that before we do anything else" (FG2, 47). Paul challenged this idea, saying that teaching that focuses on engaging students with active-learning approaches "isn't just basics done better, it's totally independent [and] different from day one" (FG2, 51).

Perhaps part of the reason why some teacher candidates felt a need to master a traditional approach to teaching before enacting unfamiliar pedagogy is that their apprenticeships of observation have conditioned them to expect teaching to look a certain way. Both Paul and David commented that traditional approaches to teaching resulted in certain default behaviours for both teachers and students on practicum. According to Paul, traditional teaching seemed to result in "kids who really aren't engaged and are mostly either just looking for marks, or not really looking for anything in particular and just sort of showing up" (Paul2, 22). By the time students reach high school, David felt, "students see it as the responsibility of the teacher to make them work" (David2, 25). Paul believed that part of the problem with encouraging students to take responsibility for their learning was not only that they were unused to that kind of teaching, but also that "people are often pretty lazy and they like getting away with not doing work a lot of the time if they can" (Paul2, 18).

The teacher candidates who participated in this study were able to theorize about the nature of both teaching and learning during this round of interviews, apparently because they had practicum experiences on which they could base many of their theories and in part because they could compare how they were taught by teacher educators in the program with how they were trying to teach their students on practicum. The next section examines in greater detail how teacher candidates learned from practicum experiences.

LEARNING FROM PRACTICUM EXPERIENCES

Each of the teacher candidates constructed narratives to share practicum experiences and to situate themselves on a professional knowledge landscape (Clandinin & Connelly, 1995). Three themes are discussed in this section. The first theme presents excerpts from the narratives the participants shared about powerful events that occurred during the practicum. The second theme interprets the nature of candidates' relationships with their associate teachers. Finally, the third theme illustrates some of the tensions experienced by candidates during the practicum.

Narratives from the Practicum

Many of the narratives about the practicum shared by teacher candidates focused on what they learned from considering the effects of particular teaching strategies on students' learning. For example, Irene learned the importance of organizing notes that she wrote on the board early in the practicum:

> I wrote things on the board and then we did the lab [based on my note]. One kid handed in his lab and he had written the note in the top half of it, but it fit in the top little margin! He just wrote it there [at the top of the page], kind of scribbled down little drawings because he wasn't sure if I wanted them to

CHAPTER 5

> write it down or not …. It taught me to … make my [expectations of] board work a bit clearer. (FG2, 21)

Max had a similar experience to Irene's, when he noticed his students creating a "jumbling half of a diagram, then writing on their pages, then the other half of the diagram" (FG2, 23) in response to the note he created using a whiteboard and smartboard simultaneously. Both Irene and Max learned that their students tended to reproduce notes exactly as they saw them, with minimal consideration for how they would later use the notes as a learning tool.

One narrative that was nearly universal among the teacher candidates was the story of how difficult it is to move students beyond their focus on correct answers. James found this tendency particularly frustrating when he spent time providing students with written feedback on their assignment: "The kids wouldn't look at the comments; they would just look at the answers to see if they got it wrong" (FG2, 79). Paul's narrative about students' focus on correct answers resonated with the rest of the candidates in the focus group:

> I had this one kid who was asking me questions [in my math class]. The question was, "Can I multiply this here, in math?" I didn't want to say, "Yes," I wanted to say, "Well, why do you think you should do that?" I wanted to lead him a bit. I tried to lead him for a while. After a while, he was like, "Can I?" and finally I said, "Yeah, you can, because …" And as I started on the "because," he interrupted me and said "THANK YOU! The answer was 'yes' to my question." (FG2, 31)

James related a similar story about an event that happened in his grade 9 science class. During his unit on astronomy, a student asked if stars varied in size. The students were content with his one-word answer (yes); James said that when he tried to explain the reason, his students "just didn't care." David contributed the same kind of narrative based on his experiences in a grade 10 science class:

> I had this activity that I used with the grade 10 applied when we were talking about acceleration …. They weren't really getting the concepts, so I put them in groups [and gave each group] a cartoon picture …. A lot of them were easy, like a dog sitting on a sled zooming down an ice slope. The whole point of the exercise was to describe, using common language, what was going on [in the picture].… [One picture], a bungee jumper, I just wanted them to look at one thing: after you initially jump off and the rope becomes initially taut just before you slow down. They all looked at different parts of the motion, either when it was speeding up, slowing down, or stopped. So when we took this [exercise] up as a class – and it went over really well, they were all engaged and talking about the pictures – when we got to this [bungee jumping] picture everyone had a different answer. It was OK, there are all of these different things, in one case this is happening and in another case this is happening. There were probably 200 solutions, and they all just wanted to know, "But what do we write down?" But what's the answer? [I said] "There is no right answer; they're all right answers." [They said] "But what do you mean they're

CANDIDATES IN CRISIS

all right answers?" I tried to calm them down by saying that if they had anything like this on the test it would be clear cut. It wasn't hard to get them engaged and talking about it, but at the end it came down to, "But what's the answer? What do I put on my sheet?" (FG2, 32)

David's narrative serves as a reminder of how conditioned most students are to seek the right answer from their teacher. He alluded to some frustration with the fact that, despite planning an engaging, open-ended lesson, in the end students were concerned only with having the right answers on their worksheets.

In a related set of narratives, some of the teacher candidates commented on the challenges inherent in asking and answering questions in a productive way when the same students always want to contribute to discussions. James found it difficult to balance questions that were slightly off topic with his natural desire to "move [his] lesson along" (FG2, 40). Irene stated:

Questioning is harder than I thought it would be. I knew it was hard, but ... I had this one class where there was one really smart kid and he meant well ... The teacher would ask a question, nobody is answering, and so he would raise his hand because he wanted the teacher to know somebody knew it. Meanwhile, I'm like, "Somebody else answer ... I know you know it." (FG2, 41)

Max had a similar experience with a student who insisted on "telling the answer as he gets up out of his desk" (FG2, 42). He went on to say, "I think that one of the hardest things I've learned that I thought was simple was asking the class a question" (FG2, 42).

The narratives that teacher candidates shared about their practicum experiences provide a window into some of the challenges they faced during their early teaching experiences. Often, teacher candidates learned about teaching when their students did not act according their prior assumptions about how people learn. Candidates were often frustrated when forced to confront the effects of their teaching on students' learning.

Associate Teachers

The relationship between teacher candidates and their associate teachers can be characterized as a dynamic interplay between the freedom candidates felt to enact their own pedagogies, the restrictions they felt to conform to their associate teachers' styles, and the extent to which their associate teachers modelled effective teaching practices. Of the teacher candidates who participated in this research, only David felt as though he was given enough freedom by his associate teacher. He characterized his relationship with his associate teacher in the following way:

I was given the freedom, not right off the bat, but certainly after a few days in, I could do whatever I wanted .... I guess that was because of the trust that was established between the two of us early on. My first day in front of the class, [my associate teacher] told me that he was very happy and surprised by how poised I was, that I didn't fumble, and that I had a good rapport with the

CHAPTER 5

> students. He said I did extremely well .... [thus] it was very easy for a quick establishment of trust which allowed me to try my own things. I know lots of candidates who weren't even given that initial opportunity to stand in front of the class early on. They ended up being placed with associates who weren't as comfortable, and had to wait as many as 3 weeks in some cases. They were very restricted ... .The first day in front of that classroom will probably have a big effect on how that associate perceives you. (David2, 12)

David also mentioned that he received feedback from his associate teacher after every class in the form of two pages of comments that gave him "a sense of timing and a sense of how often and when there was some sort of change between what we were doing and something else in the class" (FG2, 37). Of particular importance was the consistent message David received from his associate teacher: "Just do what you want. You'll make mistakes, we all make mistakes" (FG2, 37).

In contrast with David, Paul's relationship with his associate teachers was much more limiting:

> I couldn't use many of my ideas because I had two associates that were really rigid. Especially the grade 9 room where these kids were crazy and the teacher's solution – and she was great, I learned a lot from her for sure—but her solution was to just keep everything very rigid, every single lesson. So, take out homework, do examples, quiet homework time ... every single day. There was no room for anything else at all. I had to do that in her class, because of the repetition, it worked the way she wanted it to. (FG1, 54).

In his individual follow-up interview, Paul went on to say that the same associate teacher "basically wanted [him] to be her" which, although she had "a lot to teach [him]," did not allow him to "get a good sense of [his] teaching" (Paul2, 32). He expressed his frustration, saying "I feel like there's so much that I'd really like to try and it's just restricted by the fact that it's someone else's class" (Paul2, 35). The situation was not much better with Paul's other associate teacher, although "there was a bit more room to move, [the associate teacher] wouldn't give much feedback" (Paul2, 37). An additional confounding factor to Paul's practicum was his perception that "a lot of the restrictions and teaching styles [of his associates] were really opposite to what [he] was learning here [at Queen's]" (Paul2, 42).

David and Paul seemed to be at opposite ends of a spectrum between being given a lot of freedom to enact their own pedagogies and being restricted by an associate teacher who had very particular expectations. The relationships that Irene, James, and Max described with their associate teachers seemed to fall somewhere in between these two extremes. Irene spoke about how her associate teacher modelled his expectations for teaching a class. She said, "My associate teacher, he was really good. He taught more of a lecture style because he had mostly grade 12s and he wanted them ready for university" (FG2, 35). Irene also thought her associate teacher "was really great when we got to talk one-on-one ... that was wonderful to have his support" (Irene2, 11). Neither James nor Max spoke at length about the nature of their relationships with their associate teachers. During the focus group James mentioned several pieces of advice that he received from his associate teacher, whereas Max talked about the collaborative relationship that his associate teacher had with other people in the department. Both James and Max implied that they had respect for their associate teachers' style, and that they were learning a lot from the advice they were given.

The nature of the teacher candidates' relationship with their associate teachers was, not surprisingly, a significant factor in their perception of how much they learned during the practicum. At one extreme, Paul felt restricted by the lack of freedom he had to try the pedagogies he embraced as a result of his experiences in Tom's physics course. On the other hand, David was grateful for the latitude provided by his associate teacher, and he frequently commented on the high quality of feedback he received on his teaching. Interestingly, both Paul and David commented during their individual interviews that, if possible, they would advise teacher candidates to ensure they had a productive relationship with their associate teachers. Paul quipped, "I wish I could give the advice to try and get a really great associate teacher to work with, but I don't think you can really do that" (Paul2, 42). David suggested that candidates should "get out into different classrooms and different associates" (David2, 12).

Tensions during the Practicum

The October practicum was, at various points, a source of tension for the teacher candidates. The source of the tension most clearly articulated by participants was the tension between how they thought they *should* teach and the reality of their *actual* teaching. Often, this tension was framed as a conflict between the messages they were receiving about teaching from Queen's and the messages they were receiving from their associate teachers. James related an example of this issue:

> In physics class we're really focusing on making sure that the students really understand the concepts. And I found on my practicum I would attempt to have students understand the concepts but my associate teacher said, "Well, just tell students what they need to know for the test." For instance ... we were learning properties of stars, and I found myself wanting to explain to students how we understand, why we know certain stars are brighter than others, certain stars are bigger and more massive than others ... But my associate seemed to say, "Well, you know they're not really going to be tested on that so just tell them that stars are brighter and some stars are bigger and ..." So I guess that was a bit of a conflicting message because I didn't think that the students were really learning much by taking that approach. (James2, 16)

The candidates also commented on how the time constraints they were under in the practicum prevented them from enacting the pedagogies they felt would help students to learn effectively. The requirements associated with teaching everyday often superseded the lofty goals candidates had for their time on practicum. As Paul remarked, "Once you're actually in there, all this stuff you've heard [at Queen's] kind of fades. You're trying to focus on coming up with things in front of the class" (FG2, 3).

CHAPTER 5

Max commented that he did not "feel ready to try a lot of things" (FG2, 118) on his practicum. James agreed, stating "We spend so much time getting ready for the next day. We don't have time to go through a manual; we have to teach the next day" (FG2, 44). Irene called the practicum "overwhelming," which resulted in thoughts such as "Oh man, there are 25 kids here. Just do the lesson ... this works for most of the kids so I'll stick with that" (Irene2, 19). Candidates wanted to teach in a more progressive way, but felt that they had to use traditional teaching strategies as a way of coping in a stressful practicum environment.

Another source of tension for teacher candidates was the expectations they placed on themselves during the practicum experience. Irene lamented that she felt badly because "two of the other teacher candidates [in her host school] were on sports teams but ... [she] found there was enough on [her] plate" (FG2, 108); the pressure to help with extracurricular activities was overwhelming, "it added to the pressure [on the practicum] ... if I was a volleyball star in high school, I would have helped with volleyball" (FG2, 110). Frequently, the teacher candidates commented on the late nights they spent planning for the next day: "I struggled to go to bed before midnight" (FG2, 74); "There was a lot of work, I didn't sleep a lot" (David2, 16); "You're just so busy trying to get ready for the next day" (James2, 21). Paul felt that there was tacit pressure put on teacher candidates to take on more than they were ready for:

> I think I saw some people that took it, took too much on, and maybe even took the practicum a bit too seriously. Not that you shouldn't take it seriously, but a couple of people at my school were teaching three courses within a week and were incredibly stressed about it and felt like, and sort of felt maybe pressured into it. (Paul2, 43)

Max thought that the tendency to stay up late every night to plan was "not a healthy balance" for teacher candidates on practicum (Max2, 17). He argued that candidates should be careful about how much they take on during the practicum, saying "It is more important to really figure out what you want to do and how you want to do it, as opposed to just getting as much experience a possible because there is plenty of time for getting experience" (Max2, 15). Irene agreed, stating that "balance and reflecting" (Irene2, 23) were the most significant challenges she faced on her practicum. She regarded her practicum as "an opportunity to learn and think" (Irene2, 23), and tried to ensure she had time to take a step back from the hectic pace of the practicum to do both of those things.

LEARNING EXPERIENCES IN THE PHYSICS CLASS: TEACHER EDUCATORS

The perspective of the teacher educator can again be represented by one overarching theme: exploring active-learning pedagogies. During the six classes of the November on-campus weeks, Tom revisited themes that he had introduced during the first month of the program. Tom continued to develop the idea of teaching in non-traditional ways by explicitly modelling the use of active-learning pedagogies such as Predict-Observe-Explain and Rubbish Notes, both from PEEL (Baird & Northfield, 1992).

In addition to reminding students of how it feels to learn in an active-learning environment, Tom added a more explicit metacognitive component to his course by providing opportunities for teacher candidates to work with him at processing their own learning both in the physics course and in the program in general.

Revisiting PEEL

Tom began the first class by inviting the candidates to have some unstructured "time to talk" (Journal, November) in their table groups, in order for candidates to reconnect with one another and continue developing the relationships that had been suspended for the month of October. During the conversations, he made an effort to spend a few minutes conversing with candidates at each table group. After 30 minutes, he asked candidates to write a short response to the question "How did the teaching you did during September [i.e., Lesson Study] have an impact on your learning during your October practicum?" (Journal, November). Most candidates immediately began writing their responses, while some continued their conversations at their table groups for a few extra minutes. After 20 minutes of nearly silent writing, candidates got up to take the coffee break they had come to expect. Tom reconvened the class formally after a 15-minute break to make some announcements regarding the guest speakers he had invited to the class in upcoming weeks.

After the announcements, Tom directed candidates' attention to a Wimshurst machine, an electrostatic device designed to generate high voltages by manually cranking two parallel insulated disks in opposite directions. Tom explained that the output terminal arms were connected to metallic leads, which were in turn placed in vegetable oil in a clear glass dish on an overhead projector. After sprinkling grass seed on the oil, Tom asked the candidates, "What might someone predict would happen and why?" (Journal, November). After obtaining five possibilities from the class, he cranked the Wimshurst machine to generate a potential difference, and the candidates watched as the grass seed arranged itself in an electric field pattern in the vegetable oil. Two candidates offered their explanations at the conclusion of the POE.

After telling the story of the first time he used a Wimshurst machine during his own student teaching experience, Tom invited the candidates to change their focus from attending to the POE to attending to how he was teaching the class. He said:

> You've noticed that at the end of some of our classes, I've been trying to get you to ask me questions about how I am teaching. You've been at this for two months; you can now pretty well predict your classes here and what the practicum is like. How do the two modes add together to you becoming a teacher? Isn't a big part of the difference between the practicum and what you do here that you learn best when you're doing something, even in classes here? Have any of you tried to play with that notion in the school with the students? (Journal, November)

The teacher candidates seemed not to know what to make of the questions Tom asked. After what seemed like a long silence, a few of them offered comments about the lab activities they had done with students during their practicum experiences.

CHAPTER 5

At the conclusion of the first class, Tom revealed to me that he "felt better about the class than he could possibly have dreamed of" (Journal, November), even though the time that he provided for students to talk at the beginning of class was much longer than he originally planned for, a situation that would probably cause a fair amount of discomfort for many teachers. It is particularly significant that Tom did not begin the first class back, at least in a formal or traditional sense, until nearly 75 minutes after the class began. He recognized the importance of giving the candidates time to reconnect after a long absence, and trusted that their unstructured time to share some experiences would be used productively. By making an effort to sit at each of the table groups, Tom provided himself with an opportunity to reconnect with his class in small groups. The most important feature of the first class in November was the continued emphasis on the classroom community. The Wimshurst machine POE was an important reminder of the active-learning pedagogy that Tom introduced in September. The discussion at the end of class foreshadowed the Think-Aloud pedagogy that Tom was to introduce later in the November block of classes.

The second class in November began with the following prompt from Tom to the teacher candidates: "How many people asked students to copy things off of the board? How many of you had students ask, 'Are we supposed to copy this down?'" (Journal, November). After the candidates agreed that the situation was indeed familiar, Tom said, "This is going to be a silent exercise. I want you to focus on what it feels like to copy notes from the board" (Journal, November). Tom then proceeded to write the following paragraph on the board:

> The degree of rainfall for each half-year and the annual seasonal deficit are the systems which determine which areas will receive rain and which won't. However, in planning where to plan crops it is not enough to know the system; one must also take account of the different levels within each seasonal system. We much also know how much of the soil will be lost by evaporation. (Hynes, 1987, p. 30)

The paragraph is nonsense. Tom used it as an example of PEEL procedure F5, Dirty Tricks, which are designed to "demonstrate how students accept uncritically what they hear or read" (Baird & Northfield, 1992, p. 254). A few of the teacher candidates noticed that the paragraph was meaningless and shared their opinions with the class after Tom had written the note on the board.

Tom admitted to doing the exercise as a way of introducing several ideas at once. On one level, he wanted candidates to consider the implications of the traditional teaching and learning behaviours associated with copying notes from the board. He pointed out that students exhibit a wide range of reactions to copying notes, and many accept uncritically everything they write. The same range of responses was present in the physics curriculum course. Tom asked candidates, "Do you think that teachers assume that kids think when they write it down, or is it more 'Write now, learn later'?" (Journal, November). The Rubbish Notes had a particularly strong effect on James, who said during the focus group: "That little note-taking exercise was an eye-opener for me ... it definitely changed the way I think about writing notes on the board. When we were writing the note, I didn't even think about what I was writing" (FG2, 1).

Tom chose the Dirty Tricks procedure as a way of introducing candidates to the procedures contained in the PEEL database. After describing how PEEL began, he emphasized that the purpose of PEEL procedures was to "recruit students into the learning process" (Journal, November). Teacher candidates were then given the opportunity to explore the PEEL website (http://peelweb.org), with the caution that the procedures "are not an instant fix for tomorrow's lesson" (Journal, November).

During the first week back on campus, Tom used the PEEL procedures POE and Dirty Tricks as a way for candidates to revisit the theme of active-learning pedagogy that he introduced in September. In a post-class conversation, Tom stated, "Despite their early enthusiasm for doing POEs in this course, candidates rarely try a POE during practicum" (Journal, November). The data obtained from teacher candidates who participated in this study corroborated Tom's assertion. Candidates indicated that they felt too constrained to try non-traditional teaching strategies on practicum, because of the expectations of their associate teachers, their focus on getting through the next day's lesson, or a combination of both. It is likely that Tom's focus on the active-learning pedagogies of the PEEL project was intended not only to remind candidates of how it feels to learn in a more student-centred environment, but also to challenge them to try one or more PEEL procedures during practicum.

Learning about Teaching Physics from a Physicist

As a primer for Randy Knight's visit, which occurred outside of regular class time, Tom asked candidates to consider how Knight teaches about his ideas of teaching physics. During his presentation, Knight was quick to state that he is a consumer of Physics Education Research, as opposed to actually being involved in research on how students learn physics. He characterized himself as an "applied scientist" (Journal, November) who wanted to use the results of Physics Education Research to help the weaker students improve their experiences with first-year physics courses. Knight characterized the teacher candidates as "somewhere in between" (Journal, November) being experts and novices in physics, and challenged them to think about the mental models they have for a variety of physics situations. Knight's central thesis was that "misconceptions about physics are both deeply ingrained and difficult to see" and "traditional lecture-mode instruction, regardless of the instructor, has minimal impact on students' conceptual understanding." (Journal, November).

The majority of Knight's presentation to teacher candidates followed from a slide entitled "Making an Active-Learning Classroom Work for You" (Journal, November). He introduced candidates to his Interactive Lecture Demonstrations (ILDs), a teaching strategy that is similar to POEs. Candidates had the opportunity to participate in ILDs that focused on principles from optics, electricity and magnetism, and thermodynamics during the seminar. Knight concluded with a question-and-answer session, during which he challenged teacher candidates to teach less physics content in a way that would promote active learning, as opposed to teaching more physics content in a lecture style that does not result in most students developing a deep understanding.

CHAPTER 5

Comments from the five teacher candidates who participated in the study indicated that Knight and his ideas about teaching physics were well-received. James said:

> It was great to get Randy Knight in. I've read parts of his book but it was actually really nice to actually do some of the things that he was talking about in his book. Because when you read about it and actually do what he advocates, it really helps you understand how it works and why it will work better in a physics classroom. (James2, 7)

Irene admitted that she "didn't read Randy Knight's book until this past weekend ... but that when [she] read it, it started to really click that [she] was really used to lecture style" (Irene2, 1). Irene was concerned, however, that "it's still very hard to incorporate [Knight's ideas]" (Irene2, 9). Paul also felt that, because Knight "was usually working with university students," the ways in which he implemented his teaching philosophy would be "pretty different" (Paul2, 21) from a secondary school teacher. In contrast, David felt that implementing Knight's ideas was a matter of deciding to "just do it" (David2, 4) in one's own classroom.

One of the interesting things about Knight's visit was that, unlike the guest speakers who are usually invited into the physics course, Tom did not have a pre-existing personal relationship with Knight. In addition, although he obviously gives a lot of thought to the way he teaches undergraduate students, Knight was a physicist at a teaching university, not a high school physics teacher. Tom admitted to me that he "didn't have a sense what Knight was going to do with the candidates" (Journal, November) before he came, so it was fortuitous that Knight emphasized many of the same points that Tom had introduced early in the course. Before Knight's visit, Tom asked the class, "Would most of you admit to having a deep-seated fear of sending students off to university unprepared for what they'll find? You know what they'll find [lectures], so the answer must be 'Give it to them now!'" (Journal, November). It was meaningful for candidates to hear that lecturing is generally an unproductive way to teach physics from a *physicist* who teaches first-year physics courses, even though Tom had been working hard to convey that message since the course began.

Processing Learning in the Physics Course

The third and final week in the November block began with simple physics equipment: one flashlight bulb, one AA battery, and one piece of wire per teacher candidate. Tom introduced the activity in the following way:

> I'd really like you to work at this next activity on your own. Some of you will take a few seconds; some of you will take longer. That's OK. The point is whether you learn something about how to work with kids. Everyone gets one bulb, one wire, and one battery. Find how many ways you can make it light, without breaking the wire. (Journal, November)

When the candidates reconvened 10 minutes later, Tom asked them to share their perceptions about what one needs to know in order to make the bulb light. Many candidates in the class made comments about how safe they felt doing the activity.

The majority of this class was devoted to three POEs that used simple physics equipment. The first POE explored the concept of voltage in a DC series circuit by asking candidates to predict the relative brightness of bulbs connected in series. This POE was planned as a direct follow-up to one of the concepts that Knight explored during his presentation. The second POE required candidates to think about the concept of circular motion as they predicted the path that a ball would follow after leaving the curved surface of the rim of a paper plate. The third POE also followed up on a concept mentioned by Knight. Candidates were asked, in groups, to predict the shape of the magnetic field produced by a flexible fridge magnet.

At the end of the class, after candidates had spent the majority of their time exploring physics concepts using variations of the POE procedure, Tom asked the candidates to sit in a large circle around a group of tables. He switched on a digital recorder and said:

> If the recorder puts you off, you can either leave or stay silent. It's very strange to say, but we're halfway through our time together. We aren't going to see each other until January. What I am interested in hearing from you is whether you've worked out how I am trying to work with you, and if you have any questions about how I am working with you. Questions, descriptions, suggestions? (Journal, November)

A few of the candidates offered comments about Tom's focus on active-learning pedagogy in the physics course and their perception that he wanted candidates to try to use those teaching strategies during their practica. Tom went on to say:

> The standard frame of mind is: I told you, I taught you, you know it, now go out and do it. The big gap is between I taught you and you know it. The real issue isn't to slam the lecture method, but to understand it. The first year of teaching is not about applying what you learn here. This year is about learning how to track your own development, so that in those rare moments in the first year when you have the opportunity, you will take a minute and track what happens to you. The first year is hell, and there isn't a teacher education program on the planet that can change that. The buck stops with you and the textbook is novel. The nightmare is keeping up with the kids. Once you've been through a textbook once, the second time is so much easier. After 5 years, you'll know your subject inside and out. We all grow up inheriting the notion that virtually every science teacher teaches in such a way that they can tell the students, then send them to the back of the lab and verify it. Instead, give them some kind of experience, talk about it, then more experience. The first four weeks you learned the ropes. You're going back and you know where things are. You know the students' names. Did that wind anyone up? (Journal, November)

After a few minutes, Tom switched off the recorder and said, "Let's leave it at that" (Journal, November). He went on to make a few announcements about the final class of the November block.

Tom attempted to engage the candidates in a Think-Aloud, which Kosminsky, Russell, Berry, and Kane (2008, p. 197) describe as "a metacognitive strategy in

CHAPTER 5

which we [teacher educators] think publicly about our thinking processes ... and examine those processes with our student teachers." In this particular instance, teacher candidates did not take the bait; they did not choose to engage with Tom in a discussion about how he was teaching and how they were thinking about learning to teach. As Tom would later note, the "silence was awkward for some [of the teacher candidates], but several did manage to offer some personal perspectives" (Kosminsky et al., 2008, p. 199). We met immediately after the class and I offered a comment: "Perhaps the candidates are overwhelmed with the idea of going back to their host schools. They only have four more days here and their attention may already be switching to pragmatic issues" (Journal, November). We both agreed that it was important to return to the idea of Think-Alouds in January.

Consolidating November and Looking Ahead to January

The final physics class in November began with a mechanics activity for candidates to complete in small groups. Each group was assigned a set of distance-time, velocity-time, and acceleration-time graphs and given a toy car. After a few minutes of discussion, representatives from each group had to use the toy car they had been given to demonstrate to the class the motion described by the graph.

During the presentations, Tom frequently interjected with clarifying questions to ensure that candidates could verbally describe the graph they were responsible for presenting.

The majority of the final class was devoted to a presentation by a local associate teacher who was a student of Tom's many years ago. His presentation focused on showing the candidates examples of how teaching strategies such as POE and ILD might be implemented in the high school classroom, with suggestions on how to assess students' learning in non-traditional ways. His presentation resonated with James, "I like what [he] said, 'You're not going to be a perfect teacher after your first year, it takes time'" (James2, 3). The class concluded with Tom thanking the teacher for his presentation and wishing the candidates well on their practicum.

Tom and I met after the final class to discuss the November block as a whole and look ahead to the lengthy amount of time he had with the candidates in January. Tom said that he was comfortable with the way the previous three weeks had unfolded, although he admitted to feeling that "everything was spun around what Knight was doing" (Journal, November). From prior conversations that we have had over the years, I knew that Tom considered January to be the most important part of the physics course. I asked what his thoughts were as he looked ahead to January in the physics class:

> January is it. I try to keep the show going in September and November, but January is pivotal because the program is half over. Candidates have had more time to process the transition between their undergraduate degrees and their teacher education program. They've had time in schools; many have had more than one associate teacher. The challenge for me is to come across as signal rather than background noise. We [in teacher education] pay a high price if we don't work to understand where candidates are at, how they are different,

after they've had significant practicum experiences. Only in conversations with teacher candidates can we help them to see some of the big picture perspectives of what is actually happening over the course of the teacher education program. (Journal, November)

We then discussed possible activities to engage the teacher candidates upon their return in January. Tom's notion of "signal" versus "noise" struck me as an important distinction between the types of learning experiences teacher candidates were having at the Faculty. How does Tom manage to consistently be perceived as signal rather than background noise by the teacher candidates who participated in this study?

CONSTRUCTING PROFESSIONAL KNOWLEDGE
FROM TEACHING AND LEARNING EXPERIENCES

In this final section of the chapter I summarize the professional knowledge constructed and co-constructed by the teacher candidates and teacher educators who participated in this study. The themes in the data are synthesized with a view to making claims about how participants were theorizing teaching and learning during the second phase of data collection. The overarching theme of this block was the cognitive conflict between candidates' expectations of teaching and learning and the kind of teaching they themselves were enacting in the practicum and experiencing in teacher education classes.

The five participants in this study left for their October practicum placements full of ideas about how they wanted to teach and what they wanted to learn. As shown in the previous chapter, some of the effects of their long apprenticeships of observation had been named and called into question by ideas that were presented in the physics course. After four weeks of practicum experiences in host schools, working with associate teachers of varying levels of utility to their learning, the teacher candidates somewhat reluctantly returned to Queen's for the November block of classes. Their teaching experiences during the practicum had changed them. For the most part, however, they returned to a teacher education program that had not changed to suit their needs as learners.

When teachers try to improve their practice, it is possible and even likely that they will have to acknowledge experiencing themselves as a "living contradiction" (Whitehead, 1993, p. 70). The practicum experience is no exception, for the question of "How do I improve my practice?" (Whitehead, 1993, p. 69) is precisely the question that engages each teacher candidate on a daily basis. Like their more experienced counterparts in education, teacher candidates "have the experience of holding educational values and the experience of their negation" (Whitehead, 1993, p. 70) on a regular basis. Candidates' educational values have been shaped largely by their apprenticeships of observation, but they were also informed by their learning experiences in the physics course in September, the ideas they took from the Faculty of Education, and the expectations of their associate teachers. For teacher candidates, the potential for experiencing contradictions between the teacher they are and the teacher they want to be is perhaps greater than it is for either experienced teachers or teacher educators. At various points, for the candidates who participated in this study, the experience of being a living contradiction seemed to be nothing short of an existential crisis.

The experience of living contradiction began the moment teacher candidates entered their host schools in October. One of the most consistent conclusions of teacher education research is that, for teacher candidates, the practicum is the most powerful learning experience of their preservice programs (e.g., Smith & Lev-Ari, 2005). Yet powerful learning experiences are not always positive; learning can also be powerful during moments of cognitive conflict. The educational values held by teacher candidates going into their placements would eventually come into conflict with their lived experiences. The teacher candidates told narratives to situate themselves on the professional landscape of teaching and learning and to share stories of such conflicts. They shared what they learned when they experienced themselves as living contradictions arising from interactions with their students and with their associate teachers. They theorized about the kinds of pedagogies they wished they could enact, and they told cover stories to excuse why they had yet to enact them. They told stories about the constraints imposed by associate teachers, by the requirements of curriculum, and by their fear of teaching in ways that feel radically different from what they were taught by their apprenticeships of observation. The constraint of the apprenticeship of observation is salient, revealed by language such as the need to master "the basics" (Irene2, 17; Max2, 16) of teaching. The *basics* of teaching is a synonym for the traditional approach found in so many schools: teacher-centred, with an emphasis on telling students information. This is not to belittle the cover stories told by teacher candidates. The grammar of schooling (Tyack & Tobin, 1994) is a complicated set of cultural tools that are difficult for experienced teachers to navigate. It is unrealistic to expect teacher candidates to do anything other than construct cover stories as they struggle to conform to the multiple pressures of the grammar of schooling. Nevertheless, the candidates who participated in this study put considerable pressure on themselves. Their narratives of the practicum include tensions that reveal how teacher candidates experienced themselves as living contradictions.

The existential crisis begins when they are pulled back to the Faculty, perhaps having just found a rhythm to their practicum experiences. The default reaction upon returning to the university is to revert immediately to the familiar student role. However, their recent experiences teaching in schools seemed to make them much more critical of the ways in which they are taught by teacher educators. After a practicum experience full of critiques from associate teachers, it is not surprising that candidates return to the Faculty with a somewhat impatient attitude toward teaching strategies that are not having productive effects on their learning. Teacher candidates seemed to come to the Faculty of Education with expectations that were so low that teacher educators could have done almost anything and the candidates would not have questioned what they did. Practicum experiences taught candidates the questions they needed to ask: They returned to Queen's with much higher expectations of their teachers and of themselves. Although the on-campus portion of the program has the potential to relieve many of the symptoms of the existential crises associated with experiencing oneself as a living contradiction, the program seemed to fall short of its potential.

The teacher candidates continued to be strongly influenced by their peer groups, both within the physics class and in the program as a whole. Again, if teacher candidates who participated in this study experienced themselves as contradictions in varying degrees over the practicum, then it follows that the anxiety associated with the quest to answer the question "How do I improve my practice?" is amplified many times when nearly 700 candidates return to the Faculty in November. The "negativity, negativity, and more negativity" (David2, 17) could be seen as a natural consequence of so many candidates simultaneously trying to resolve inner conflicts about the nature of teaching and learning. Although the candidates who participated in this study did not, by and large, have the same perceptions of their peers in physics as they did of their peers in the overall program, it could be that the frequent silences and perceived lack of co-operation that was so frustrating to Paul were symptoms of the same kinds of anxiety being experienced throughout the program.

Tom's pedagogy resonated with the teacher candidates because *how* he teaches generally matches *what* he teaches. The candidates' frequent descriptions of Tom's emphasis on teaching the importance of relationships in teaching by focusing on relationships in the physics course provides clear evidence that the candidates are sensitive to the consonance of his pedagogy of teacher education. The low-risk, trusting environment offered in the physics course seemed to provide a sense of relief for the teacher candidates, even though they were largely unable to articulate Tom's overarching goals for teaching the course. They trusted him as a teacher and, for now, that seems to be sufficient for them to have productive learning experiences in the physics course.

The perspective of the teacher educator reveals Tom's focus on using active-learning pedagogies, a focus that he began in the first class in September. Tom implicitly recognizes that the needs of the teacher candidates change when they return to campus in November; his response is to strengthen the message he began in September. The candidates' experience of themselves as living contradictions is exacerbated in the physics course. Tom maintained a safe environment where candidates were forced to confront the fact that it is possible to consistently teach and learn in non-traditional ways, despite the traditional views of teaching that encourage candidates to master the *basics* before trying anything risky on their practicum. Tom provided experiences that encouraged candidates to live at one end of their lived contradiction, the end where their educational values were challenged and encouraged through PEEL procedures, guest speakers, and Tom's commitment to his relationship with the members of the physics class. Knowing that candidates would return to another practicum experience where educational values and optimism are likely to be implicitly or explicitly negated by the rigours of daily teaching, Tom focused on the opportunity he had to create an environment where candidates were engaged in their own learning, even when they responded to a Think-Aloud with silence. There is no way for a teacher educator to control or mitigate the fact that teacher candidates will experience themselves as living contradictions on practicum. It is possible and, as the data suggest, far more preferable, to engage candidates in conversations about the teaching and learning that occurs in a methods course. The narratives that candidates construct on and about practicum are important and necessary for the development of their professional knowledge about teaching and learning. The metaphors that teacher candidates use to theorize about teaching and learning offer a far richer potential for teacher educators to help candidates to navigate the treacherous waters of their existential crises.

For the first time in the data, the teacher candidates began to articulate their theories of teaching and learning. Candidates theorized that traditional, transmission-based approaches to teaching fall far short of the goals they hold for the quality of students' learning. They also realized that they did not learn about teaching by being lectured. Candidates theorized that relationships were a specific component of how they approached teaching students. They also realized that they responded to teacher educators who attended closely to their needs as learners. Perhaps most importantly, the teacher candidates who participated in this study realized that there were parallels between how students learn curricular content and how they were learning to teach. The corollary is that teacher candidates could begin to see parallels between the way Tom taught them and the way he hoped they would consider teaching in their host schools and in their future careers as teachers. Tom encouraged them to see as real the possibility of remaining true to their educational values and to embrace rather than ignore experiencing oneself as a living contradiction.

CHAPTER 6

CREATING A CLEAR SIGNAL AGAINST A NOISY BACKGROUND

[Physics is] that class where you know you're not going to have to show up and do something trivial ... it's been sort of that place of refuge where we know we can go.... and focus on what I feel is important and of value. (David3, 7–9)

In addition to the regular schedule of coursework, a 8-month teacher education program needs to deal with the challenge of finding the appropriate time to include the extra requirements of a professional certification program. In the Ontario context, these extra requirements include finding time for presentations by the teachers' unions and for the Ontario College of Teachers. In both cases, candidates are required to complete an application form to ensure they become certified Ontario teachers and are paid at the appropriate rate once they complete their degree. At Queen's, there are also many opportunities for candidates to engage in various workshops related to finding a job, including a popular recruiting fair for candidates interested in teaching overseas. Teacher candidates' thoughts naturally begin to drift to the job search and the possibility of teaching in their own classroom.

Unfortunately, the practical stress of finding a job can often coincide with the mid-point of a 8-month teacher education program. Teacher educators, particularly those who feel it is their responsibility to give candidates as many resources as possible in the name of preparation for the first year, might feel a new push to cover as much content as possible. There might be an increased pressure to complete assignments, particularly if candidates are about to embark on their final extended practicum. The previous chapter revealed that some participants felt that the November on-campus portion of the program did not do enough to help them resolve the existential tensions they arose during their first month of practicum. Candidates who participated in this research experienced themselves as "living contradictions" (Whitehead, 1993, p. 70) as a result of their practicum experiences. If these tensions were exacerbated during their second practicum, in December, then it is possible that candidates returned to the on-campus weeks in January feeling more unsettled than they did in November.

In short, there are a considerable number of distractions in a 8-month teacher education program, particularly at the mid-point when candidates are compelled to consider applying for jobs, possibly while coming to terms with increased requirements from course work and feelings of insecurity about their practicum experiences. These distractions may well add up to a considerable amount of noise in a program that might make it difficult to focus on the broader challenges of learning to teach. It becomes a major challenge, then, for teacher educators to send a clear signal against the noisy background of a busy teacher education program.

CHAPTER 6

The first section of this chapter describes the major events that occurred during the physics course in this block of classes. The data obtained from the focus group and individual interviews are then analyzed to provide insight into how teacher candidates constructed professional knowledge from learning experiences in the physics course. Selected narratives of the candidates' practicum experiences are then presented in order to reveal many of the tensions associated with constructing professional knowledge during the practicum. The next section provides the perspective and voice of the teacher educator as I analyze the discussions Tom and I engaged in during January classes. Finally, the chapter concludes with a summary of the professional knowledge constructed and co-constructed by the teacher candidates and the teacher educators.

CONTEXTUAL FEATURES OF THE PHYSICS METHODS COURSE

Tom began this block of classes by engaging candidates in group work designed to help them set goals for their learning in January. At the end of the first class, he formalized the self-directed learning (SDL) assignment that would become the focus of the term. Candidates were asked to come to the second class prepared to form groups around common interests. These SDL groups would each be responsible for producing an "exemplary teaching resource" (Journal, January 7) to share with peers in the final class. The rest of the January classes alternated between two patterns. On Mondays, a guest speaker presented to teacher candidates for approximately half the class, and Tom used the other half of the class to both debrief the presentation and to guide candidates in processing the effects the program was having on their learning. Thursdays were designated as self-directed learning classes, where candidates were free to work on the projects on which their groups had decided. To emphasize the point, Tom stated that candidates need not attend class on Thursdays if their group's time could be spent more productively elsewhere. The physics courses concluded on Thursday at the end of January with 13 presentations of exemplary teaching resources from both groups and people who had chosen to work individually.

LEARNING EXPERIENCES IN THE PHYSICS CLASS: TEACHER CANDIDATES

The data provided by the participants during the focus group interview and the individual follow-up interviews were analyzed with a view toward understanding how the teacher candidates were constructing knowledge from learning experiences during their physics methods course. Four themes are explored in this section: Learning from the Program, Learning from Tensions, Learning from Tom, and Theorizing Teaching and Learning. The first theme focuses on how teacher candidates learned from the structure of the program, with particular emphasis on the transitions between the end of the extended fall practicum, the winter holiday break, and the return to Queen's in January. Unlike the previous two chapters, in which candidates spoke at length about how they learned from peers in both the physics classroom and the program, this set of data contributing to this chapter gave little mention of the effect that other teacher candidates had on participants' learning. Instead, the idea of candidates' experiences as living contradictions is further revealed by the extent to which candidates articulate the tensions they experienced during the teacher education program. The ways in which participants learn from Tom's pedagogy are interpreted in the third theme. Finally, the last theme explores the theories about teaching and learning that participants constructed from their experiences.

Learning from the Program

Teacher candidates who participated in this study indicated two major ways in which they learned from the program. First, the rhythm of the program continued to play an important role in their professional learning as they compared their experiences and expectations for learning on the practicum and at the Faculty. Second, candidates articulated a perceived lack of coherence in the teacher education program, largely due to their teacher educators' diverse pedagogical approaches and expectations, many of which contradicted their expectations of learning at the Faculty. This section interprets both aspects of how candidates learned from the program.

Teacher candidates returned to the Faculty of Education at Queen's after their December practicum and a 2-week winter holiday break. As James noted, "I would definitely rather come back [to the Faculty] than go back to the classroom. I needed that time to reflect and prepare for things like the job search" (James3, 30). Irene felt that coming back in January was "kind of relaxing because you have less hours, less responsibilities being a student again," adding that by the end of the final week of practicum, "it was just like trying to slog through marking and get things done, not a lot of critical reflection going on" (Irene3, 37). The space for analysis of experience provided by the return to campus was also mentioned by James: "Coming back here gives us the opportunity to reflect and really reminds us the importance of reflecting on our practice and thinking about how we teach and the theory behind it" (James3, 15). Paul also enjoyed the transition back to the Faculty, although his enthusiasm was more due to feeling that "going back for practicum has had a lot of negative parts" (Paul3, 5), many of which made him question his desire to enter the teaching profession. For Paul and David, the physics classroom acted as a kind of "safe haven" (David3, 6) from many of the external pressures and frustrations of the practicum; the transition to the Faculty was a welcome one for both of them. Max was unaffected by the transition: "Back to school, back to placement, no real difference to me" (Max3, 19).

The previous chapter explored how candidates' expectations of the program changed as a result of their first practicum experiences. Participants' experiences teaching in October taught them to be more critical of the kinds of teaching they experienced on their return to the Faculty in November. This result was magnified in the January data set; the teacher candidates who participated in the research were more critical of the pedagogical approaches of their teacher educators in January. In particular, candidates perceived a lack of coherence in the program. David perceived the pedagogies used by teacher educators as a dichotomy:

> There's a camp that believes it should be a theoretical Faculty of Education, versus the other camp that believes it should be more practical and building

up a "toolbox of skills," if you will, for students before they go into placements. (David3, 23)

The lack of coherence in teacher educators' approaches to pedagogy made many candidates' January learning experiences frustrating. Often, frustrations in one or two courses in the program led to a general sense of malaise. Paul said that his frustrations with some courses were the result of his perception that "no parts of it [the course] seem to match up" (Paul3, 27). He was also critical of the fact that some courses became too student-centred: "I just keep hearing the opinions of my classmates who have never been teachers before; it's all just individual or group presentations for the entirety of the course" (Paul3, 27). Paul stated that he learned the most when teacher educators used a coherent approach to teaching: "The reason I'm liking certain classes is because the profs do what they mean, what they say we should do, so there's no contradiction" (Paul3, 28).

Max felt that the sheer number of "silly workshops and fairs" (Max3, 17) was distracting and contributed to an overall lack of coherence in the program. Irene found the program confusing from a learner's perspective: "I can never put in words what I feel like I'm learning [at the Faculty]" (FG3, 115). Returning to an idea that he articulated earlier in the year, James stated that while the program was somewhat incoherent, it was up to individual candidates to help shape the quality of their learning experiences:

> I would tell students to really take advantage of the time spent at the Faculty of Education to learn about areas of teaching and learning that they want to learn about, and to try and gear all their assignments towards areas they're interested in. (James3, 26)

At the same time, however, James was frustrated by the lack of time to pursue the elements of the program that were of interest to him:

> I would like to have a bit less class time and more time to do individual work ....
> It seems like in a lot of classes, we're told to 'Go learn this or go do that, learn about what you think you need to learn about' ... [but] pretty much our whole day is spent in class! (James 3, 27)

Again, teacher candidates' learning was affected by the mixed messages they received from the program. By January, the teacher candidates had learned which elements of the program to focus their attention on and which elements of the program did not provide meaningful learning opportunities. For the teacher candidates who participated in this study, the meaningful opportunities for learning coincided with the parts of the program they perceived as the most coherent.

Learning from Tensions

The tensions that candidates expressed in the data fell into two categories: tensions experienced as a result of lack of coherence in the program and tensions created as a result of looking ahead to the February practicum. The tensions associated with candidates' analyses of the experiences during the December practicum are explored along with their narratives of experience in the second section of this chapter. In both cases, the tensions described by teacher candidates exacerbated their experiences as living contradictions. In most cases, the candidates lived contradictions as a tension between conflicting messages received from their teacher educators and associate teachers and their developing pedagogical vision.

Several candidates expressed frustration with the fact that learning experiences at the Faculty tended to magnify, rather than resolve, the tensions that had been developing over the course of the preservice year. Irene felt that each of her classes had a different emphasis, leading to her perception that "there are just too many most important things [in teaching]" (Irene3, 35). Max agreed, stating that every teacher educator has a "slightly different idea of what a teacher should be like" (Max3, 13). In particular, Irene and James framed the different emphases from teacher educators as a tension between teaching subject-specific curricula and teaching big picture issues such as inclusion, social justice, and literacy skills. As James said,

> A conflicting message we're getting here is that we're told to teach to curriculum [and] at the same teach certain skills like problem-solving skills and at the other end writing skills. But like I said, we're told that we have to teach to the curriculum, so one of my big concerns is just how do we reconcile those two different areas? (FG3, 59)

Irene picked up on the same issue:

> It seems like the curriculum classes focus on teaching the class as a whole … but then other classes are really focused on the individual learner … [but then] you have to incorporate social justice and do whatever you can to make everyone feel welcome culturally … and then [there are] the exceptional learners …. In theory it's all really important, but in practice I don't see how I am ever going to manage to do it all. (Irene3, 28)

Even though candidates returned to the Faculty in January with significantly more teaching experience than in November, they continued to feel overwhelmed by the requirements of teaching in secondary schools. By emphasizing the importance of different elements of teaching, teacher educators apparently contributed to candidates' sense of malaise.

David and Paul articulated the tensions they felt as a result of a perceived disconnect between how they were being taught at the Faculty and how they were expected to teach in the schools. David believed that "telling us [candidates] how to teach as a teacher but not doing that yourself [as a teacher educator] was the most obvious conflict [in the program]" (David3, 26). Paul took David's concern one step further, stating that some teacher educators found it difficult to have a "balance" between teacher-centred and student-centred pedagogy, with the result that he had to "listen to student presentations for hours on end" (Paul3, 29). The result, according to Paul, is that some teacher educators were "not doing what they want us [candidates] to do very well" (Paul3, 29).

The most consistent and significant tension described by teacher candidates concerned the upcoming February practicum. Candidates' experiences in the December

CHAPTER 6

practicum, combined with the conflicting messages they perceived from the Faculty to create anxiety about their return to host schools in February. The candidates were concerned that the internal contradictions between the pedagogy they wished to enact and the pedagogy they felt they had to enact would become more pronounced in the upcoming practicum. The main source of the pedagogies they wished to enact continued to be the ideas with which they had identified at the Faculty of Education.

Irene believed that many of the ideas concerning active-learning pedagogy that she embraced were in direct conflict with the more traditional teaching advocated by her associate teacher, framing the challenge as one of "teaching for coverage versus teaching for learning" (Irene3, 18). This tension was particularly pronounced when she considered how well she was preparing her senior physics classes for university. Although Irene wanted to "focus on concepts," she was concerned that the traditional lecture style her associate teacher used "would help students more [when they get to university]" (FG3, 63). Irene was frustrated by the disconnect between what she learned at the Faculty and the challenges of teaching secondary school students: "It feels like we can talk about having active-learning classrooms and really engaging students [at the Faculty] ... but then you just hope that [kind of teaching] transfers into skills for university" (Irene3, 5). She worried that if students "have a really good high school experience, then that will just really let them down in university" (Irene3, 7). The tension between the active-learning pedagogies advocated by the Faculty of Education and the traditional teaching style of her associate teacher caused Irene to feel like a living contradiction. She wanted to teach for conceptual understanding, yet she felt that she would leave her students unprepared for university if she made that choice. The messages that she received from the Faculty of Education in January did little to help her to resolve this tension.

Paul perceived himself as a living contradiction because he was restricted by his associate teachers during practicum: "I just felt like I was doing things as a part of what was required of me to get the teaching done or to please my associate teachers" (Paul3, 3). Although Paul was "passionate" about using active-learning pedagogies, he often felt, "I had to be somebody I didn't want to be" (Paul3, 3). Paul believed that teaching in a way that did not suit his identity resulted in more resistance from his students, noting that "there was always the tension between what they [students] wanted to be doing and what you [as the teacher] were making them do" (Paul3, 22). Thus Paul had "bad associations with teaching" as a result of the limited freedom he experienced on practicum. Paul's tension toward the February practicum was so significant that he stated: "I don't even want to go" (FG3, 98).

David articulated feelings of tension toward the upcoming practicum because he perceived that he was not meeting his goals for implementing active-learning pedagogies. Although David readily admitted during the focus group that he had more freedom from his associate teacher than Paul had, he was quick to point out that "I don't have the freedom I thought I would have, so I can't just take the risk and then take the blame ... I just find myself not wanting to go back for that reason" (FG3, 102). He felt that his use of active-learning pedagogy would not progress much further with "someone watching over my shoulder the whole time" (FG3, 101).

David was also concerned about the tension associated with the expectation to teach a full course load during the third practicum: "If that's where I am, just make it September, give me a class, let me go with it" (FG3, 101). David's experience as a living contradiction arose largely from his belief that the kind of teaching he wanted to enact was restricted by the fact he was teaching someone else's class during practicum, "however lenient they are" (FG3, 100).

Max's experience as a living contradiction was a mixture of the identity concerns expressed by Paul and the concerns about teaching full-time expressed by David. Max admitted that, during his practicum, "I noticed that when I was out there doing my thing, I was not sure where I should draw the line of what of me I could put into [teaching], I guess I ended up being a little reserved because I wasn't sure" (FG3, 95). A message from a guest speaker in Tom's class helped Max to clarify one of the tensions he felt as he looked ahead to the February practicum:

> He said for your first year of teaching what you want to do is get through so you still want to teach so it's like survive so you still want to teach. But we're going out doing, essentially, a first-year of teaching for the 5 weeks but we're also doing other things [such as active-learning pedagogies]. If you're not expected to do that during your first year, why would we be able to do it now? Why would you want us to do it now? (FG3, 104)

Max did not understand how he was supposed to enact the active-learning pedagogies he had embraced against the background of just trying to make it through a full-time teaching load. The experience of being a living contradiction helped him to call into question the taken-for-granted assumptions surrounding teacher candidates' learning.

Learning from Tom

The teacher candidates who participated in the research continued to explore how they were learning from Tom's pedagogy during the January focus group and individual interviews. Significantly, comments about Tom's pedagogy were the most frequently coded items in the January data set. Although candidates continued to comment on the nature of Tom's relationship with the class, they focused their attention on trying to name *what* they learned from Tom's class while theorizing about the big picture of Tom's pedagogy.

The issues of naming the content of Tom's class proved challenging for candidates, particularly because the focus of the physics classes in January alternated between guest speakers and self-directed learning. If anything, Tom was up in front of the class *less* often than he was during either the September or November on-campus weeks. As Irene noted, "It's hard to say [what I've learned from physics] just because we've had a weird month ... we haven't had a Thursday class in a little while [because of self-directed learning time]" (Irene3, 23). David also found it hard to articulate the content of the physics course:

> My perception is that because there's little, or seemingly little ... physics content covered in that course, that I have the sense that we're not doing too much. But at the same time I recognize that a different approach is being

taken there and I think the payoffs are coming in other classes. So that's why I'm, sort of, having a difficulty answering with respect to physics. I've certainly taken from this course the idea of self-directed learning and focusing on what I feel is important and of value. And I guess what I'm doing is I'm taking that idea and extending it to other classes. (David3, 8)

Interestingly, David's idea of course content is *physics* content, not his newfound focus on self-directed learning that was reinforced by experiences in physics class. During the January focus group, the candidates had the following discussion (FG3, 31–35) about the role of physics content in the physics class:

David: To make a point, and this isn't a negative although it may come across that way, …. Based on what I've observed in that class, I couldn't provide evidence that he necessarily knows much more than a layperson about physics and that's not a bad thing.

Paul: About physics. Yeah, that's weird.

David: About physics. And that's not a bad thing necessarily. Instead of focusing the course on physics content, which we all know and, if we don't, it's in our heads and we'll refresh ourselves with it when we get there. He's focused on theories and practices in education. But if you think about it, some of the demos he's done he could have rehearsed or just read up a little bit and a lot of the answers come from us anyways. He hasn't once stood up there and taught a physics lesson.

Paul: He almost never wants to get into it.

David: Yeah. I mean I'm not saying he doesn't know his stuff, I'm sure he does. But just think about it. There's no evidence from that class or the interactions that I've had that would necessarily show that he knows anything more about physics than someone off the street.

Irene: What about POEs?

James: I agree with you but I think he knows a lot about teaching and learning.

David: Absolutely.

This excerpt from the focus group shows how the teacher candidates who participated in this research understood the role of physics in the physics curriculum course. Later in the focus group, Paul noted that there was probably a reason that Tom shifted the content of the course away from physics: "I feel like Tom does everything so deliberately in this class … for some reason I can't figure out, [he] is really trying to never tell us anything about physics" (FG3, 53). Although candidates acknowledged that the POEs required physics knowledge, they felt that the physics course was more about big issues in teaching and learning, and they acknowledged the thought that Tom put into issues of teaching and learning.

Ironically, one of candidates' complaints about the content of the physics class is the fact that Tom rarely made his opinion explicit. The following exchange

(FG3, 35–36) took place in the January focus group almost immediately following the preceding discussion:

James: I wish he would sometimes talk a bit more about his experiences in [teaching physics]

Irene: Yeah. I agree.

David: Oh, I find myself wishing that too. Not that he'd lecture but when he makes those firm statements because ... I think there's a real trust there and he isn't forcing ideas on us, he's sort of providing them; if we want to agree we can. So I think when it comes around to time when he does make a strong statement, that might be some of the reason why I'm more inclined to want to hear that and say, "You know what, I bet what he has to say is important." And he does it so infrequently that it sort of means something as opposed to saying "This is how it is" or "What I believe is" every day.

Tom's tendency to carefully pick when he makes a "strong statement" to the class made candidates more likely to attend to his comments about teaching and learning. The candidates decided on the reason why Tom chose to keep his opinions about teaching and learning to himself in the next section (FG3, 40–50) of the January focus group interview:

Paul: But the way that he's teaching is just doing it.

Irene: Yeah.

James: Um-hmm.

Paul: As opposed to saying "This is what I'm doing" and you know "Now I'm going to do this and watch."

David: So the way we teach is the method?

Paul: Yeah. He actually does that, you know. It's shocking but he does. And that's what I've found so impressive about it is that he hasn't ever once told me what to do and yet I've learned so much from him.

Max: I think one of the things is we all know teaching is impossible to perfect so even if someone who is an amazing teacher is coming out and telling us, "These are amazing things that work, and you can just do these and you'll be a great teacher." But how are you going to get better if you are just told what a great way is?

Paul: Yeah. And he said himself that that won't work. He said that we can do as many workshops as we want with great ideas and it won't work.

Together, the candidates came to the conclusion that *how Tom teaches is the content of the physics course*. They also realized that Tom's message of the importance of active-learning pedagogies would be ineffective if he simply told candidates to use active-learning pedagogies.

CHAPTER 6

The discussions about Tom's pedagogy that occurred during the focus group provided a framework for candidates to theorize about the overarching theme of Tom's pedagogy. James emphasized the importance of relationships in Tom's pedagogy:

> Tom is a great role model. He cares a lot for his students, just by showing how much he values our opinion and how the course is run and how the program here at Queen's is run and that's a thing I have learned, or I value very much as a teacher, caring for students. Tom shows that it's definitely effective. He stresses POEs a lot and active learning. I've tried to incorporate that in my classroom as much as I could ... I think it's had a positive effect on the students' learning. They seem interested in things like POEs and demonstrations and hands-on learning as opposed to just me up there, for instance, talking or writing notes on the board. (James3, 1)

James' comments suggest that he was encouraged to try active-learning pedagogies based on his experiences as a learner in Tom's class. David also picked up on the importance of relationships in Tom's class, arguing that the relationships formed a platform from which Tom could introduce a variety of concepts:

> My take on how Tom's running things is that he's sort of throwing things out, many things during a class ... everyone isn't going to pick up on exactly what he's doing each time but if you pick up on a good idea, you can sort of run with it or create a new repertoire or put it in the vault for later use. Just in modelling how he shows genuine concern for us and ... the course and the program, how ... [he] takes what we want to look at and what we want to learn and tries to incorporate that. (FG3, 15)

In his individual interview, Max also commented on the variety of ideas that Tom presented in the class:

> The main thing is just the way we run the class and how we go about learning just by kind of doing whatever we find appropriate and finding interesting things that Tom thinks or we think will help us learn, and just looking at them and seeing what's good about them ... more the ideas and getting them into us, so eventually I'll be able to pick up these ideas, hopefully, and bring them in [to my teaching], but not really forced to [incorporate them right away]. (Max3, 1)

Paul picked up on David's and Max's ideas, commenting on the subtlety of the way he learned from Tom's modelling of good teaching practices: "Some stuff [teaching strategies] you pick up from him and you don't know you're picking up ... that he's been doing the whole time [during the preservice year]" (FG3, 16). Paul also suggested that it takes time to recognize Tom's subtle style:

> After the two blocks [of classes], I liked the course. I thought, "This is going well" but I couldn't really think of anything I'd learned in that class. POEs, and that's about it. I couldn't really think of anything else I'd learned. Then I went to teach and I found myself getting it, I found myself getting everything he'd been trying to teach us. I could articulate "Tom's philosophy of

teaching physics." I had this conversation with my friend the other day. She asked, "Well, so what do you think about teaching physics?" I just talked to her for 15 minutes and I said, "Basically these are my physics professor's ideas." (FG3, 43)

For Paul, Tom's implicit and explicit modelling of pedagogy became clearer after he had both time to consider what he learned and teaching experiences on which to anchor his developing ideas.

The teacher candidates who participated in this research devoted a considerable amount of time to analyzing and interpreting the way they were being taught in the physics course. At first, it was difficult for candidates to name features of Tom's pedagogy beyond the obvious value he placed on the relationships he had with candidates in the course. During the focus group, however, teacher candidates came to the conclusion that the content of the physics course was the pedagogy that Tom used to teach the course. Importantly, Tom gave the candidates' space to process their learning and resisted lecturing the class about physics concepts or issues in teaching and learning. How he taught was the message.

Theorizing Teaching and Learning

Overall, participants' comments were much more delineated between theorizing about teaching and learning during the practicum and theorizing about teaching and learning at the Faculty of Education than in September or November. Candidates' theories about the nature of learning focused on how students in their host schools learn curricular content rather than how teacher candidates learn to teach.

During his practicum, Max noticed that students in his classes did not all learn in identical ways:

One thing I've really noticed is how different all the students are. In my math class, there's some people you'd explain them a concept and they go, "Oh," and then others, you'd draw it a couple of times and find some sort of manipulative for them to hold and look at that has to do with it, and that will get them to figure it out. And then other ones you have to approach in a completely different way. It was always a bit of a surprise for me, since, just tell me something and I'll generally figure it out. And I guess I'm always surprised how little students get out of a class most of the time. (Max3, 4)

Like many teacher candidates, Max's experiences learning his subject matter were quite different from the experiences of the majority of students he taught. Because he was someone who could "figure out" mathematics with minimal instruction, it was surprising for him to learn that most of his students were leaving mathematics class feeling confused. Max said that he wanted to learn "different techniques and strategies for dealing with an applied [level] class, how you want to teach them, and how you can assess them" because he had "never known many people who went in the applied stream" (Max3, 15).

James articulated similar thoughts, stating that the fact that "there are a lot of different learning styles" has "been hammered home pretty much throughout the

CHAPTER 6

whole year in both practicum and during the time spent here" (James3, 6). During his individual interview, James spoke at length about the importance of using a variety of teaching approaches to engage the different learners in his classes:

> You've really got to continually change your approach to teaching ... based on your class. So an important thing is, before you just start teaching ... find out as much as you can about the students you're teaching and try to adjust your teaching styles according to who you're teaching and what you find out. And that's hard of course because these days if you can have three classes with almost 30 students, it's hard to find out exactly the interests and learning styles, for instance, of each student in your class. (James3, 9)

For James, the importance of thinking about the different ways in which people learn was one of the strongest messages of the program.

The five teacher candidates emphasized the importance of building relationships to the quality of students' learning. Irene stated that "a good relationship really helps" (Irene3, 13) in the teaching profession. Max offered: "If, as a whole, the class gets along and enjoys each other, then they'll be OK to say things they might not say elsewhere" (Max3, 6). Max linked the importance of relationships on practicum to his own experiences as a learner: "I've noticed that the teachers I actually learn from are normally the ones that I'd stop and talk to outside of class .... You pay more attention to someone you'd want to actually talk to" (Max3, 5). Irene was quick to point out that developing relationships with students can take time, citing her recent experiences on practicum: "At the end of December ... they [students] were more engaged [compared to October]" (Irene3, 15). She characterized her relationships with students as a critical feature of her practicum: "To become a good teacher, I've really got to know all my students and be able to connect with them, because without that I'm just a student teacher who comes in every so often and talks ... and I don't want that" (Irene3, 30). James agreed: "Getting to know my students as much as possible is a big issue [on practicum] ... the last two practica I didn't spend enough time trying to address the special needs of certain students" (James3, 21). David found that the importance of building good rapport with his students was emphasized in the December practicum: "I would have told you before the course started that it would be important to establish a good relationship with all the students ... as a classroom management strategy ... [The last two practica] reinforced what I probably could have said already" (David3, 13).

Teacher candidates made more comments theorizing the nature of teaching than they did theorizing the nature of learning. During this January phase of data collection, the candidates discussed both how they thought about teaching and what it means to be a part of the teaching profession. James offered that "teaching is incredibly difficult" (James3, 5) and "there are definitely ways of teaching that are effective but there is no right way to teach; it depends on a lot of circumstances" (James3, 8). For James, the idea that there is not *one* right way to teach was "an eye-opener" (James3, 8). The idea of multiple ways of teaching closely aligns with James' earlier comments about the importance of teaching students in a variety of ways. When asked to give advice to future teacher candidates, James acknowledged the time that it took to become a teacher: "It's going to take a while to become the teacher you want to be, and by 'a while' I mean several years ... so take it one step at a time" (James3, 25). Irene echoed James' sentiment, warning future teacher candidates "not to expect too much out of the teaching practica" because "the more you teach the more you realize you're really just starting out learning something" (Irene3, 31).

James, Irene, and Max felt that establishing good relationships with other teachers was an important part of the teaching profession. James said: "I've learned that [establishing] relationships with colleagues is very important ... it's probably the best way to go about getting advice" (James3, 10). Irene made a similar comment: "If I didn't have a supportive department, I would have had a lot of trouble ... they were really friendly and really helpful. If I was all on my own it would have been tough" because other teachers provide "insights" (Irene3, 16). Max noticed that significant differences in pedagogical approaches might exist even if relationships between teachers are cordial: "On my practicum, most of the teachers got along ... but there would still be things they'd argue pretty heatedly about" (Max3, 7). The candidates agreed that it was important to interact with other teachers, for both pedagogical and moral support.

Paul took a different approach to thinking about the nature of the teaching profession. Although he was quick to say that "doing the actual teaching was a lot of fun" (Paul3, 1), Paul felt that there were elements of the profession that were unappealing. Paul related the lifestyle of a teacher to character acting:

> So I love teaching. I really do. There's a lot of what I like. The lifestyle isn't what I'm looking for right now. The sort of character of the teacher, I just don't like playing that character every day. I don't like telling people what, I don't go through my everyday life telling people what to do, so I don't know why I go and do that every day at school. I don't know what's best; I'm still trying to figure that out myself. (FG3, 107)

Paul's experience of himself as a living contradiction reached a peak in January, to the point where he questioned whether or not he should enter the teaching profession: "I just don't want to be in a school in Ontario next year" (FG3, 7). When prompted by another participant in the focus group about whether or not he wanted to enter the teaching profession in general, Paul responded: "I don't know. I don't feel great about it" (FG3, 9). He was concerned about the effects the lifestyle of being a teacher might have on him: "I just picture myself as being an actual teacher next year and there's a lot of stuff I don't like about it: the lifestyle and what it does to you" (Paul3, 4). Despite his misgivings, Paul believed that "it's not impossible" (Paul3, 4) to think of himself going into teaching next year. Looking ahead, he stated that he believed the final February practicum could change his mind: "Maybe it will make me want to be a teacher again" (FG3, 108).

The participants continued to theorize about the nature of both teaching and learning during this round of interviews. Their theories about how students learned from them continued to develop as a result of the extended fall practicum experience. Candidates' theories about teaching tended to focus on how they fit into their

CHAPTER 6

conceptions of the teaching profession, rather than on articulating visions of the kinds of teachers they wanted to be. Overall, candidates' comments reflected more careful thinking about the nature of teaching and learning, as a result of the December practicum and more time to process how they learned to teach at the midpoint of the teacher education program. The next section examines in greater detail how teacher candidates learned from practicum experiences.

LEARNING FROM PRACTICUM EXPERIENCES

The narratives that teacher candidates began about their practicum experiences during the November data collection were continued during the interviews held in January. Given that January was the midpoint of the teacher education program, teacher candidates were in a unique position to analyze their experiences during the fall practica while looking ahead to the final practicum in February. The previous section noted some of the tensions that candidates felt as they considered their next practicum placements; this section of the chapter focuses on what candidates learned from looking back and considering the fall practicum experiences. The candidates' narratives of experience during practicum were much more personal during this round of interviews. Perhaps a reason for the more personal nature of candidates' narratives is that relatively little was said about the practicum during the third focus group interview. When the practicum was discussed during the focus group, it was usually in the context of looking ahead to experiences in February. The focus group also had a feeling of shared resignation to the inevitability of the February practicum. Candidates were more forthcoming with their analysis of practicum experiences during the individual interviews. For this reason, the narratives of each of the participants in the research are considered in turn. Each participant's section describes and interprets major events during the fall practica, the relationship between associate teacher and teacher candidate, and tensions that the candidate felt as a result of prior practicum experiences.

James' Narrative of Fall Practicum Experiences

James was enthusiastic about his fall practicum experiences, but admitted that by the end of his December practicum he was "getting stressed out because [he] had three lessons to prepare and [he] had to learn the material" (FG3, 93). James also stated that he "was feeling tired" (James3, 29) by the end of December. At the same time, however, James felt that his teaching had improved considerably by the time he finished his December placement:

> I was becoming more organized and more confident in the classroom, but at the same I was teaching two different classes as opposed to – well three classes, two courses – so the workload was greater but I was able to handle it better because I had that much more experience, even if it was just an extra month. But I realized that there were certain things I thought I did pretty well, classroom management, for instance. (James3, 29)

James felt that it was important for him to "not take [the practicum] so seriously" in February because he wanted to "go and just try to have fun teaching" (FG3, 93). His major goal for improving his practice in February was to explore the question "What can I do to engage my students in the courses I'm teaching?" (James3, 23). James believed that it would be easier for him to learn how to engage his students in February because the practicum coincided with the beginning of the second semester of high school. He looked forward to that chance to "start a new class with the associate teacher" rather than "stepping into a class that's already been started" (James3, 21).

At the midpoint of the program, James characterized the relationship between the practicum and the on-campus weeks in the following manner:

> I definitely learned the most at my practicum, because I think the best way you learn how to teach is to actually teach. But at the same time I think it's important to step away from the classroom from time to time and learn about the theory of teaching, because although there's definitely a difference between what you learn on the job and what you learn back here, it's important to be reminded of the theory and stay on top of the theory, and try to apply the theory to your practice in the classroom. (James3, 12)

Overall, James' narrative of his fall practicum experiences is a positive one. He believed that the practicum was a powerful learning experience and did not name any specific problems, other than concerns that he was not meeting the learning needs of all of the students in his classes. He did not make any comments about the nature of his relationship with his associate teacher. James looked forward to his February practicum as an opportunity to explore some of his questions about teaching and learning, but at the same time he wanted to try to avoid feeling overwhelmed by responsibilities.

Max's Narrative of Fall Practicum Experiences

Max viewed his fall practicum experiences as an opportunity to practise "some of the basics of teaching" such as "maintaining control of the class" and "learning how much [information] the class can handle a certain day" (Max3, 8). He implicitly named the effects of the apprenticeship of observation on his pedagogy during the fall practica, "I guess in October and December [I was] still teaching like I've seen teaching all my life" (Max3, 8). Looking ahead to his February practicum, Max felt that he would continue "trying to get away from [the kind of teaching] I've seen my whole life," although he acknowledged that it "was not really a goal [he] could perform in one practicum" (Max3, 14). Max also wanted to "survive [the February practicum] and come out like he still enjoys teaching" (Max3, 14).

Although Max did not refer specifically to the nature of his relationship with his associate teacher, he did say that "the practicum is always fun but it's kind of awkward having that other person [the associate teacher] there sometimes and being in someone else's class" (Max3, 18). Like James, Max looked forward to the prospect of starting a new semester with his associate so that he could "start out teaching a

CHAPTER 6

different way [from traditional teaching] ... and be ready to try things [such as active-learning pedagogies]" (Max3, 9). Upon consideration of his development as a teacher at the midpoint of the program, Max characterized the fall practica as the place where he learned the basics of teaching and looked ahead to the February practicum as a space for him to enact active-learning pedagogies. He freely admitted that is was difficult to shake off the default teaching moves that he learned from his apprenticeship of observation. When prompted to comment on why it was hard to move beyond the basics, Max had this response:

> I guess just making sure I know all the basics well enough to be like, "All right. So I can do all these other things." And I don't really have to worry about, you know, making sure the class is awake, and, you know, taking attendance and yelling at kids, and writing tests, and whatever else. Because one thing I noticed is, if I'm thinking a bit too hard on what question I'm going to ask next or what is coming next after I finish this one statement, I won't notice if someone, has their hand up or is asleep or punching the kid next to them, or whatever. So, you know, just being able to keep that level head while still paying attention to what I'm doing. (Max3, 9)

Max's narrative of practicum experiences was one of naming his default teaching moves, and struggling to move beyond them. He felt that he needed to master basic teaching behaviours, such as simultaneously attending to multiple classroom events, before he would be able to enact different pedagogies. Max was hopeful that his February practicum, which began at the start of a new semester, would allow him to try different teaching strategies right away.

Irene's Narrative of Practicum Experiences

Irene experienced considerable tension during the December practicum because she was unable to enact active-learning pedagogies upon returning to her host school. Irene felt constrained by the curricular expectations set out by her associate teacher:

> December was kind of frustrating for me. I had all these great plans for active learning classrooms. It was going to be great ... but then I got there and my teacher had just finished a unit and ... he wanted to do the lab portion of the test, or of the unit. That was just his way of teaching, do the stuff [theory] and then do the hands-on. I don't know if I agree with that but that was just the way it worked.... Then the labs took 2 weeks and that was kind of frustrating ... I didn't feel like I had a ton of ownership over what I was teaching for those first 2 weeks. Then [I taught] planetary mechanics [which] was a whole lot of history and stuff, which I found a lot of fun, but then I found like I was just making excuses for not trying new things like active learning. (Irene3, 18)

Irene stated that she always has "all these great ideas when [she] goes on practicum" yet they don't "really work out that way, just because ... [she] feels like [she] needs more practice" (Irene3, 18). For Irene, the gap between her pedagogical vision and her enacted practice was a powerful factor in her narrative of the fall practicum. Despite her frustrations, Irene described her practicum experience as "good" because she "liked the length of it" and the rhythm of the program: "It helps to go back and forth [between the Faculty and the host school] to be able to see things from two different perspectives" (Irene3, 36). For Irene, the time spent at the Faculty was welcome because "it provides a different perspective and brings me back to the theory ... otherwise [she] could be quickly falling into learning the rote style of teaching" (Irene3, 19).

Irene had considerable respect for her associate teacher, describing him as "great" (Irene3, 14) even if he was "a bit disorganized" (Irene3, 20) when it came to assessment. One feature of his teaching that had a profound effect on her was the "lectures" (FG3, 62) he gave to his Grade 12 physics class. At first Irene "was scared" by the prospect of lecturing Grade 12 students, but she soon bought into the idea that "they need to be prepared for university" (FG3, 62). During the focus group interview, Max challenged her assertion: "I don't think that an extra four months of getting lectured will help you at all when you get to university" (FG3, 65). Irene responded that a lecture-based Grade 12 physics class "might help to ease the transition [between high school and university] a bit" (FG3, 66). During her individual interview, Irene returned to the idea of lecturing grade 12 physics students and defended her associate teacher's style, stating that students in his class know university physics "is going to be hard, and more what [classes] are going to be like in university" (FG3, 8).

Irene looked forward to her February practicum but, like James, she wanted to "find more balance" (FG3, 96) in her many responsibilities as a teacher candidate. She was "stressed" (FG3, 97) by the prospect of using active-learning pedagogies with her students during the February practicum, even though she was disappointed and frustrated when she was forced to teach using traditional methods in December. Irene wanted to "be more of an engaging teacher" but was concerned that she did not "have a lot of experience yet to be able to have a lot of good ideas for how to do active learning" (Irene3, 29). At the same time, Irene felt that excusing herself from trying active-learning pedagogies due to inexperience was inappropriate: "I keep saying, 'Well, I don't really know what I'm doing so I'll worry about it when I'm teaching full time. Right now I'll just get through this unit.' And I don't want to do that because it's always going to be like that" (Irene3, 29).

Irene's narrative of her fall practicum experience was filled with the tension between the kind of teacher she wanted be and the kind of teacher her associate teacher wanted her to be. Compounding the issue was her respect for her associate teacher's pedagogy, even though it was contrary to the messages she was receiving from the physics course. Irene was trapped in a kind of vicious circle: She wanted to enact active-learning pedagogies during her practicum, but she felt that her inexperience prevented her from finding creative ways to engage the class, and subsequently she felt guilty about using inexperience as an excuse.

David's Narrative of Practicum Experiences

Of the teacher candidates who participated in the study, David was the only one who indicated that he had almost complete freedom during his fall practicum. Given that

CHAPTER 6

many of the other candidates struggled with the fact that they had to teach within clear boundaries established by their associate teachers, it might be somewhat surprising to learn that David said he was "dreading going back [to practicum in February] and having to do the same things [he] was doing before" (FG3, 100). For David, the practicum meant he had to "work under someone else's shadow," which was a frustrating prospect for him, regardless of how "lenient" his associate teacher was (FG3, 100). During his individual interview, David was asked what he learned from his fall practicum experiences. He replied:

> I don't know that I'm learning a whole lot, because I'm not really able to do what I want to do, which is what was getting my frustration levels up. I don't really want to go back to this next practicum, not because I don't enjoy it, but because I just want it to be September already .... It was communicated up front that I could try whatever [teaching strategies] I want. At the time it's nice to hear that, and I didn't think too much about it, but I just knew that that was wrong.... You can't really just do whatever you want. There are pressures of always knowing that you're being evaluated and, sure, I can try whatever I want, but if I fall flat on my face and I'm not able to recover, well, it's going to reflect in the assessment, which, as much as they say "Don't worry about these [teaching assessments]," hiring [school] boards are clearly asking to see these. We come into a classroom that's been set up already and ... we know full well that when we leave, we're handing it back, so we can't make the changes or operate really as we may want to. (David3, 18)

David believed that, no matter how much freedom he had during his practicum, there was a limit to what he could learn from the artificiality of teaching in *someone else's* classroom. He pointed out that associate teachers implicitly create boundaries for teacher candidates out of necessity, because associate teachers are ultimately responsible for the course after the practicum is finished: "As much as he [the associate teacher] says 'Try whatever you want, try this, try that,' I realized, well, he's still making me cover all of this [curricular material] and I don't have the freedom that I thought I did" (FG3, 101).

David's dominant narrative of the practicum was his feeling that the practicum is an artificial learning environment. Problematically, David perceived that "the ante seems to go up" each practicum, with the result that he was going to be "swamped" with responsibilities during the final February practicum (David3, 30). Although David was quick to say, "I feel like I must be learning something [on practicum]" (David3, 18), he seemed to struggle with the whole concept of learning to teach from the practicum. David characterized the idea of learning from practicum in the following way:

> You go to the practicum and you hope to be exposed to all of these different situations and as you go through a situation, you kind of tick it off and you've then, quote-unquote, "acquired" that skill for dealing with whatever it may be. There may or may not be a finite number of situations and once you've been through them all, you're good to go. (David3, 29)

David's metaphor of ticking off learning experiences during practicum is telling. At this point in the program, David regarded the practicum as an experience to get through, rather than an experience from which he could learn productively.

David's narrative of his fall practicum experiences focused on the tension he felt because of the implicit restrictions of the practicum placement. Although he had freedom to try a variety of teaching strategies, he ultimately felt like he had to teach in a certain way in order to avoid falling "flat on his face" (David3, 18) and getting a poor assessment. David also believed that he was confined by the curricular constraints placed on him by his associate teacher. A recurring feature in his narrative was the realization that, although he had some freedom to try different pedagogies, he did not have freedom to truly experience what it is like to be a teacher because he did not have final authority over what happened in his classrooms.

Paul's Narrative of Practicum Experiences

On his fall practicum, Paul experienced tension between two different sets of experiences working with two different associate teachers. His associate teacher for physics gave him "a lot of freedom" (Paul3, 16) to use a variety of teaching strategies, whereas his associate teacher for mathematics made him adopt her pedagogy, which according to Paul was "formulaic: taking up the homework, doing a lecture, and then having time to work on the homework" (Paul3, 17). When planning his mathematics course, Paul felt that he had "no freedom to do anything interesting" (Paul3, 17) with his students. The dramatic contrast concerning freedom that he had to plan and enact pedagogies resulted in two different sets of feelings for Paul. He elaborated on this point during his individual interview:

> In the physics class it felt like everything that I was doing that was along the lines of what we've been talking about [in the physics curriculum course] felt really in tune with how the class was working. We would do this POE [Predict-Observe-Explain], for example, just a basic one, and it just sort of made sense [because] people wanted to be sort of talking, thinking, discussing, and then figuring out how they were wrong based on something they were seeing .... It was successful because it was in line with them, you know. It was in line with just people. Whereas in this math class, it felt like every time I was struggling or getting discipline issues or they were getting bored .... I mean, every second of that class was a struggle ... because in that class I was always specifically working against the grain. These crazy Grade 9 kids [in the math class] had all this energy and wanted to be out of their seats and talking to each other, whereas in physics class a lot of the time those activities were really built around just channelling that into more productive stuff .... In the math class, it always felt like you were ... making them sit and be quiet and work on homework, you know.... Even just having them sit there and listen to me talk, that just didn't feel like a natural thing, even for 10, 15 minutes, in math. (Paul3, 16).

Paul felt a tension between the active-learning pedagogies that he could enact during his physics class and the traditional, teacher-centred pedagogies he was required to

CHAPTER 6

use during his mathematics class. He felt that active-learning pedagogies were "in line" with how students learned and he "could see the power of what [Tom] is trying to teach in [physics] class" (Paul3, 16). He also believed that the classroom management issues he encountered in math were a result of trying to control rather than teach students. "I could sort of be myself in that physics class, and in the math class there was always the tension between what they [students] wanted to be doing and what you were making them do" (Paul3, 23). The tension that Paul experienced between the physics and math classes showed him "the difference between doing the basic style [of teaching] ... and really thinking about what's going to help the class learn" (Paul3, 21).

During both the focus group and individual interviews, Paul frequently mentioned that he had "bad associations with teaching" (Paul3, 9), largely due to "some really unpleasant teachers" (FG3, 105) at his associate school. The tipping point for Paul seemed to be a time during the fall practicum:

> There was a stretch of 2 or 3 days when I heard every single teacher in my department, except for my two associate teachers, speak loudly enough for me to hear about how much student teachers suck ... about how student teachers aren't how they used to be [and] when they [the experienced teachers] were student teachers, they would bend over backwards to please their associate teachers. (Paul3, 7)

This experience made Paul "dread" (Paul3, 6) the thought of having to share an office with the other teachers in his department, to the point where they "made [him] not want to go to school every day" (FG3, 105).

Paul's narrative was filled with tension for two reasons. The first was the conflict he felt between teaching using active-learning pedagogies in his physics class and the lecture-based teaching of his mathematics class. As Paul noted, "In the physics class, when things were going well it just kind of happened" (Paul3, 23). He was given the space to teach in a way that aligned with his pedagogical vision in the physics class; the math class was frustrating because he was forced to teach in a way that felt unproductive for both his students and him. The second reason for Paul's tension toward the practicum was the "negativity towards teacher candidates" (Paul3, 8) that he perceived from members of his host department. The net result of Paul's narrative of fall practicum experiences was that he looked to the February practicum as something to "get through" (Paul3, 34) rather than to learn from.

Summary of Narratives of Fall Practicum Experiences

The teacher candidates who participated in this research shared a variety of "secret stories" (Clandinin & Connelly, 1995, p. 5) during their individual interviews. Each candidate named and described tensions experienced during the fall practica. The tensions that James experienced during the fall practica were relatively benign; his experience seemed to be positive overall and the only issue that he raised was one of finding a balance in his workload upon returning to the February placement. Max experienced tension between his desire to master what he named "the basics" of teaching and his desire to move beyond the effects of his apprenticeship of observation. Max looked to the February placement as an opportunity to try and enact unfamiliar active-learning pedagogies, although he acknowledged that changing his default pedagogy would be challenging. Irene found herself in a cycle of wanting to enact active-learning pedagogies, feeling confined by the requirements of both time and curriculum, and then feeling frustrated with her tendency to find excuses not to challenge her default teaching strategies. Although he seemingly had more freedom than any of the other participants, David experienced tensions during his practica as a result of his perception that the practicum is an artificial learning environment. He found it difficult to move beyond the idea that he was, ultimately, a stranger in someone else's classroom. Paul found himself questioning his place in the teaching profession for two reasons. First, he felt uncomfortable in one of his host classrooms because he had to teach in a way that contradicted his beliefs about how students learn. Second, he was discouraged by the negative attitude toward teacher candidates in his department.

LEARNING EXPERIENCES IN THE PHYSICS CLASS: TEACHER EDUCATORS

The perspective of the teacher educator during the January on-campus weeks is described and interpreted in this section, in a chronological format using quotations and observations taken from my research journal. Data include the notes I took during each physics class and the notes I kept during conversations with Tom over the month of January. In keeping with the requirements of the ethics board, my observations focused on features of Tom's teaching. The quotations listed in this section are based on transcriptions that I created in my journal and hence are cited as (Journal, January). Where appropriate, some of the comments from teacher candidates who participated in the research are included in order to provide additional insight into specific events in the physics methods course. In these cases, the citations follow previously established conventions.

The perspective of the teacher educator can again be represented by one overarching theme: creating a clear signal against a noisy background. During the eight classes of the January on-campus weeks, Tom revisited the mandate that he set at the end of the November block, namely, to ensure that his message came across as a signal for candidates to think carefully about their own learning rather than as more background noise. The previous section of this chapter interpreted the considerable evidence that the process of learning to teach is one filled with tensions and contradictions. Tom had long felt that January was the most important time in the program. His major goal was to create a productive learning environment, rather than one that faded into obscurity as candidates struggled to contend with the tensions carried over from the practicum and the new challenges posed by the emphasis on finding a job for September.

Setting the Stage for Self-directed Learning

Teacher candidates arrived to their first physics class of the winter term to find the physics units in the Ontario curriculum listed on the front board. Tom invited candidates to mix themselves up, as they had predictably returned to the same seats

CHAPTER 6

they grew accustomed to during November's classes. He introduced the first activity in January in the following way:

> My idea is to try to set up today for you figuring out what you want to spend your time doing over the next seven classes. Thursdays are going to be essentially your own days, and I have arranged for guest speakers to come in on Mondays. I want you to have the time between now and this Thursday's class for you to figure out what it is that you want to do. (Journal, January)

Tom then reminded candidates to get reacquainted with one another at their tables and distributed white boards so that the candidates could record salient features of their discussion. He repeatedly emphasized that the focus of the January classes would be up to the teacher candidates to pursue individually or in groups.

After about 30 minutes of discussion, each group of teacher candidates presented the results of its conversation. There was a diverse range of issues in teaching and learning presented. Tom wove together the large-group discussion by calling attention to the inherent complexities of teaching:

> It seems to me that there wasn't a whole lot of overlap. Each of the groups could understand where everyone is coming from. It is important to point that out so that you realize why becoming a teacher feels like you have the world on your shoulders. You just get better at one thing, and you have 15 other things to worry about. (Journal, January)

Tom took the opportunity to call candidates' attention to a variety of resources (e.g., the PEEL website, the PSSC physics textbook, and Hewitt's textbooks) that they might wish to use in order to pursue some of the issues raised during the discussion. At the conclusion of the discussion, Tom provided more detail on the self-directed learning assignment for the month of January:

> I am interested in you having a plan for how you want to spend your time in physics class. *That can include not coming to class.* That raises the temptation to work on all of the things where someone else is telling you what to do first. I would simply like you to have that experience. I would like you to come to class on Thursday so that different people can negotiate what they want to work on. I am not going to hit the beach for the next month; it's just that, particularly on Thursdays, I don't see myself as action central. I want to be here to jump in when you want me to. (Journal, January)

The teacher candidates in the physics course asked a variety of questions that suggested some disbelief about how little structure had been provided for the self-directed learning part of the physics course. Tom clarified that he had two requirements for self-directed learning: candidates were to come to Thursday's class prepared to form groups around common interests, and each group would be responsible for having something to share on the last Thursday in January.

Learning from Self-directed Learning

At the beginning of the second class in January, the teacher candidates quickly organized themselves into groups around issues that they wanted to pursue during their self-directed learning time. A few of the candidates chose to work individually. Tom reminded candidates that self-directed learning meant that they could choose to spend two consecutive Thursdays however they wished. Approximately 70% of the candidates turned up to work in class on the first Thursday; none came for the second Thursday. Tom was present for each of the SDL classes and had computers available for candidates to use.

The focus group interview and the individual follow-up interviews that I conducted with teacher candidates took place in the last week of January, in the middle of the time candidates were encouraged to pursue self-directed learning both inside and outside of the physics course. For this reason, the perspectives of the teacher candidates who participated in the research shed considerable light on the self-directed learning activity. As teacher educators, Tom and I had little idea of what to expect for the final class because most candidates had worked independently.

Comments about self-directed learning from the teacher candidates who participated in the research fell into two categories: observations about how Tom structured the self-directed learning time in the physics course and candidates' individual experiences using the self-directed learning time. The candidates unanimously commented on the fact that Tom had "taken [self-directed learning] to a new level" (FG3, 22) because "there are no guidelines" (FG3, 24). Paul stated, somewhat tongue-in-cheek, "Tom's basically removed every single restriction, I can't think of a single restriction he's placed on us at all. I feel like I could leave town and show up in April" (FG3, 26). James also brought up the freedom of self-directed learning, "We don't have to show up to a Thursday class, right? That's one unique thing" (FG3, 22). David theorized at length about the unique approach Tom took to self-directed learning:

> Tom is actually giving us the time to do self-directed learning ... it seems like he's recognizing that we have all this work and everything else to do so he's also giving us time in which to tackle the self-directed learning, as opposed to just "Well, here's an open-ended assignment. Make sure it's due at the end of the week." In which case, sure it's open-ended but you do the first thing that comes to mind to get it done and move on, whereas here Tom is sort of trying to foster the desire to do something meaningful and substantial [with our time]. (FG3, 23)

For teacher candidates who participated in the research, the issue was not that Tom chose to make self-directed learning a part of the course because, as James noted, "self-directed learning is a theme here at the Faculty" (FG3, 22). The defining feature of self-directed learning in the physics class was that Tom provided class time for candidates to "focus on what they feel to be important" (FG3, 20).

Although the candidates were appreciative of the time provided for self-directed learning, they also felt, in retrospect, that they could have used their time more wisely. Irene summed up the group's feelings when she said, "I've learned that you don't always spend self-directed learning time wisely" (FG3, 55). In her individual interview, Irene admitted that she let "other courses take precedence" (Irene3, 3) during the self-directed time. Paul said he "hadn't worked hard enough on it" (Paul3, 14).

CHAPTER 6

Max said that, at first, he was "a little apprehensive" about self-directed learning but "that it ended up being good because [there was] no pressure, just exploring" (Max3, 2). James agreed that it was "great to have the option of doing pretty much whatever we wanted" but felt that his choice of activity resulted in "not really learning a whole lot" (James3, 4).

By the time the deadline came, all the teacher candidates in the physics course seemed quite enthusiastic about sharing the results of their self-directed learning time. The final class did not begin until 15 minutes later than scheduled, because candidates were informally discussing the various resources that they had brought in for the occasion and Tom chose not to interrupt their discussions. Thirteen presentations later, Tom asked the candidates, "Did most of you find that surviving the program interfered with self-directed learning?" A few candidates in the class admitted that it was hard to focus their attention on self-directed learning with the stresses associated in light of the job search that had begun in earnest.

Learning from Guest Speakers

The other major feature of Tom's pedagogy during the month of January was the guest speakers that he invited into the physics classroom. The speakers were diverse: a first-year university student at Queen's, a superintendent from the local school board, and a local science department head. After each speaker, Tom engaged the class in a discussion to process the issues raised by the presentation. The candidates who participated in the research appreciated the diverse perspectives offered by the guest speakers. David said that he "enjoyed the guest speakers who came in … [because he] could compare their biases or beliefs [about teaching and learning]" (David3, 1). James said that he "took something different away from each speaker" (James3, 2).

The perspective of the first-year Queen's student enrolled in a physics course was particularly interesting to the teacher candidates because he was able to draw comparisons between how he learned in high school and how he learned at university. James noted that it was "good to hear his perspective, as he was fresh out of high school" (James3, 3). Irene appreciated hearing from "a first-year student how much they felt they were prepared [by high school]" (FG3, 2).

The perspective of the department head of science from a local school was by far the one that resonated most strongly with the teacher candidates who participated in this research. For Paul, the department head's talk was particularly powerful, "It seemed like hearing him talk somehow just 'made the link' I guess, is the only way to put it. You see how you can really just do actual things" (Paul3, 12). Paul went on to say that an earlier talk in November from the same teacher helped him to "crystallize a lot of what we'd been talking about in physics class" (Paul3, 10), because the teacher shared Tom's commitment to using active-learning pedagogies in the physics classroom. The science teacher also made a strong impression on Max and James, both of whom mentioned his realistic advice about the first year of teaching: "What you want to do is get through so you still want to teach, so it's like survive so you still want to teach" (FG3, 103).

CREATING A CLEAR SIGNAL AGAINST A NOISY BACKGROUND

Processing January Classes

At the conclusion of the January classes, Tom and I met to process the self-directed learning activity that was the central feature of his teaching in January. When I asked Tom for his reaction to the self-directed learning presentations that occurred during the final class, he replied:

> I think the fact that it worked; that there was a product from everyone said something. I found myself pleased that it wasn't a month of students doing presentations to each other, which I've never really liked because it always seems like passing the teaching role over to the students, particularly when you tell them what to present on. If everybody just came away with a sense of what might be different about self-directed learning in terms of how it feels, I think that's the point of it. I think the difference from when I first started trying self-directed learning is that I've now accepted that it will work. I have to give it warning, lead up to it, and then just go ahead with it and not back off and change my mind at the last minute. (Journal, February)

I then asked Tom to comment on his conception of January as the lynchpin of the program. He replied:

> Here in the building the program is its own worst enemy. It seemed fairly important to keep listening to them in terms of how they were experiencing the overall pressure. In a sense, while January may look like the lynchpin, in a sense the program makes it something other than that. (Journal, February)

Tom's comment reminded me of the tensions and pressures that candidates who participated in the research had articulated during both the focus group and individual interviews. In particular, I recalled David's comment that physics class served as a "safe haven" (David3, 6). I asked Tom if he was intentionally setting up the learning experiences of the physics class as a contrast to his perception of candidates' learning experiences in the program:

> *Shawn*: Are you setting this environment up to be very different from the program they are experiencing? They are getting told a lot about, for example, job applications. There are many workshops to go to. Then, in physics, every other class is self-directed: Come if you want, stay at home if you want. Was that intentional?
>
> *Tom*: It is not accidental. If I have the sense that the program is going berserk, and is violating a lot of the basic ideas that are across the front of the room up there [e.g., Explore First, Explain Later or How I Teach is the Message], then I want to do what I can to keep the experience of those ideas alive. So, yes, anything I can do to make my course look and feel better than the rest of the program, I will always try to do, because really I think that's what everybody in the building should be trying to do. I haven't thought of it this way before, but teaching in a school doesn't require you to think about what other teachers are doing. They are in a 4-year high school program, so to speak, but each

subject does stand more or less on its own. Whereas here, every student is a part of an 8-month program, all of which is supposed to focus on becoming the best teacher you can become. I guess I'd have to say that the program loses sight of that fact. (Journal, February)

From Tom's perspective, making self-directed learning the focus of January had two main pedagogical purposes. The first was to provide teacher candidates with the opportunity to have a learning experience that was different from both the potentially frantic pace of the program in January and their previous experiences as students. The second purpose was to step back and provide an opportunity for candidates to think about some of the main ideas of his teaching. As Tom said, "We're not going to come up with many more 'big ideas' for teaching, we've got a pretty rich list as it is. I think the self-directed learning is consistent with those ideas" (Journal, February).

Looking ahead to April, Tom thought aloud about the "best way to put a bow on whatever we've got so far [in the physics curriculum course]" (Journal, February). From his perspective, much of what candidates end up taking from the physics course depends on how they relate learning experiences in the physics course to "what they do in other pockets of the program" (Journal, February). Instead of "urging candidates to be super-teacher in their first year," Tom hoped that candidates were getting the message that the big ideas he was modelling and promoting are "ideas that you have to work your way into" (Journal, February). As he surmised at the end of the discussion, "Good teaching is rocket science, and you have to teach yourself that; no one can do it for you" (Journal, February).

CONSTRUCTING PROFESSIONAL KNOWLEDGE FROM TEACHING AND LEARNING EXPERIENCES

The professional knowledge constructed and co-constructed by the teacher candidates and teacher educators who participated in this study is discussed in this final section of the chapter. The themes in the data are synthesized with a view to making claims about how participants were theorizing teaching and learning during the third phase of data collection. The overarching theme is captured as a contrast between noise and signal. The tensions experienced by teacher candidates in their practicum experiences and the perceived incoherence of the teacher education program seemed to contribute to a sense of unfocused noise. The learning experiences provided by the physics course seemed to contribute a focused signal for their learning to teach.

During a meeting in late November, Tom characterized January as the "pivotal" (Journal, November) point in the program. Teacher candidates have completed 8 weeks of fall practicum experience and 7 weeks of coursework. The tensions described by teacher candidates in November are heightened at this point in the program. Without exception, the candidates who participated in this research looked forward to returning to the Faculty for classes in January. Feelings of relief quickly gave way to feelings of tension, however, as the contradictions they experienced in the fall term seemed to be magnified and compounded by experiences during the January on-campus weeks. Scientifically, noise may be defined as competition between dissonant sounds. This definition is also an apt way to characterize the interactions between old and new tensions experienced by teacher candidates during the month of January.

The first instance of noise occurred upon candidates' return to the Faculty of Education. Although they welcomed the change, candidates quickly perceived a lack of coherence in the program. The major cause was the variety of pedagogical expectations espoused by teacher educators, a variety that David characterized as a competition between rival "camps" (David3, 23) at the Faculty. As Tom noted in our January wrap-up meeting, candidates are bound to perceive a program as incoherent when teacher educators are sending mixed signals in a program that is ostensibly supposed to have one goal, the preparation of future teachers. The perceived over-abundance of job-related fairs and workshops did little to assuage candidates' frustrations with the program.

Candidates did not expect teacher educators to use identical teaching strategies, only to recognize the competing demands placed on how they think about teaching and learning. The lack of coherence in the program was perceived both as "too many most important things" (Irene3, 35) and a tension between teaching subject-matter curricula and teaching big picture issues such as social justice and inclusion (FG3, 53). Perhaps most significantly, teacher candidates perceived a lack of program coherence when they were taught in ways that did not coincide with the ways in which they were encouraged to teach. How they were taught seemed to matter more than what they were taught.

The second instance of noise was the tension surrounding practicum experiences, both those already completed and those that were to happen in February and March. The teacher candidates said little about their fall practicum experiences during the third focus group interview in January. Their narratives seemed to become "secret stories" (Clandinin & Connelly, 1995, p. 5), told during individual interviews and underscoring the tensions that were magnified during the fall practicum experience. The secret stories of the fall practicum further reveal a major tension between candidates' pedagogical vision and enacted practice. For the most part, this tension remained unresolved. The implicit and explicit restrictions placed on candidates by their associate teachers were a primary source of this tension. Perhaps Paul felt this tension more strongly than the other candidates because he had two different associate teachers, one who allowed him to teach in a way that was in accord with his pedagogical vision, and one who did not. David raised the issue that, regardless of how flexible an associate teacher is, a practicum is ultimately an artificial learning environment because candidates are learning to teach in someone else's classroom. Looking forward to the February practicum, candidates expressed concern that their responsibilities would increase to that of a full-time teacher. They expressed concern with the idea that they were supposed to impress their associate teachers with the way they handled a full-time teaching schedule, yet first-year teachers may be expected to do little more than survive their first year of teaching.

Against this backdrop of noise in candidates' experiences, both on practicum and in classes, Tom's major pedagogical challenge was to become a signal that candidates could recognize and respond to, rather than another dissonant background sound.

CHAPTER 6

By taking a step back from the front of the classroom and turning the physics course over to the self-directed learning project and guest speakers, Tom provided a space for candidates to think about their learning. During the third focus group interview, participants puzzled over several pedagogical issues in the physics course, such as the role of physics content in a physics curriculum course and Tom's tendency to avoid lecturing candidates on how to teach. Teacher candidates who participated in the research came to the conclusion that *how* Tom teaches is the essential content of the course. During the individual interviews, each candidate discussed ways in which they were thinking about teaching as a result of Tom's physics course. Paul felt that it required time to process how he learned from the physics course, an idea supported by the fact that most of the candidates' conversations about teaching and learning in the physics course revolved around course experiences in September and November, as opposed to January.

The perspective of the teacher educator reveals the pedagogical decision-making process behind a significant teaching move: Tom's decision to provide a space for candidates in the physics class to engage in self-directed learning. By this point in the year, Tom had introduced all of his big ideas about teaching and learning to the class, so stepping back and engaging candidates in self-directed learning was the biggest signal that he could send amidst the chaos and noise of January. Prior experience had made Tom consider the importance of listening to his students about the effects that the program is having on their learning, particularly during the month of January when their attention is divided between the upcoming final practicum and the pressure of the job search. In a way, providing candidates with more freedom and control over their own learning was a way for Tom to help them relieve the tensions associated with incoherence in the program and also encourage candidates to refocus themselves on issues that he saw as important. It would be far less effective to tell candidates to focus on the big picture of learning to teach. Instead, Tom showed them one way to focus on their own learning through self-directed learning.

Comments from the candidates revealed that it was particularly important for Tom to make self-directed learning classes optional. The degree of freedom given to the physics class around the self-directed learning activity was met initially with a certain degree of incredulity. Candidates felt trusted and appreciated the space they had to make decisions about their own learning, although in hindsight most felt that they would spend their time differently given another opportunity to engage in self-directed learning. From Tom's perspective, providing the experience so candidates could feel what it was like to direct their own learning was more important than any end product they may have created.

The participating teacher candidates continued to theorize about the nature of teaching and learning. The importance of developing productive relationships with both students and other teachers was a dominant theme in the data. For the teacher candidates, it was important to have freedom to form their own rapport with their students in order to learn how to best meet their needs as learners. Perhaps a part of their emphasis on the importance of relationship arose from their perceptions of teaching as a difficult and challenging profession. There was considerable evidence that the teacher candidates were beginning to think about the first year of teaching and what their lifestyle would be as first-year teachers. They looked toward the February practicum with a certain amount of trepidation because of the requirement to take on a full teaching load. For some candidates, such a requirement underscored the artificiality of the practicum learning experience and made them wish they were beginning in their own classrooms, rather than in someone else's. At the conclusion of January, candidates left the Faculty of Education for two months of practicum experiences, one month in their host schools and one month they had arranged themselves in an alternative educational setting. Looking ahead to April, the challenges for Tom and the teacher candidates who participated in the research were significant. How would they name and interpret the knowledge they constructed and co-constructed over the course of the teacher education program?

CHAPTER 7

CONSOLIDATION AND LOOKING AHEAD

Every time I go into Tom's class, I am thinking about, "What is teaching?" I do reflect upon that sometimes in other classes, but every time in Tom's class I am thinking about that for a good part of the 2 ½ hours. He does give lots of practical advice, like POEs, but I just think he hammers home the big picture.

(James, FG4, 69)

A great deal happens in a preservice teacher education program, particularly one that lasts just 8 months. Candidates come in to a program such as the one at Queen's University with at least an undergraduate degree in hand and a lifetime of experiences witnessing teaching at the elementary, secondary, and post-secondary levels. They have well-developed, if tacit, assumptions about what teaching and learning should look and feel like. Some candidates may be unsure about what to expect in a teacher education program, aside from the promise of practicum experiences in at least one school and professional certification upon successful completion of the degree. Upon entering the program, it is highly unlikely that candidates have given much thought to the discipline of education, if they are even aware of its existence.

Yet by the end of the same teacher education program, several profound changes have occurred in teacher candidates. The most obvious change is as a result of their practicum experiences; they have spent considerable time in a school environment learning the cultural routines associated with being a classroom teacher. For many candidates, experiences related to the practicum are the most visceral learning experiences in the program. Some candidates may have decided that teaching is no longer their preferred career. Others have had a lifelong dream affirmed and eagerly await the opportunity to teach in their own classrooms the following September.

It would be a mistake, however, to ignore the experiences that teacher candidates have during the on-campus portion of their program through coursework and interactions with teacher educators and other teacher candidates. Considerable evidence has been presented in the education research literature underscoring shortcomings of preservice teacher education programs. Many of the sharpest criticisms come from the field, including practising teachers who may believe that extended classroom experience is the only relevant way to learn to teach, school administrators who may wonder why new teachers are not better prepared for the realities of everyday teaching, and recent graduates of teacher education programs who are frequently frustrated with the quality of their programs. Most of the criticisms presented in the literature are valid and should be of considerable concern to those who care about preservice teacher education. The literature also abounds with potential solutions to the problems raised both by researchers and those in the education system.

CHAPTER 7

Clearly, experiences in the on-campus program are worthy of consideration, and the data presented so far indicates that these experiences can have a profound impact on how teacher candidates construct professional knowledge about teaching and learning. One of the main challenges for a teacher educator at the end of a teacher education program is to find ways to help teacher candidates consolidate their learning. A part of this consolidation process will naturally include looking toward the future, as candidates think about the kinds of teachers they want to be.

The first section of this chapter provides a brief overview of events during the final six classes of the year. The data obtained from the focus group and individual interviews are then analyzed to provide insight into how teacher candidates constructed professional knowledge from learning experiences in the physics course. Unlike the previous three analysis chapters, the teacher candidates' experiences on practicum were not a significant part of the data. Instead, the participants spoke at length about what they had learned during the preservice teacher education program, with particular emphasis on the difference between their prior assumptions about teaching and learning and their theories about teaching and learning in April. Selected narratives of the candidates' learning experiences during the year are presented in order to illustrate many of the tensions associated with constructing professional knowledge during the teacher education program. The next section provides the perspective and voice of the teacher educator as I analyze both the features of Tom's pedagogy during the month of April and our discussions as we thought about our experiences with the physics methods course over the year. Finally, the chapter concludes with a summary of the professional knowledge constructed and co-constructed by the teacher candidates and the teacher educators who participated in this study.

CONTEXTUAL FEATURES OF THE PHYSICS METHODS COURSE

The physics class reconvened for the final six classes on the first Monday in April. The teacher candidates were welcomed back to the physics course and provided with an opportunity to have informal discussions about their most recent practicum experiences. Tom then raised the issue of the role of content knowledge in teaching physics by encouraging candidates to consider physics texts favouring a conceptual approach to understanding physics (e.g., Einstein & Infeld, 1966; Hewitt, 2006). Each of the remaining classes had two key features. First, Tom introduced an idea from the literature on physics education research, such as cognitive dissonance or assessment, and facilitated a discussion that encouraged candidates to link the ideas to their experiences teaching students on practicum. Second, Tom provided opportunities for the teacher candidates to analyze how they learned from the physics class, the practicum, and the overall teacher education program. During the penultimate class, candidates were engaged in small- group discussions about their learning for the majority of the class. The physics methods course concluded on the final Thursday in April with Tom revisiting a theme he introduced during the first class of the year: the importance of minding the gap between theory and practice.

CONSOLIDATION AND LOOKING AHEAD

LEARNING EXPERIENCES IN THE PHYSICS CLASS: TEACHER CANDIDATES

This final analysis of how teacher candidates constructed professional knowledge from learning experiences in the physics course interprets both the learning that occurred during the April classes and, more generally, the learning that occurred in the physics class over the course of the year. The four themes that were discussed in the previous chapter are again used in this section: Learning from the Program, Learning from Tensions, Learning from Tom, and Theorizing Teaching and Learning. The first theme names and interprets candidates' impressions of how they learned from the structure of the teacher education program. The second theme revisits candidates' experiences of themselves as living contradictions by further exploring the tensions they experienced during the program. Although there is some mention of the teaching strategies used by Tom during the month of April, the Learning from Tom theme focuses on participants' comments about how they learned from Tom over the course of the entire physics methods course. Finally, the Theorizing Teaching and Learning theme interprets candidates' assertions about the nature of teaching and learning

Learning from the Program

The comments that participating teacher candidates made about the teacher education program fell into two categories. First, the candidates characterized the program as an overall positive learning experience, despite the frustrations they had articulated over the year. Second, the candidates believed that it was important to learn how to learn from the teacher education program, acknowledging that the program was very different from their prior learning experiences. This section discusses both of these ideas in detail.

During the final focus group interview, the candidates agreed that they were better teachers for having gone through the teacher education program at Queen's, "despite everything [that was] negative" (FG4, 124). Irene said: "I look back and I've really enjoyed this year. There have been some things that have felt a bit useless, but for the most part, I look back on the year and it was a good time and I learned a lot" (FG4, 43). James appreciated the teacher educators at the Faculty of Education: "A lot of them gave me good practical advice about how to teach in the classroom" (James4, 9). Although David found it much easier to articulate the negative elements of the program than the positive ones, he was quick to point out that he learned a lot from the program:

> I am or will be a much better teacher for having gone through this year than I would have if I had somehow been allowed to teach without going through this year of experience and just gone straight into a high school, without a doubt. Despite not being able to list things that are positive about the program, which is in itself, I think, a very positive statement to make about the program. (FG4, 171)

Paul also felt that completing the teacher education program was more beneficial to his learning than going straight into a school. The coursework of the teacher

CHAPTER 7

education program gave Paul a "focus" that was slightly different between each class "but with some real commonalities" (Paul4, 29). Paul theorized: "If I was teaching, I would feel a bit more like I was trying to constantly improve but without a focus ... it would feel a bit more like treading water" (Paul 4, 29). The program provided Paul with "specific goals to think about" and "real ways to critically analyze" how he learned to teach (Paul4, 29).

Max agreed with David's and Paul's assertion that it was better to go through a teacher education program than to start teaching right away in a high school. Max thought that he would "be better at quite a few things like lecturing, controlling a classroom and projecting [his] voice" if he had spent the previous 8 months teaching in a school, but went on to say that it would only "take a year or so to catch up on those things" (Max4, 10). For Max, the most important part of the program was that it challenged his assumptions about teaching and learning:

> I don't think I would ever move on from doing demos to making them interactive like that [P.O.E.s] and just other things in the classroom, like just having discussions versus talking [at the students]. I don't think that [alternative ideas about teaching] would ever be brought out unless I somehow decided out of nowhere, but I can't picture any school really convincing you to do [something different]. (Max 4, 12)

The teacher education program helped Max to consider different ideas about teaching and learning, with the end result that he felt, "In the grand scheme of things I'll be a better teacher for doing this" (Max4, 10).

The teacher candidates frequently commented that the B.Ed. program required them to re-think how they approached learning in a university program. Irene noted that the on-campus courses were, in general, "pretty relaxed" but that she got "tense" when course expectations were unclear (FG4, 74). The following comment during the focus group interview elicited empathetic laughter from her peers: "In September, I was working super-hard and worrying about pass/fails for everything. *And then I caught on* [italics added]" (FG4, 74). David was quick to add: "And then I caught on. I could say that about so many things this year" (FG4, 75). Irene later commented that she was uncomfortable with the pass/fail assessment until the middle of the teacher education program: "Every so often ... you suddenly worry that maybe this one is different ... it's this kind of panic ... Will they fail me on this if I make a mistake?" (FG4, 134). Irene revealed that she came to terms with the assessment scheme of the program by taking control of her own learning: "You have to jump through hoops to pass. But that's to pass. To actually learn you've got to do more than that ... most of us have been responsible about trying to actually learn" (FG4, 112).

David reported that the on-campus portion of the program involved "a lot more work" (FG4, 109) than he expected; before attending the Faculty of Education he was not aware that there was "teaching theory" (FG4, 121) and so he was surprised to learn there were many ways to approach teaching and learning. He characterized the program as a dichotomy between theory and practice, saying "You're not here [at Queen's] to get that practical experience, that's what practicum is for ... this is

CONSOLIDATION AND LOOKING AHEAD

a university, you're here to get the theory" (FG4,121). Irene also conceptualized the teacher education program in "two chunks where there's the theory and the practice, so basically on campus in class and practicum" (Irene4, 18).

Paul also characterized the program as a dichotomy, although in a very different way than David and Irene:

> I would divide my courses into maybe half and half, in terms of ones that really worked for me and ones that really didn't. For me that would also have to do with the messages [from the classes]. I have a couple of courses where the whole class is just focused on class presentations, student presentations with almost zero input from the teacher ... [There are] the lecture classes that everyone complains about where there's not really any choice but for it to be completely teacher-centred. There are a couple of classes, including Tom's, where it's a good balance between student-driven and teacher-as-a-coach type of thing. So I feel like there have been three spots on the spectrum. Although the messages are often the same in terms of what a teacher's supposed to be and what students in a great classroom might be doing, in terms of actually following through on it, there are just enough classes that do too much of either side. [They are] either too teacher-focused or too student-focussed. Or not *too* student focused, just not enough actual guidance from the prof. (Paul4, 20)

According to Paul, there were few courses that used an appropriate mixture of teacher-centric and student-centric pedagogies. Although he acknowledged that many of the messages about teaching and learning were similar across the program, it is clear that he felt he learned best from courses that found an appropriate pedagogical balance.

Learning from Tensions

The teacher candidates who participated in this study continued to articulate the multiple tensions created both on practicum and on campus and the effects of those tensions on their learning. The nature of the tensions described by candidates focused on how they thought of themselves as teachers. Candidates' experiences of themselves as living contractions continued to dominate the discourse, pointing to both the disconnect between their intended and enacted pedagogy and the tension they perceived in the nature of the teaching profession.

For better or worse, the practicum experiences serve to indoctrinate teacher candidates into the well-established cultural norms of the schools, which Tyack and Tobin (1994, p. 453) called the "grammar" of the schools. The candidates were concerned with becoming lost in "all of the little pieces of teaching" (FG4, 20), everything from attendance to the politics of being a member of a teaching staff. Candidates' experiences on practicum showed them that politics could be particularly "annoying" when conflict occurred between teachers in the same department (FG4, 71). Often, they noticed that the conflicts resulted in colleagues who "didn't talk to each other," which contributed to "unnecessary stress" in the department (FG4, 71). James mentioned that he was surprised to learn that there was "a lot of heat between different departments and the administration," because he "didn't experience [the politics] in high school ... [because he] was on the other side of the fence as a student" (FG4, 72). David expressed concern about his desire to "start questioning" (FG4, 48) the status quo of the schools, and the potential political ramifications of his questions. Politically, he felt "pulled" in different directions by the Faculty of Education, the Ontario College of Teachers, and the Ontario Secondary School Teachers' Federation. David identified the positions of these groups as "politically charged, them-focused, and them-biased" (FG4, 80), a situation that resulted in a significant source of tension surrounding his entrance to the teaching profession.

The teacher candidates continued to focus on the tensions they experienced as a result of not being able to enact pedagogies that were in line with their pedagogical vision. They offered the dominant culture of teaching-as-telling as part of the reason for the difficulty in implementing active-learning pedagogies. For example, David believed that an active-learning approach to teaching was "so completely different" from what he saw during his practicum that teaching for active learning "would be like swimming against the current, making waves" (FG4, 17). Enacting active-learning pedagogies was not an easy task, even for candidates who felt that they were in environments that would support an alternative approach to teaching and learning. Irene admitted that during her practicum experiences, "I wasn't doing what Tom recommends, but I wanted to and my associate teacher was open to it" (FG4, 31). She believed that her inability to use a novel approach to teaching was due to "cognitive dissonance" between her experiences as a student in high school and what she was being told at the faculty: "It's hard to learn something [from the apprenticeship of observation], then unlearn something that you thought you knew" (Irene4, 10). She went on to say that "there's so much involved in teaching, you can't do it all at once" (Irene4, 14), a perception that was tacitly reinforced by the tendency of coursework at the Faculty to "throw all these things at you like you have to treat everyone as an individual and [yet] teach the whole class" (Irene4, 15).

Paul continued to express concerns about adopting what he perceived as the familiar, authoritarian persona of a teacher. The cultural forces that expected him to act like an authority figure were not aligned with his pedagogical vision of sharing control of the classroom with his students:

> How much is it actually safe to do that [share control of a classroom with students] as someone who is supposed to be and who is an authority figure? You know, like, you can't really get away from that.... I would never be able to get out of the fact that I could probably get a kid suspended and fail them and all kinds of stuff .... At the same time part of the teaching strategies, part of the teaching, sort of, philosophy that I've personally come towards does involve giving up control and does involve trying as hard as you can to interact with students on the basis of mutual respect and mutual learning, in which case maybe not being an authority figure would be a bit of an asset. But there were certainly a number of times in my practicum where that started to seem a bit idealistic and I did wish that I had the ability to, you know, even just the ability to get mad. I don't really know how to get mad and yell. (Paul4, 16)

Paul was also concerned that his vision of teaching and learning was so different from the traditional ideas about how teachers should behave that he wondered whether students would be able to learn in the kind of classroom environment he wished to create. Paul perceived that students in schools are used to attending classes where "they just sit there, the teacher tells them stuff, they write it down, and then they go home" (FG4, 19). On his practicum, he felt a tension whenever he tried something that students "weren't used too" and wondered if it was even possible to change "the way they actually learn, in just these one-hour blocks [of classes]" (FG4, 19).

During the final focus group interview, David (FG4, 24–26) raised a source of tension that seemed to resonate with many of the other teacher candidates:

David: I starting thinking [about] what kind of tone I want to set [at the beginning of my first year of teaching] and then what kind of tone can I responsibly set .... If I do what I want to do [teach using active-learning pedagogies], am I going to have the time and the resources and the wherewithal to follow through with that all year long? If I don't think that I am going to be able to do that in my first year teaching, would it be irresponsible of me to start it that way? If I don't think I could continue, does that make sense? Might I be better off just doing, well, not just the standard sort of teacher thing, but with some sort of positive and try and pace myself? Say [to myself] "OK, I am going to do it almost the regular way because this is my first year teaching, but the whole year long, I'll concentrate on implementing little bits here and there." So I will kind of get used to it and then I'll know what to do, I'll have the endurance to sustain that the following year .... Can I start that way? Is it responsible of me to do that if I don't think I can sustain [an active-learning approach] to teaching?

Paul: Because then after two months you look back at that first day, when you told them they would be really engaged ...

David: ... and I haven't done it, not since the first week! What's the point?

James: That's a good point.

David was concerned about the ethical implications of starting with an active-learning approach to teaching when he was unsure whether or not he could sustain the approach over the long term. David wondered how he would feel if, at the end of his first year of teaching, he realized: "I started well and I just wasn't able to hold onto it" (FG4, 32).

Learning from Tom

Unlike the other themes that have been discussed in this and previous analysis chapters, the teacher candidates who participated in this research have consistently named and interpreted the ways in which they learned from Tom. Comments about Tom's pedagogy were again among the most frequently coded items in the April data set. After establishing that the teacher candidates unanimously agreed that they learned how to teach from the way Tom implicitly and explicitly modelled his

CHAPTER 7

pedagogy, this section goes on to explore the ways in which the individual participants theorized how they learned from Tom.

One of the most revealing moments during the data collection occurred during the final focus group interview when I asked the teacher candidates to describe what they learned from the physics class that was distinct from what they learned from other elements of their preservice teacher education program. Paul and David (FG4, 55–57) immediately responded:

Paul: How to teach. [All laugh].

David: Yes. How to teach. Next question. [All laugh]

Paul: Seriously, that's why I answered that question. How to teach.

Almost immediately after this brief exchange, which generated approving laughter from the other participants, Paul qualified his answer somewhat: "I've had some good classes and I've learned some great stuff" (FG4, 61). Irene added: "It is the class that actually got me thinking about my learning" (FG4, 58). The following discussion ensued (FG4, 62–70):

Paul: Anyways, so all I was trying to say is that everything we've done in physics class is about how to be a good physics teacher.

David: Or just a good teacher.

Paul: You're right, a good teacher in general. Specifically, a good physics teacher I think. That's the only class I find that has really done that. I've learned a lot here [at the Faculty of Education], but that's the only class that's like, "Here's how to be a good teacher."

James: I think most other classes are good, but it's practical advice like teaching strategies. The big thing about physics class for me is that we're encouraged to focus on the big picture and constantly reflect on the big picture. That's one of the main things I am taking away.

David: I was just thinking the same thing. "What's the big idea?" We're getting used to sort of, just thinking about what's going on. I am going to use the term "character development." I don't know if that quite encompasses precisely what I mean. But this class is a little bit more about that as opposed to some classes which are a little bit more about the knowledge and the theory, the definitions and the terms ... whereas physics class is less about the content. The assumption there is that you know it [physics content], or you know enough to know what you don't know and you'll catch up on that in the summer. So let's focus on big ideas, thinking, maybe even sort of character development.

Paul: How do people learn? Who are they?

David: Yes, more on relationships, like I said.

James: Every time I go into Tom's class, I am thinking about, "What is teaching?" I do reflect upon that sometimes in other classes, but every time in

Tom's class I am thinking about that for a good part of the 2 ½ hours. He does give lots of practical advice, like POEs, but I just think he hammers home the big picture.

Max: In Tom's class you make your philosophy of education, in other classes you write it down.

Taken with the comment that Irene made just before this discussion, it becomes clear that the teacher candidates perceive that they learned a lot from the physics course because they were encouraged to analyze their thoughts about teaching and learning and focus on big picture issues in education.

Although the teacher candidates agreed unanimously that they learned a lot from Tom, the ways in which they characterized their learning differed somewhat. Irene mentioned that she initially found Tom's pedagogy "a bit frustrating" because "it didn't always feels like we were moving fast or covering much" (Irene4, 8). She felt uncomfortable when "Tom would ask questions and then there would be silence" (Irene4, 3). Eventually, though, Irene realized that Tom was "teaching the way he's telling us about teaching" (Irene4, 8). During the final focus group interview, Irene said that although "practising what you preach" was a critical feature of Tom's pedagogy, it took a while for her to realize "what [she] was learning all along" was how Tom taught the class (FG4, 58). In her view, the way that Tom taught the physics course showed her that she "learned without knowing it" during the teacher education program (FG4, 13). In her individual interview, Irene said that learning from Tom was not "a specific event," but a "build up" of the "collaborative stuff" during the physics course (Irene4, 3). Although Irene remembered "cool" moments from the physics course, such as POEs (FG4, 93), she "can't picture a specific time … [the message from physics class] just eventually sunk in" (Irene4, 4). Overall, Irene believed that Tom's pedagogy was "like a blur that caused [her] to think about thinking and [cognitive] dissonance" (Irene4, 4). Irene offered a statement to sum up how she learned from Tom: "I may not remember what you said but I'll always remember the experience" (FG4, 15).

Tom's pedagogy made an impression on Max right from the beginning of September, because "half the time you're working in a group or having discussions with the rest of the class; there always seems just to be a good flow going on" (Max4, 2). Like Irene, Max found it difficult to recall particular events in the physics course that had an effect on his learning, instead naming learning from Tom as "osmosis" (Max4, 2). Max had a lot of faith in Tom's ability to direct the learning in the physics course: "I guess he's figured out how most of these things [learning activities] will end up, so he'll know what the flow will be at the end and he can lead into it" (FG4, 100). Max also praised Tom for realizing that "no one is going to accomplish anything new in April" and ensuring that "he's already done all of the big things" (FG4, 14) by the end of the year. Max felt that the physics classes in April helped to "bring it all together" (FG4, 14). In particular, Max was excited by the activity that encouraged candidates to plan what they would do during the first four days of school next year. He thought: "I was thinking about how I can actually do all of the things [during the first week of school]" (FG4, 14).

CHAPTER 7

Overall, Max stated that Tom's pedagogy had a greater impact on his learning than any specific activity during the physics class: "I think it was probably just the atmosphere and how we did things [that had an effect on my learning], not actually specifically what we do, just the way we go about class" (Max4, 1).

Tom's pedagogy encouraged James to "constantly reflect on the big picture" (FG4, 65). The physics course "changed the way [he] thought about what it is to teach, what it means to teach, what teaching is exactly and how students learn" (James4, 10). According to James, the most important message from Tom's class was "personal reflection ... on how [he] teaches and how students learn" (James4, 2). Although James felt that he "always understood the value of reflection," he felt that Tom "hammered home" the importance of "reflecting on the big picture" (FG4, 9). James linked "Tom's focus on active learning" to the way he "approached Grade 9 and 10 science classes" during practicum (James4, 1).

By the end of the preservice teacher education program, David felt: "I've come to respect and believe what we've talked about in the physics class" (David4, 6). David went on to say: "'Explore first, explain later' is something that feels right to me" (David4, 8) and made a link to the lesson study pedagogy that Tom enacted in September:

> Maybe it's the way it [lesson study] was set up. It was open-ended and we could tackle it how we wanted. You know, choose the subject matter we wanted, that had to be part of it. Part of it was the open time frame; we didn't have a strict deadline for that. We could choose to finish it earlier or later depending on what we wanted to get it out of the way with ... There was a sense of ownership and a sense that it was for us. And it was certainly the first time in the program for me that I had an opportunity to, you know, model a lesson or try out a lesson .... In terms of lasting effects, one that will stay with me ... Tom made some comments afterwards that were just very positive. I'm sure he did for everyone. (David4, 21)

David's comments indicate that he "bought into ... the ideas that we've discussed in [physics] class" (David4, 12) early in the year. One of the reasons that David identified so strongly with the messages associated with the physics course was the trust that Tom showed to the teacher candidates early in the program.

During the final focus group interview, David admitted to wondering how often Tom improvises his lesson plan: "Does he just pull this stuff out? Does he know what we're going to do in a class beforehand?" (FG4, 95). By the end of the year, however, David believed that Tom's pedagogy was carefully thought out, even if it seemed otherwise:

> I give him a lot of credit. I think the way he's gone about doing things, he lets us think he is going with the flow. I am not saying he's not, but I think there is so much more to what he's doing than what first glance indicates. (FG4, 96) .... There is way more behind what he is doing, which is really good to know. Not that I doubted it before, but it's good to know that he's not just sort of stumbling on to things that are working well for us. There is a lot of thought

and experience behind what he is doing, which validates for me that these methods are worth striving for. (FG4, 99)

The effects that Tom's pedagogy had on David's learning were powerful. David trusted Tom early in the year and appreciated the incremental way that Tom built up the overarching themes of the physics class, noting that "Tom modelled what he thought was good teaching" (FG4, 59).

Tom's pedagogy of teacher education encouraged David to try and use similar approaches with his students in schools: "Because we've done it in that class ... it's given me that push I think to try it when I get out there" (FG4, 6). David commented on three specific features of Tom's pedagogy that he wished to enact in schools:

> It's OK to be calm as a teacher. It's OK to have silence or not to have anything to say at a particular moment. It's OK, in the middle of a class, to stop and think about what's going on and completely change directions if you need to. (FG4, 59)

David perceived Tom's pedagogical approach as "swimming against the current" (FG4, 16) of what he had noticed in the schools, although he was quick to add: "If I could incorporate a bit of [Tom's pedagogy] into how I teach, I think it would benefit the students and I think it would benefit me" (FG4, 61).

Paul continued to theorize at length about Tom's pedagogy, although at times he felt like "the Tom cheerleader in the group" (FG4, 10). Paul acknowledged the impact that POEs had on his learning: "What I mostly learned from physics class was just the way Tom taught" (Paul4, 1). For Paul, how Tom taught was more important than what he taught. Paul believed that, from a very early point in the course, "I feel like I've been able to understand what Tom was trying to do" (FG4, 8). His empathy and enthusiasm for Tom's pedagogical approach to the physics course was also a source of tension throughout the year, as he often felt his classmates were not engaging with Tom as much as they could have:

> I really don't think that they [some of the other candidates] stepped up to all the potentiality of what Tom was doing. I think they were too quiet, not willing to take risks, and generally not interested in really taking him up on doing something interesting most of the time. Not that I necessarily blame them for that .... If they weren't that interested in learning it, then that's fine (Paul4, 2).... It got a little bit better [later in the year], people sort of came out of their shells ... I feel like he'd always suggest some kind of activity ... that if the class as a whole really wanted to run with it, it could be great ... even just a discussion topic .... I remember there were a few times in class where I asked questions ... [such as] "I'm trying to figure out how to deal with this question and I'd like to hear what everyone has to say about it." And there would just sort of be not really anything. Tom would just sort of give up on helping me get an answer for it. But anyway, it changed a bit in the way that people became less quiet and a bit more comfortable with each other. I think at least having the classroom community sort of worked. But in terms of "let's all

work with what Tom's given us and maybe add our own things to it and get to some really interesting new places," it just didn't really happen. So a lot of times Tom would have these ideas that he'd want to try, and they would just go pretty short because it would just have to be aborted because people wouldn't really take it anywhere. (Paul4, 3)

Although Paul was adamant that he did not "want to set [himself] up as the knowing person who had things figured out and knew what was best for everyone" (Paul4, 3), he obviously felt that Tom's pedagogy depended a great deal on how much the candidates were willing to engage in different kinds of learning experiences. He stated that there was "a bunch" (Paul4, 3) of other candidates in the class who were willing to engage in the same way that he was; nevertheless, the resistance that he perceived from some members of the physics course was an obvious source of continuing frustration for Paul.

Paul perceived that the success of using active-learning pedagogies was largely dependent on the degree to which students chose to engage with the learning experiences provided by the teacher. He saw parallels between the challenges that Tom faced teaching the physics methods course and the challenges that he faced teaching students in schools:

There's something about the kind of teaching that Tom does, and that I hope to be able to do, obviously not exactly like Tom's but, you know, that kind of teaching, which, in a really funny way, I found actually makes you feel like you're losing control as a teacher, which I was actually not expecting. I feel like in the other kind of old-fashioned methods, as I think of them, I've seen and felt that there's a lot more control and that you can really direct things how you want them to go. But when you try to do the kind of teaching that gives kids control over their own learning, you're inherently losing some control over that. And I think that relates also to what I was thinking of the class, which is that Tom gave us control, you know, and at some point he couldn't [exert any more control]. If he was teaching a different way, he could say, "OK, I want you guys to hand this in now." And then he would get these assignments and, you know, but there's obviously all these problems with that kind of method that he's talked about, which is about people not having control over their own learning and what kind of learning actually happens in that case. And so when you do try to give kids control, then there's this, for me, unexpected aspect which is that something might happen like in Tom's class, where you say, "Here's control over what we're doing here, or some of it anyway" or a lot of it in Tom's case, and he didn't necessarily get what he was hoping for. I'm sure, you know. I'm sure he's said this to you, to some extent, which is that, if he was hoping at least that more would happen with the independent study, for example, and then it didn't, that's sort of just a funny offshoot of the method, of the methods. I found that myself, you know, you can make the class, and obviously I wasn't giving them as much control as what happens in physics, but every time I did, it was like the class was sort of now out of my hands and it was up to them to do something with it.

You had to have that hope if you were going to teach like this. You had to have that hope that they were going to really take that and do something with it, but there were times when there was just nothing you could do. (Paul4, 9)

According to Paul, using pedagogies that support active learning requires a teacher to give up some control of their class. More significantly, a teacher who enacts student-centred pedagogies has to be willing to let their own teaching fail to a certain extent. Ultimately, in an active-learning environment, students must make the choice about whether they want to engage with the learning experiences: if they choose not to, then a teacher cannot simply fall back on familiar, teacher-directed routines lest they destroy all features of a student-centred learning environment.

The student-centred focus of Tom's pedagogy held particular appeal for Paul, even though the learning behaviours of some of his classmates often frustrated him: "Tom is willing to step in and guide and give his opinion, and profs ... that really let students drive the class but connect as a really solid guide sometimes, those are the profs that I've really respected" (Paul4, 22). Paul also felt that Tom "has a really good skill at the kinds of questions he asks ... they're always very insightful .... He always has this much more productive line of thinking that he draws you towards" (FG4, 10). Like David, Paul appreciated Tom's flexibility while he was teaching: "Tom has never been afraid to get sidetracked by something that seems like fun" (Paul4, 31). Upon consideration of his time in the physics course, Paul had the following to say about the effects of Tom's pedagogy on his learning:

What I've really learned in that class is because I feel like I've been able to understand what Tom was trying to do. And so I've taken from that a lot of really great ideas. Even if it hasn't worked all the time and even if people haven't taken him up on it, I feel like I've really thought about it and been able to see all his great little ideas and just the atmosphere he cultivates and stuff. That's what's given me this inspiration and ideas. (Paul4, 8)

Paul learned from *how* Tom taught the class more than from *what* he taught. He gauged the effects that Tom's pedagogy had on his learning during both successful and unsuccessful moments in the physics course. Throughout the physics methods course, Paul showed considerable evidence of thinking about how what he learned from Tom could be applied to how he wanted to teach students on practicum.

The active-learning approach to pedagogy that Tom enacted in the physics class had varied, but powerful, effects on the participants' learning. The candidates who participated in the research noted that much of what they learned from how Tom taught was implicit, especially at the beginning of the course. They praised Tom's ability to use pedagogies that were in line with his messages about education; in colloquial terms, he practised what he preached. Irene admitted to some frustrations when she did not understand the direction that the course was taking, but eventually came to believe that she had been implicitly learning from how Tom taught over the course of the year. James appreciated how Tom encouraged teacher candidates to focus on big picture issues in teaching and learning. Max, David, and Paul all indicated that they trusted Tom from early in the course and hence did not become concerned when features of Tom's pedagogy became unclear. Max noted that Tom had named all of the important messages in his course by the end of September, so that he could continually return to building on and reinterpreting the big ideas that he wanted to develop. David appreciated how Tom modelled a pedagogy of stillness and calm, which stood in sharp contrast to how he experienced traditional pedagogies in the school system. Although Paul noted some of the limitations of a student-centred approach to teaching and learning, he believed that the benefits of the pedagogy that Tom explicitly modelled outweighed the drawbacks. Paul strongly believed in the power of creating a different set of learning experiences for students in a context based on shared intellectual control over the course.

Theorizing Teaching and Learning

During the final data collection phase, the teacher candidates who participated in this research theorized teaching and learning in dichotomous terms. They contrasted traditional ideas about teaching and learning, such as teacher-centric approaches that require students to listen to lectures and copy down notes, with the alternative approaches to teaching and learning characterized by shared intellectual control over a classroom and a focus on student-centred, active-learning pedagogies. In general, participants did not discuss specific instances from their practicum experiences when they theorized the nature of teaching and learning. Most of their comments indicate that they have developed broad philosophies about the nature of learning and teaching.

To varying degrees, the candidates challenged the traditional notion that students learn best by listening to an expert lecture on a given topic. Irene felt that "if you're just listening, you don't learn much," contrasting lecturing with "things like learning by doing" (Irene4, 9). Paul was concerned that his students learned "how to learn" (Paul4, 33) because "those are the kinds of things that you don't forget as easily from year to year, as opposed to some formula for physics" (Paul4, 45). David was taken with the idea of "metacognition and students being responsible for their own learning" (David4, 1). James defended lecturing somewhat by pointing out that his associate teacher was good at giving lectures and that candidates had "all seen in university and high school that lecturing works" (FG4, 128) for some students. In response to James' assertion, David immediately wanted to know: "Is that because he is a good lecturer or because [the students] are learning? .... I could listen to someone for 75 minutes, but maybe he is just very entertaining" (FG4, 129). James countered: "There was definitely some learning going on for a lot of students" (FG4, 130), but stated in his individual interview that "it really helps to use different methods to differentiate teaching [and] teach in different learning styles" (James4, 3). James acknowledged the importance of using a variety of pedagogical approaches and felt that using a traditional lecture was equally valid to other options.

Candidates theorized that both teaching and learning were more conceptually complicated than they originally thought. For example, Irene said: "I've learned that learning doesn't make a lot of sense" (Irene4, 9). Max said that he had "never even thought of" teaching and learning as "theory-type things" (Max4, 14). Perhaps a part of the reason that the candidates had not thought deeply about the nature of teaching and learning before their B.Ed. program was due to the fact that they were, for the most part, comfortable and successful with traditional models of school:

> I learn by someone telling me something, I assimilate it, and then it either agrees or disagrees with me and then it's part of my knowledge base. So I assumed that's how students would learn and how I would teach them. And I don't know, I guess I've seen that not everyone is like that. It seems about half of our physics class works that way, maybe a bit more, and we're the academic physics or math people. (Max4, 5)

Max's comments reveal how difficult it can be for candidates to conceptualize how people might learn physics and math differently from the way that he learned. Like Max, James acknowledged that he learned successfully from traditional, transmission-based pedagogies. James' success in school had a profound impact on how he approached teaching and learning:

> I didn't really understand how complex it was until I came to Teacher's College [sic]. I thought there was pretty much just one way to teach: you know, you go up and you give your little lecture, you give students work to do, and then you wrap it up and you give students tests at the end of units, or some kind of lab if you're doing science, or sometimes an essay if you're doing an arts class or something like that. I guess that's the way I went through high school, that's the way most of my teachers were .... But that's the way I went through university. I mean, pretty much every course you do in university is just a lecture course, right. I didn't really realize teaching was so complex and there's so many different ways to teach. (James4, 16)

The traditional forms of teaching experienced by the teacher candidates made it difficult for them to conceptualize the intricacies of teaching and learning until they experienced first-hand the difficulties students had learning from lecturing. As Paul noted: "the really important stuff I do isn't just explaining stuff really well, because they will forget it pretty quickly" (Paul4, 37).

The teacher candidates who participated in the research felt that teaching was even more challenging when they tried to adopt an active-learning approach to pedagogy. David noted that "students have been more engaged" when he used active-learning approaches, but worried that he "wasn't there long enough to see if there was any learning done [long-term]" (David4, 9). He went on to theorize that active-learning pedagogies are "difficult to do in a short amount of time ... even if you're able to teach a whole unit, including whatever summative units you have at the end, I think you need more time to find out if students have really learned the benefit of what you've done" (David4, 10). According to David, the use of active-learning pedagogies requires "swimming against the norm" (David4, 28), a situation which enhances the already intricate set of demands placed on teacher candidates.

Paul also felt that using active-learning pedagogies helped to engage the students, with the qualifier that even if "you do it well, it would just feel like a piece because you only had them for those 5 minutes where they were active and engaged"

CHAPTER 7

(FG4, 20). The instances where Paul engaged his classes using specific teaching strategies that support active-learning were fleeting:

> The stuff we've been working on in Tom's class is just a piece of the picture …. You can't just do POEs …. It'll work for, like, 10 minutes and then you've lost them again. So unless you have a really good sense of the whole scope of the course in terms of content, all the little things that teachers do if you have a really good handle on those, you can keep in mind what to do if someone's absent and if you're thinking about that test you're going to write in 2 weeks …. Once you've got the sense of all of that, I feel like it'll be a lot easier to bring it all together. And so you can have POEs, not just working as something that will work for 10 minutes, but as something that will actually affect the way the rest of the class goes. If your whole class is built around keeping kids engaged and active and reflective and critical, that's what I'm working towards, is that big picture. Because I would do POEs and then I would do think-pair-shares but then sometimes I'd also be doing a boring lesson on the board and my assessment wouldn't really match what we talked about in POEs and so it really lost sort of some of that momentum. And then the next time we'd do a POE there would only be a dim recollection of that energy and that kind of learning that was happening. (Paul4, 18)

Paul names one of the unstated challenges for teacher candidates who adopt a non-traditional approach to teaching and learning. Most of the teaching witnessed by the candidates who participated in this research was traditional and teacher-centred, as shown throughout the analysis chapters. Thus it is not surprising that, even when candidates try to enact active-learning pedagogies, any perceived success is short-lived. Paul mentioned during the focus group: "I can only get a sense of [using active-learning pedagogies]. I didn't have it down" (FG4, 22).

Using an active-learning approach to teaching and learning requires teacher educators to manage several layers of cognitive dissonance, because such a non-traditional approach requires a re-conceptualization of how to approach teaching and learning. It requires teacher candidates to frame teaching and learning as conceptually complicated. It challenges teacher candidates to go beyond a reliance on lecturing with the occasional POE. By the end of the teacher education program, the candidates had begun to develop big picture theories about the nature of teaching and learning. Often, their theories had implications for the challenges that lay ahead for their own teaching. As Paul noted, traditional teaching "comes sort of naturally, just write stuff on the board and they copy it down … you can really control how the class is going to work" (Paul4, 11). In addition, non-traditional approaches to teaching and learning "might be a fair challenge" (David4, 4) for students, so candidates face the additional difficulties of enacting theories that challenge the students' expectations of school.

The teacher candidates who participated in this research theorized about the philosophical nature of teaching and learning in dichotomous terms during the final phase of data collection. In many ways, their theories represent a clearer articulation of candidates' pedagogical visions than was evident in prior analysis chapters.

Although their theories are still fraught with tension, the focus of the tension has shifted from one of identity to one of enactment. Instead of theorizing about the kind of teachers they wanted to be or how they fit into the teaching profession, candidates theorized about how their personal philosophies of education would help them to navigate the culture of the school system. They have reasons for wanting to enact particular pedagogies and they look forward to having their own classrooms.

LOOKING AHEAD TO FUTURE TEACHING EXPERIENCES

These five teacher candidates did not make significant comments about the role that practicum experiences played in their learning during this round of data collection. Perhaps part of the reason for the scarcity of comments about practicum experience arises from the structure of the preservice teacher education program at Queen's. Upon concluding winter coursework at the end of January, teacher candidates returned to their host schools for their winter practicum from the beginning of February until the end of the first week in March. After a week-long March Break, teacher candidates dispersed to a variety of non-traditional educational settings for the alternate practicum placement. Often, teacher candidates use this opportunity to obtain overseas teaching experience or to teach in a non-school setting such as a museum. The alternate placement ran from the third week in March to the end of the first week in April. Teacher candidates then returned to the Faculty of Education for the final 3 weeks of classes.

The final focus group and individual interviews were conducted during the last week of classes in the teacher education program. By this time, the teacher candidates who participated in the research had been away from their host schools for 6 weeks. The final school placement may have become a distant memory, especially given that candidates had a 3-week alternate practicum placement that may have been very different from their school placements. I believe that another reason for the scarcity of comments about the practicum is that candidates are inevitably focused on the prospect of becoming full-time teachers in the near future. The previous analysis chapter described and interpreted the tensions that candidates felt when they looked ahead to their February practicum experiences. It is possible that the February practicum became, for some of the participants, an experience to be endured rather than learned from. Framed in this way, it is not surprising that the candidates' thoughts tended toward their future careers as teachers rather than their past practicum experiences as teacher candidates.

This section explores the state of candidates' professional knowledge as they looked ahead to the kinds of teachers they wish to be and the nature of the pedagogies they wish to enact. As in the previous chapter, I use comments provided by each of the participants to construct individual narratives of how they viewed their future careers as teachers. In each section, I attend to participants' prior assumptions about the nature of teaching and learning, the new teaching and learning behaviours they developed as a result of the program, and their goals as new members of the teaching profession.

CHAPTER 7

James' Narrative of his Future as a Teacher

Based on his conversations with graduates of the Faculty of Education, James had the mindset coming into the teacher education program that "education is not that hard [a program]" (FG4, 105). He felt that "teaching was going to be pretty easy" (FG4, 103), although he soon found out that teaching is "a lot of work" (FG4, 107). During the final focus group interview, James articulated the reasons behind his prior assumptions about the program:

> I thought coming in that I knew what teaching was. I've been in school for pretty much all my life. I'm just going to get some good, hands-on teaching strategies that are going to help me. I didn't actually think about the whole idea of what teaching is. (FG4, 113)

James was surprised that the teacher education program had a profound effect on him: "I didn't think I'd actually change the way I think about teaching" (FG4, 118). Looking ahead to his first year of teaching, James wanted to have "good performance tasks, good summative assignments because ... it's important to establish those in your first year" and stated that his focus on meaningful assessment "definitely came from here at Duncan MacArthur" (James4, 14). More broadly, James named the use of active-learning pedagogies as a specific goal for his early years of teaching:

> I want to foster an active learning environment as much as I can. I think it's going to be difficult to do on a consistent basis my first year, maybe even my first couple of years. I learned that in physics class and I learned it in some of my other classes, so I guess you could say I learned it here at the Faculty of Education. I think it's very important to have students that trust you and respect you. So I want to try to establish an environment of trust and respect in my first week ... I think that came from here at the Faculty of Education but also my practice teaching I learned that that's important. (James4, 13)

Again, James' comments reveal that he developed broad perspectives on teaching and learning from courses that he took at the Faculty of Education. Although he acknowledged that his practicum experiences were also an important source for his development, it is significant to note that both the physics methods course and other courses had a profound effect on the way he approached teaching and learning.

James did admit to feeling some tensions around beginning a teaching career. Specifically, he worried about "the workload" and "how to keep ahead" (James4, 15). He was not worried about classroom management, saying that "it really depends on the type of students" and that "it's something you learn over time, it can't be taught, you've just got to go and learn it" (James4, 15). James felt that his major concern would be "trying to find the time to get everything done" (James4, 15); beyond that he was excited to begin a career in teaching.

Max's Narrative of his Future as a Teacher

Max claimed that he approached the Faculty of Education with no prior assumptions about what he would learn: "I hadn't even expected classroom management ... I was like, 'I'm going to teachers' college [sic], I wonder what they'll do'" (FG4, 119). Unlike the other participants in the study, Max did discuss his time on February practicum, likely because he felt more freedom to use active-learning pedagogies with his new associate teacher. The result was that Max felt he had "the general idea" (FG4, 27) of what he could do with active-learning pedagogies. Max's associate teacher taught from an active-learning framework and thus had his classroom set up in ways that supported student-centred approaches to teaching. Although Max admitted that he still struggled with making the "actual material interesting," he felt that "it was a good push" to be in a classroom that was set up to support active-learning pedagogies (FG4, 28).

In addition to continuing his exploration of using active-learning pedagogies, Max wanted to "get a lot of feedback going both ways" (Max4, 13) during his first year of teaching. He was mindful of the temptation to treat secondary school physics as another math course: "I think just making sure that I keep away from algebra problems because it's really easy to fall into that" (Max4, 13). Max characterized himself as being "brave" with his willingness to try new teaching strategies, but was concerned about the difficulty he had indentifying the nature of the challenges that his students were likely to encounter with physics (Max4, 6). For this reason, Max said that he relied heavily on Knight (2004), particularly "at the beginning of a new section" because it was useful to consider questions such as "What problems will they [students] have? How long should I be putting in for these things [concepts]? And what are the good ways to introduce them [concepts]?" (Max4, 4). Max resolved to try to implement the active-learning approaches articulated in Knight (2004), "even though they aren't ... easy" (Max4, 13).

Irene's Narrative of her Future as a Teacher

During the final round of data collection, Irene did not articulate the prior assumptions that she had coming into the teacher education program. Instead, she spoke at length about the profound effect that her associate teacher had on her hesitation to implement active-learning pedagogies:

> My associate was an amazing lecturer. He could fill a blackboard and it was amazing and it was concise ... and the kids were with it because you raised the bar so high they had to stick with it. I wasn't doing much active learning so I wasn't doing what Tom sort of recommends. But I wanted to, and my associate was open to it, I just think I kind of felt ... trying to balance all of the other stuff with teaching with also keeping them engaged ... I just kept on putting it off. Once I get used to taking attendance, then I'll work on that. Most teachers were good at my school but they weren't active learners. So I kind of modelled after them a bit too much. More than I wanted too. (FG4, 27)

Although Irene wanted to use active-learning pedagogies, she found it difficult to enact teaching that was not in line with the culture of teaching and learning at her

CHAPTER 7

host school. Irene was unique among the candidates because she was unsure about making high school teaching her career:

> I don't really know what I want to do. I guess my problem is, when I think about seeing myself teaching, I can definitely see myself teaching for a year or two, because I want to try, and I can see myself coming back to it. But I don't see myself being 30 years straight in a classroom. I might, that might change ... [but right now] I'm not one of those people who's ready and set to get a job and teach for the rest of my life. (Irene4, 22)

Irene was adamant that her uncertainty about entering the teaching profession was not because she was uncomfortable with being a teacher: "It's more because I want to try other things. I don't see it as giving up because I don't like it" (Irene4, 24). Regardless of her feelings toward the prospect of being a life-long teacher, Irene had definite goals for her pedagogy and future classroom environments:

> I'd want an inclusive classroom .... When I think about myself teaching, I think so much about the academic side of it ... [and not as much about the] just helping kids get through the stuff side of it, which I don't know if that's right. I never planned on being a social worker ... but I just hope that I can build up one of those classrooms where people are honestly enjoying the learning, whether its physics or math .... That'd be a big feature, just hoping the kids like the learning and getting them through tough years and stuff like that. But I mean active learning would be nice and I think, sort of, integrating things a bit more if possible. I mean, physics and math are so close it's frustrating when they're different, but, I mean, you're stuck by the curriculum. (Irene4, 26)

Irene admitted: "I still feel like I've got that [cognitive] dissonance" around "all the active learning and everything we've done in physics" (Irene4, 25).

Although Irene felt ambivalent toward active-learning pedagogies, largely because she witnessed her associate teacher successfully use lectures with his senior physics and mathematics classes, Irene reconceptualized her idea of teaching and learning as a result of the teacher education program:

> Learning when I got here meant passing tests ... getting the information so that you can look it up later and it's in your head a bit. It was just about kind of like the transfer of information, not about the, it actually sticking with people .... To me learning was teacher stands at the front of the class and gives their nice lesson and the students have learned it. And now it's more like, "Well, it doesn't really work that way." So I guess that's a change. It's hard to put in words what I feel it's changed to, but it's definitely changed from that. Same thing with teaching, I guess. You know, teaching was standing delivering a lesson and now it doesn't feel that way. I know there's so much more to it. Teaching as a profession I'm definitely changing my thought because there's so much more with it, like, social working .... So it's kind of a circular definition saying that teaching is about learning to teach but I think I changed my mind. I thought teaching was just passing on the information on some cool stuff, like math. So that's definitely changed .... because hearing the different ways people learn and stuff, it's still sort of changed for me because it's not

just telling somebody something. I hate to think I thought of it as telling before but I think relative to now anyway I did. (Irene4, 27–29)

It is noteworthy that Irene's experiences in the teacher education program helped her to reframe a view of teaching as transmitting information to one of teaching and learning as complicated, related acts that require careful consideration of a number of contextual factors.

David's Narrative of his Future as a Teacher

During the final focus group interview, David said that he "had no expectations for this [teacher education] program" because of conversations with graduates who said that the Faculty of Education was "just jumping through hoops" (FG4, 108). Coming to Queen's, David hoped to "get something out of it" but really just was looking for "the stamp that would allow [him] to register with the OCT [Ontario College of Teachers]" (FG4, 108). David was confident about his ability to succeed in the teacher education program because he used his high school physics teacher as a barometer for teaching:

> I think I can explain things pretty well to other people. I can do what he [high school physics teacher] did ... I don't think it's actually going to be hard if I get physics classes [during practicum] ... I still have his notes from high school. (FG1, 123)

Later in the focus group interview, David stated that his experiences during the preservice teacher education program taught him to question the teaching strategies used by his high school teacher: "If I wasn't in an academic class in that school, if he had taught that way to anyone else, it would have been a disaster" (FG4, 127).

After experiencing a few weeks of the teacher education program at Queen's, David was forced to confront two realities: he "actually had to do something" (FG4, 111) during coursework and "there's all this theory behind teaching" (FG4, 120). Both realizations stood in contrast to David's prior assumptions about the teacher education program: "If I gained something, it would be that practical 'how to do things'" (FG4, 120), such as "strategies" he could "input" when on practicum (FG4, 114).

During his individual interview, David expressed some concerns about his first year of teaching:

> I have this idea of what I want to get to eventually, but I don't know that that's achievable in first year. So I'm really wrestling with what to introduce and certainly, you know, how to be, how to run a class, and sort of not have a letdown during the year. I don't want to start something I can't finish. I've had too many of those experiences myself ... [when I thought] this class, this experience, this trip, this something "is going to be fantastic" ... [based on] that first day, that first couple of days, and then you know, it just inevitably shifts. The pendulum swings right back to the middle. I'm not at a point where I know what I want to incorporate in my class in September ... it's something I'm thinking about and I will continue to think about and I'll have to figure out. (David4, 26)

CHAPTER 7

At other points during both the focus group and individual interviews, David signalled his enthusiasm for enacting active-learning pedagogies. Yet this comment reveals his concern for setting the bar too high during the opening weeks of his first semester of teaching. David was concerned about sending mixed messages to his students if he started using active-learning pedagogies at the beginning of the year but then was unable to sustain his practice and had to resort to a more traditional approach.

David expanded on his concerns, citing some of the difficulties that he perceived in using active-learning approaches in traditional school environments:

> I see value in the techniques and the ideas that we've discussed in this physics class. Generally speaking, we're swimming against the norm with a lot of these things, you know, they're difficult to implement for various reasons … one being, we have a set curriculum: This is what you need to do, better race through it as quickly as you can…. Getting it all right that first year would be nice and has to be a goal of mine. I've got to set that lofty goal, not that it will be reached … In thinking about what will I be able to sustain over a semester or a year, it's got me thinking, and I don't have answers yet, as to what I will do or what I will try … It's a good place anyway to be, knowing that it's a concern for me and I'm thinking about it. I'll find some answers. I'll figure it out. But I don't have them right now. (David4, 27)

David seemed resigned to the idea that it would take time for him to become the kind of teacher that he wants to be, particularly given his perception of the demands of the curriculum and the culture of the school.

When asked whether his experiences in the teacher education program created any new learning habits, David replied: "I'm going about things differently" (David4, 33). He saw the learning behaviours that he exhibited during the teacher education program as a natural extension of prior learning habits:

> High school for me was very little work and excellent grades and then university hit … First semester was the same as OAC so there was no incentive … and then second semester hit in second year and … I made this change from completely mark-driven and trying to exude this air of excellent marks for no effort … until the undergrad when I started appreciating a little bit more the content and learning for the sake of what I'm learning …. I think that transition has sort of continued into this year … I guess I learned that I could choose what to put my energy into and what not to put my energy into and be able to justify it … [in a way that] felt honest to me …. I feel more in control [of my learning]. (David4, 31)

The major concept that David learned from his time at the Faculty of Education was the importance of "taking control of your own learning" (David4, 3). He linked the influence that self-directed learning had on him with the ways in which he wanted to teach his future students: "I've probably applied it equally to myself as I have in terms of how I can apply it to teaching the students when I end up teaching" (David4, 3). Perhaps this realization is part of the reason David felt comfortable admitting that it would take time to become the kind of teacher he wanted to be, as he realized that learning to teach means engaging in self-directed learning over a lengthy period of time.

Paul's Narrative of his Future as a Teacher

Paul encapsulated his initial thoughts about entering the teacher education program at Queen's in the following way: "I thought I knew physics really well, I was really good at explaining it, [and] what I was going to get here were specific strategies for kinds of assignments, kinds of activities, and classroom management" (Paul4, 24). In particular, Paul felt that coursework at the Faculty of Education would provide him with "an activity that will work" (FG4, 115) for given situations. During his final individual interview, Paul discussed his conception of teaching and learning when he entered the program:

> When I came into education, I thought one of the reasons was because I just love explaining physics. I'm a big geek and you get really passionate about topics and you love about talking about them. And I think I'm pretty good at explaining. I love coming up with random analogies and stuff. Learning, for me, was having someone tell you the answer ... and then going home and thinking about it and then coming back with questions. So for me, that was learning, but my experience with teaching was that that's sort of all you needed to do, was give them the answer and then they'll go and think about it. (Paul4, 36)

Paul's prior conceptions about teaching and learning were similar to those articulated by the other candidates who participated in the research. By the end of the teacher education program, however, Paul's theory of teaching and learning had changed significantly. It "had become not giving answers and hoping they [students] will think about it," but "teaching kids how to learn" (Paul4, 37).

Despite the tensions that Paul articulated in earlier interviews, by April it was clear that he wanted to enter the teaching profession after finishing the B.Ed. program. Paul had two major pedagogical goals for his first year of teaching: He wanted to create a safe classroom environment and he wanted to find ways for his students to take active roles in their own learning. Paul expanded on both of these points during his final individual interview:

> What do I want to include in my teaching? The obvious answer would be "fun" and just a nice classroom to be in. People want to be in it. Tom has never been afraid to get sidetracked by something that seems like fun; I think that's a pretty careful thing he's done .... I don't like just being focused on science as a teacher, it seems kind of morally problematic to me. So I think that I kind of reconciled that by thinking that ... when you're doing this sort of active learning we talked about, it is the kind of learning that'll serve you well in a lot of different places ... [such as] curiosity in processes and curiosity and enthusiasm for the process of finding the answer as opposed to just interest in an answer itself. Because that's something that you learn pretty quickly once you leave high school, that there pretty quickly ceases to be an answer to pretty much anything, which is terrifying. So I think if you can instil that, a

> comfort in the process of finding an answer and an excitement in and a love for that process, I think that's a huge part of active learning. But I think there are also aspects of self-confidence, [such as] confidence in your own ability to say things that will be of use to a larger group like the classroom. So anyway, all that is to say that what I want to bring into the class is all these active learning things … those things specifically have all come from Tom's class. There are [also] a number of strategies and ways of thinking about teaching and about relationships and ways of developing, sort of, philosophies of teaching that have come out of the other two classes I said I really liked. (Paul4, 30)

The importance of active learning was central to Paul's theories about teaching and learning. He felt that the decision to use active-learning approaches went beyond enacting particular teaching strategies. For Paul, a non-traditional approach to teaching was a moral choice that helped him to think about the overall role of a teacher in schools, beyond the confines of traditional subject-matter boundaries.

Given that Paul's conceptualization of teaching had changed so dramatically, it is not surprising that he also reported: "I've changed my idea of what learning might be" (Paul4, 32). A major catalyst for Paul's conceptual change was due to his observation that students in his practicum classes did not learn the same way he did while he was in school:

> I've seen the students come into my classes without really having taken much information from their other classes sometimes, you know, like they don't remember how to do the little math stuff or whatever, and that can be pretty frustrating. But then there was always this challenge that of trying to get them to learn it again. You were always working to sort of get this piece of information stuck in there, like kind of wedged into their brain again so they could use it …. And it comes back to active learning. It comes back to POEs. The main goal of the POE isn't understanding why the thing went down the tube. It's developing the community, it's developing the class, the framework from which we can share ideas without fear of being wrong, and it's about getting kids really engaged in what's going on. You put all that together, and I think that's also really about "This is how you learn," you know … If you want a safe environment for teaching it's because learning is about taking risks. And if you want kids engaged, it's because not just, I don't know, not because they'll remember facts better, it's because you want them to understand that being engaged, that is the learning … You can't just hear the answer and write it down and then that's learning. So a POE or as, or even just a POE as sort of like a good example of all the active learning stuff we've talked about, again, not changing the subject, just, you know, teaching them how, "This is how you learn stuff." You know, bring it to them. Let's get good at giving it. Let's get good at learning how to learn. (Paul4, 32)

Paul's plan to enact active-learning pedagogies stemmed from his belief that teachers should focus on helping students to learn how to learn, rather than on trying to transmit curricular information. He believed that even powerful teaching strategies such as Predict-Observe-Explain are means to an end, rather than ends in themselves.

The goals of Paul's developing pedagogy were to help students both develop a conceptual understanding of the material and critically analyze how they learned.

LEARNING EXPERIENCES IN THE PHYSICS CLASS: TEACHER EDUCATORS

The overarching theme representing the perspective of the teacher educator is one of consolidation. During the remaining six classes of April, Tom revisited each of the four big ideas he had introduced over the course of the year. The four big ideas are, in order of reintroduction to the teacher candidates in April: Learning from Literature, Predict-Observe-Explain, Processing the Program, and Relationships in Teaching and Learning. This section begins with a consideration of a conversation that Tom and I shared just before the first class in April; it sets the stage for many of the final learning experiences created in the physics course. Instead of using the chronological reporting method from previous chapters, the data are organized and interpreted according to how Tom revisited each of the ideas from the physics course during the month of April. The section concludes with discussion of a post-course meeting that Tom and I had to process what we learned from the physics class in the year the data were collected.

When Tom and I met before the first class in April, he named some of the issues that he wanted to pursue during the final weeks of the program. Tom wanted to engage the candidates with Einstein and Infeld's (1966) book and had arranged for a local intermediate science teacher to come in as a guest speaker. The major focus of the issues that Tom raised for April, however, was providing candidates with an opportunity to process the way they learned, both in the physics course and in the program as a whole. I asked Tom to explain how he planned to make the physics courses in April relevant for the teacher candidates. Tom replied, "I've got this sense that there is more than enough to mess with and, in the end, it probably doesn't matter what I do as much as work everything to the big picture" (Journal, April). Tom believed that there was little point to introducing new concepts at this point in the year; the challenge was to help teacher candidates to construct meaning from the big picture that he had painted in various ways throughout the year. Each of the big picture issues is now considered in turn within the context of the six physics classes in April.

Learning from Literature

Tom referred to research literature during the April classes more often than in any of the previous three blocks of classes. He read aloud from *The Evolution of Physics* (Einstein & Infeld, 1966) during the first class to call attention to the possibility of explaining physics without relying on mathematical formulae. He introduced the idea of "cognitive dissonance" (Tavris & Aronson, 2007, pp. 11–39) as a way of thinking not only about why students persist in believing prior assumptions despite being presented with conflicting evidence, but also about why it is so difficult to teach in ways that are different from our experiences during the apprenticeship of observation. Tom linked this last point to the difficulty candidates expressed

CHAPTER 7

implementing some of Knight's (2004) ideas about teaching physics, despite their best intentions. Finally, Tom asked candidates to read an article about assessment and physics instruction (Dufresne & Gerace, 2004), a request that provided an opportunity for him to revisit the power of using POEs in physics.

Predict-observe-explain

Tom began the penultimate class with a discussion about the ways that teachers tend to behave when confronted with a student who provides the wrong answer to a question. The discussion was grounded in the argument presented by Dufresne and Gerace (2004), who illustrate several ways to use assessment as a way of helping students learn physics concepts. The teacher candidates were caught up short, however, by one of the conceptual examples provided in the article (Dufresne & Gerace, 2004, p. 430). The example asked students to predict how a scale might read if a block of wood, a small metal block, and a container of water were arranged on it in different configurations. The example tested students' conceptual understanding of the force of buoyancy.

When Tom asked the teacher candidates to consider the example, it became apparent that there was considerable confusion surrounding the nature of the buoyant force. Tom went to the back of the physics classroom and quickly set up an apparatus that resembled the question posed by Dufresne and Gerace (2004). He asked candidates to draw a free-body diagram of the situation and to make predictions about how the scale would behave. After conducting the impromptu POE, Tom reminded the candidates: "Imagine how frustrated you would have been if you left this class without knowing the answer ... be mindful of your students next year" (Journal, April).

This final POE was important for several reasons. First, it provided Tom with the opportunity to remind teacher candidates of the procedural elements of the POE pedagogy, which is particularly relevant to candidates who did not do a POE during any of their practicum experiences. Second, it encouraged candidates to revisit how it feels to struggle with a physics concept from a learner's perspective. Tom drew attention to the candidates' behaviour as learners when he suggested that they were "hedging" (Journal, April) their comments about the physics of the POE, showing how easy it is to fall back on default learning behaviours. Third, it allowed Tom to demonstrate the importance of flexibility in teaching. The candidates in the physics class saw that Tom felt it was important to set up a POE on the spot, despite the fact that it was not a part of his lesson plan. Again, Tom taught the candidates a lesson about pedagogy by enacting practices that resonated with his overall message.

Processing the Program

Over the course of the year, Tom used a variety of strategies to engage the members of the physics class in conversations about their learning. Although these activities met with varying degrees of success, Tom continued to find ways for candidates to analyze the quality of their learning in the class. Halfway through the April classes, Tom asked the teacher candidates to "think about what we've done this year and come up to the board and write a significant event that happened in the class"

(Journal, April). More than half of the teacher candidates in the class rushed up to the board to record their thoughts in one of the circles that Tom had drawn for purposes of the activity. Candidates were then invited to draw a connecting line between any two circles, and place on the line a connecting word that explained the reason for their choice. Members of the class enthusiastically engaged in the activity. Tom then asked the group: "Given that you're going to be a school teacher next year, what does doing something like this mean to you?" (Journal, April). He encouraged the teacher candidates to make links between the learning experience of summarizing their time in physics class and the possibility of using a similar teaching strategy with students in schools. By creating a concept map with the candidates, Tom provided an opportunity for the members of the physics class to see a visual representation of their learning experiences over the course of the year.

Tom devoted half of the second-last class to another activity designed to help candidates analyze their learning. After asking the class to arrange themselves in groups of four, Tom displayed four open-ended questions that asked candidates to articulate some of the features of their learning during the teacher education program. Candidates then discussed the questions in small groups with very little prompting from Tom. I noted: "The atmosphere is almost cathartic, as it seems like the candidates needed this additional time to unpack the year in small groups" (Journal, April). The class ended with a whole-group discussion about the highlights and challenges of learning to teach. It seemed unlikely the discussion would have succeeded without the opportunities Tom provided previously for candidates to talk about their learning throughout the year and the time Tom invested in developing relationships with the members of the class.

Relationships in Teaching and Learning

The teacher candidates who participated in the study consistently discussed the importance of their relationship of trust with Tom. Early in the data collection, each of the participants named Tom's focus on relationships as a significant feature of his pedagogy. Given that Tom began the year by calling attention to the relationship-building aspects of Predict-Observe-Explain pedagogy, it was particularly appropriate that he began the final block of classes by sharing a personal narrative about the importance of developing relationships with students.

Tom asked the candidates to read through a page of responses from physics students that he taught 41 years ago with the following caveat: "I want to try something that makes me a little uncomfortable because it is personal" (Journal, April). After candidates finished reading the comments and had a chance to ask some questions, Tom said:

> The particular reason for mentioning this is 2 weeks ago, I had dinner with one of the respondents. The message in this is that it is worth keeping some class lists, particularly if you felt a strong connection to the class. Since having dinner with this person, I have been in email contact with several people from this class ... It is kind of fascinating to see that some people still remember their Grade 12 physics teacher. (Journal, April)

CHAPTER 7

This was a highly personal moment between Tom and the physics class. It required Tom to share a part of his past experiences teaching physics, something that he had not done until this point. While many teacher educators are tempted to share teaching tips from their personal experiences, the one story that Tom shared from his time in the secondary school classroom centred on the nature of his relationships with students. Tom's personal story had an effect on two of the participants in the research. James stated in the focus group: "I really like the personal stories Tom told .... It just made me think about how much of a positive impact you can have on people's lives" (FG4, 92). Paul referred to the moment as "touching" (FG4, 93).

The other way that Tom brought the focus of the course to the importance of relationships in teaching was to invite another guest speaker to the class. With the exception of Randy Knight, each of the guest speakers in the class was a former student of Tom's from either the B.Ed. or M.Ed. program at Queen's University. In April, a local intermediate science teacher visited with the class to share his experiences using active-learning pedagogies with students in Grades 7 and 8. Not surprisingly, the candidates who participated in the study felt that the guest speakers reinforced the messages that Tom gave during the physics course, particularly the message that cautions candidates: "Don't try to become good at everything all at once" (FG4, 33) during the first year of teaching. Tom felt that inviting former students to be guest speakers in the class sends the message that he "values maintaining relationships far beyond graduation" (Journal, April). Thus guest speakers served two purposes, namely, to provide candidates with an opportunity to interact with experienced school teachers and, more tacitly, to encourage candidates to maintain contact with Tom during their careers.

The relationship between Tom and the members of the physics methods course was perhaps most evident during the final class in April. A group of teacher candidates took it upon themselves to film each of their classmates responding to a series of prompts. These responses were edited together to provide a short movie designed to be a memento for everyone in the class. The final class began with a screening of this 8-minute film, much to the delight of the class. Proving that turnabout is fair play, the teacher candidates asked Tom a series of questions about what he has learned about teaching teachers over his career, in order to include Tom in the class video. Tom used his time in the interview to emphasize the importance of finding different ways to listen to students and of being willing to modify your lesson to take students' feedback into account. Judging by the candidates' decision to ask Tom questions about teaching and learning for their class movie, it would appear that Tom's message about the importance of relationships was collectively taken to heart.

Processing the April Block

Toward the end of the April, Tom and I met to discuss our experiences with the physics course over the month of April. When I asked Tom to describe how the April classes were fitting in with his overall themes for the year, he responded:

> Right away, I needed to focus this course on learning: theirs [candidates], mine, and their students [on practicum]. I said it in the first class and I said it

often .... My goal is to try to make this course as coherent as possible. There is a strong tendency [among candidates] to avoid talking about their learning, mostly because they have gone through school for so long without being asked to talk about it ....When candidates find out that teaching and learning are hard, it doesn't fit with the cultural notion that teaching is easy ... there is a strong cognitive dissonance. (Journal, April)

Rather than provide answers to try to minimize the cognitive dissonance that candidates still felt in April, Tom planned to revisit each of his main themes to remind candidates that the dissonance existed for good reason. Many of the learning experiences that Tom provided during the physics course were different than the experiences many of the candidates were used to from school. In a way, "trying to close things too dramatically might sent a contrary message to Tom's focus on keeping the lines of communication open and his message about the importance of understanding learning to teach as a process that begins, but doesn't end, during the B.Ed. year" (Journal, April). Thus it seemed appropriate for the physics class to end not with a definitive conclusion, but with a series of gentle reminders about active-learning pedagogies, relationships, and relevant literature. Each reminder was grounded in a set of learning experiences within the physics class itself.

CONSTRUCTING PROFESSIONAL KNOWLEDGE FROM TEACHING AND LEARNING EXPERIENCES

In this final section of the chapter I summarize the professional knowledge constructed and co-constructed by the teacher candidates and teacher educators who participated in this study. The themes in the data are synthesized with a view to making claims about how participants were theorizing teaching and learning during the final phase of data collection and over the course of the academic year. The overarching theme is one of consolidating and framing learning while looking ahead to future teaching experiences.

After a 2-month hiatus for the February practicum and the alternate practicum experience in March, the physics class reconvened in April for six classes. During this final round of data collection, the candidates tended to discuss how they learned over the course of the year, not limiting their discussions to events that occurred during April. The participating teacher candidates unanimously felt that they were better teachers for having experienced the preservice teacher education program at Queen's University. Candidates learned to focus their attention on particular elements of teaching and learning as a result of coursework; in many cases they were encouraged to challenge their prior assumptions about how to teach and about how students learn. In addition to providing several catalysts for thinking about teaching in different ways, teacher candidates re-learned how to learn in a university context as a result of the contrasts between the teacher education program and their undergraduate degree experiences. In all cases, the B.Ed. program required more effort than candidates had been led to believe. Most participants framed the preservice teacher education program in familiar, dichotomous terms that placed the university as the obvious home of theory and the practicum as the obvious home of practice. Paul characterized the program slightly differently, framing the program in terms of pedagogies that did and did not engage him and thinking about teaching and learning. Overall, the candidates summarized their learning from the program by acknowledging that it provided a worthwhile set of experiences, both on- and off-campus, that were valuable to their development as teachers.

In many ways, the tensions articulated by candidates over the course of the academic year remain unresolved because the data indicate that participants were looking ahead to teaching careers with many of the tensions they had articulated during earlier interviews. They did consolidate their perceptions of themselves as teachers to the point where they were able to clearly and consistently articulate the kinds of pedagogies they wished to enact. Looking ahead to their first years of teaching, the dominant source of tension for participants was the perceived disconnect between how they wanted to teach and the contextual factors that threatened to trap them in traditional, default modes of teaching. This tension was a natural extension of the tensions they experienced during the practicum, when many of the candidates were unable to enact active-learning pedagogies despite their best intentions. A few of the candidates expressed concern about being able to teach using active-learning approaches at this early stage in their career particularly upon realizing that such approaches require unfamiliar conceptualizations of teaching and learning.

It seems particularly noteworthy that the candidates who participated in this research chose to spend the majority of their April interviews discussing and interpreting how they learned from Tom's pedagogy. The learning effects associated with the practicum experiences went almost unmentioned, perhaps in part due to the fact that the alternate practicum placements made the memories of the February practicum more distant. It seems reasonable, however, to point out that the learning experiences associated with the physics course were more chronologically distant than either of the winter practicum experiences, yet the teacher candidates continued to make their experiences in the physics course a primary focus of their discussions. Although the candidates universally acknowledged that they learned from other elements of the program, the consolidated understanding of the group was that Tom's pedagogy encouraged them to think about how they learned to teach while focusing on broad issues of teaching and learning.

This is not to suggest that the teacher candidates all learned from Tom in the same way. For Irene, the effects of Tom's pedagogy were slow to take hold and came into focus only at the end of the program. Max trusted Tom to lead the class in an appropriate direction right from the start because he appreciated the collaborative, trusting atmosphere that Tom created with the members of the physics course. James was strongly affected by Tom's focus on the importance of carefully analyzing various features of teaching and learning. David noticed the incremental way that Tom built up themes over each of the on-campus blocks of classes, and came to believe in the importance of each of those themes. Paul articulated a strong empathy and enthusiasm for Tom's pedagogy, to the point where he was frequently frustrated by what he perceived as missed opportunities when other members of the physics class failed to fully engage in various learning experiences. Paul's frustrations seemed to lead him to additional insights into the challenges of active-learning approaches to pedagogy, such as the requirement to trust the learner even when he or she is not engaging with a learning experience.

The five teacher candidates consolidated their view that teaching and learning are more complicated than the simplistic cultural ideas of a subject-matter expert telling students, seen as blank slates, the information required to pass a test. Traditional notions of teaching and learning are conceptually difficult to challenge due to a lifetime of experiencing the socializing effects of the apprenticeship of observation. Adopting an active-learning approach to teaching requires a major conceptual shift in how one approaches teaching; it is not sufficient to simply add active-learning strategies such as Predict-Observe-Explain to a dominant classroom culture of lecturing.

Overall, the participants were quite focused on the challenges they faced in becoming full-time teachers in the near future. James was concerned that the workload of first-year teaching would prevent him from using active-learning approaches to teaching and learning. Max expressed confidence in his teaching abilities, due in large part to a positive practicum experience with an associate who also used an active-learning approach, but he was mindful of the temptation to treat physics as an applied-mathematics course. Irene was unique among the participants in that she was unsure of her future as a teacher, although she was quick to note that her understanding of learning had been changed as a result of experiences in the program. David too was convinced of the benefits of using active-learning pedagogies, but looked ahead to his early years in teaching with a certain amount of trepidation. Specifically, he was concerned about starting the year with an unsustainable focus on active-learning. He did not want to disappoint his students by emphasizing active-learning at the beginning of the year, only to have to return to a more traditional approach in order to manage his workload. Paul saw active-learning pedagogies in the broader context of the productive, safe learning environment that he wished to create with his future students. He acknowledged the challenges associated with such a non-traditional approach, but was optimistic nonetheless.

Having articulated all the major issues that he wished to explore, Tom's main task for the month of April was one of consolidating what candidates had learned from both the physics class and from the program as a whole. Tom directed candidates to relevant literature on physics and physics teaching and introduced the concept of cognitive dissonance as a way to help them process their learning. Tom provided a way for the candidates to live comfortably with the dissonance arising from their experiences in the preservice education year. Factors contributing to dissonance included the tension between what they had learned about teaching and learning and their prior assumptions and the discrepancy between the kinds of teachers they are and the kinds of teachers they want to be. Tom resisted the familiar temptation to frame a tidy conclusion with the teacher candidates in the physics course. Doing so would have contradicted his message that teaching and learning are intricate and messy and require more than an 8-month professional program to understand. Instead, Tom acknowledged candidates' tensions by touching on the four major themes of the course and, at the end of the final class, encouraging them to take their dissonance forward into their teaching careers:

> One of the reasons that make the transition into this place difficult is that you are all of a sudden a teacher and you have to learn how to pay attention to learning. You have to learn how to learn, rather than learn how to get the highest marks. By the time you've taught something a few times, you will have mastered the content ... Every teacher should always have two agendas: a content agenda and a learning agenda. (Journal, April)

Throughout the physics course, Tom encouraged the teacher candidates to think beyond teaching students right answers about physics. It seemed appropriate to end the course with a reminder that the real challenge of teaching is not just developing subject-matter knowledge for teaching, what some might call pedagogical content knowledge, but also constructing knowledge of teaching and learning from personal experience.

CHAPTER 8

DISRUPTING THE APPRENTICESHIP OF OBSERVATION

The apprenticeship of observation undergone by all who enter teaching begins the process of socialization in a particular way; it acquaints students with the tasks of the teacher and fosters the development of identification with teachers. It does not, however, lay the basis for informed assessment of teaching technique or encourage the development of analytic orientations toward the work. Unless beginning teachers undergo training which offset their individualistic and traditional experiences, the occupation will be staffed by people who have little concern with building a shared technical culture. In the absence of such a culture, the diverse histories of teachers will play a cardinal role in their day-to-day activity. In that respect, the apprenticeship of observation is an ally of continuity rather than of change. (Lortie, 1975, p. 67)

This book set out to analyze how teacher candidates and teacher educators construct professional knowledge from teaching and learning experiences during a preservice teacher education program. Several decades ago, Zeichner and Tabachnick (1981) published an article with a title that many seem to take as suggesting that school experiences overwhelm or "wash out" the effects of preservice teacher education programs. A closer reading of the paper suggests that the authors are posing the possibility that there may be few, if any, effects of teacher education coursework to be washed out by the culture of the school during practicum experiences. One of the major findings of this study, however, is that the manner in which the physics methods course was taught had a substantial impact on the nature of the participants' learning about teaching.

This analysis of one preservice course reveals that disciplined attention to how a teacher education course is taught can produce significant learning effects, contrary to many common assumptions about the utility of coursework in teacher education. The interview data indicate clearly that the five teacher candidates who participated in the study formed coherent pictures of teaching and learning that are different from the traditions they experienced during their apprenticeships of observation. Participating in the focus group and individual interviews added a unique element to the preservice program experiences of the five teacher candidates. The self-study data provided valuable insight into naming and interpreting the challenges of teaching candidates in ways that are distinctively different from traditional, teacher-centred approaches to teaching and learning.

This concluding chapter begins with a discussion of the findings of the research in light of the literature on teachers' professional knowledge, with particular emphasis on understanding the data in terms of the narrative perspective (Clandinin & Connelly, 1995) and the reflection-in-action perspective (Munby & Russell, 1990) on the

CHAPTER 8

epistemology of professional knowledge. Next, the questions posed at the beginning of this book are revisited and three guiding principles of teacher education are offered as ways of summarizing the data analysis. Excerpts from a interview with Tom Russell, which occurred after the data were collected and analyzed, are then presented to reveal how thorough analysis of his teaching and of the ways in which five candidates learned to teach encouraged him to reframe his pedagogy. The concept of the authority of experience (Munby & Russell, 1994) is then discussed with a view to understanding how and why participants in the study came to think about their professional knowledge in new ways. Finally, the chapter concludes by describing the ways in which the physics methods course challenged the candidates' apprenticeships of observations.

THE DEVELOPMENT OF TEACHERS' PROFESSIONAL KNOWLEDGE

The literature reviewed in Chapters 2 and 3 developed the argument that a purely propositional approach to theorizing how teachers learn is inadequate for a deep understanding of how teachers' professional knowledge develops. While teacher candidates can and do learn from propositions, I argued that consideration of how teacher candidates learn from experience offers a more productive way of thinking about the intricacies of learning to teach. Indeed, a purely propositional approach to thinking about the development of teachers' knowledge tends to result in conceptualizing a knowledge base for teacher education that is predicated on the assumption that new teachers can be told how to teach by experts in both the classroom and the university.

The knowledge gap between expert, experienced teachers and novice teacher candidates is readily apparent both to teacher candidates during their practicum experiences and to teacher educators as they teach methods courses. As Shulman (1986, 1987) argued, knowledge of subject matter alone is a necessary but not a sufficient requirement for becoming a teacher. Teachers must develop knowledge of how to teach their subjects, knowledge that Shulman named *pedagogical content knowledge*. The idea of pedagogical content knowledge proved to be a tempting one for researchers and many studies were conducted with the aim of providing descriptions and interpretations of the nature of teachers' pedagogical content knowledge.

Ultimately, documenting pedagogical content knowledge has proven to be an elusive goal (Berry et al., 2008). The difficulty arises because teachers typically do not use the language associated with pedagogical content knowledge and because teachers' pedagogical content knowledge is highly dependent on the contexts in which they teach (Barnett & Hodson, 2001; Loughran et al., 2001). In the context of this study, it appears that pedagogical content knowledge is more a convenient way for researchers to name teachers' expertise than a productive line of reasoning for thinking about the development of teachers' professional knowledge. It seemed unproductive to frame the knowledge that the participants constructed over the academic year in terms of pedagogical content knowledge because they rarely discussed how they taught a specific physics concept, even though one could say that the candidates had more pedagogical content knowledge at the end of their teacher education program than they had at the beginning. In contrast, the next sections demonstrate that the epistemology of experiential knowledge, represented by the narrative and reflection-in-action strands of research, offers considerable insight into the process of learning to teach for these five teacher candidates.

Narratives of Experience

The data show considerable evidence that the teacher candidates created multiple narratives as a way to interpret their developing professional knowledge. Each of the three kinds of narrative posed by Clandinin and Connelly (1995) was evident in the data as the teacher candidates attempted to navigate their professional landscapes. The sacred story of theory-into-practice was particularly evident in participants' prior assumptions about what they would learn during a preservice teacher education program. During the first round of interviews, for example, the participants indicated that they expected both to learn and to be taught in traditional ways. David said that he expected the B.Ed. program to help him "polish" (FG1, 14) the teaching behaviours he had witnessed as a student, Irene wanted professors to tell her "how to improve" (FG1, 88) on lecture-style approaches, and Paul "expected to be taught traditionally" (Paul1, 3).

An intriguing dynamic concerning the candidates' cover and secret stories of practicum experiences appeared in their considerable discussion of the practicum during the second round of interviews, which occurred after the first 4 weeks of practicum experiences. Consideration of the narratives shared during the second focus group (November) reveals that candidates were likely telling cover stories to one another. This is not to suggest that the narratives were in any way false; it only underscores that candidates avoided rich descriptions of how they taught. Instead, they discussed the challenges presented by their students and their associate teachers. James, David, and Paul contributed stories of frustration when their students cared more about right answers than about understanding fundamental concepts. Another major narrative was a description of candidates' relationships with their associate teachers. They talked openly to one another about the varying and (in four of the five cases) somewhat limited freedom they had to try a range of pedagogical approaches. Both strands of discussion allowed the candidates to talk about features of their practicum that were, to a certain extent, safe because they did not reveal anything that was particularly personal about their own teaching. The candidates appeared to be using cover stories with one another in a manner similar to many experienced teachers: to cover up feelings of personal discomfort and to situate themselves on a common professional knowledge landscape with deeply embedded cultural traditions.

In the third focus group (January), candidates spoke at length about how they perceived they were learning from the physics methods course, but made no mention of their practicum experiences. Instead of telling cover stories, they revealed their secret stories of classroom practice to me during the individual interviews that followed the focus group discussion. The conversations in the third round of individual interviews felt intensely personal, perhaps because the participants had become more comfortable with me or were eager to make sense of the increasing incoherence of the program as a whole. Each of the individual interviews offered a

CHAPTER 8

collection of secret stories revealing the complicated relationships between teacher candidate and associate teacher and the tensions candidates experienced during practicum. For example, even though he had the most consistently positive attitude throughout the B.Ed. year, James revealed concerns about his ability to balance workload during the practicum. Max admitted to feeling trapped by a perceived need to master traditional, teacher-centred pedagogy before moving on to strategies that encouraged students to take an active role in their learning. Although she was comfortable with and impressed by her associate teacher's ability to lecture senior physics students, Irene felt guilty for finding reasons to fully adopt her associate's style in place of attempting to enact some of the ideas she explored in the physics methods course. David described his frustration with the artificial learning environment of the practicum and his desire to have his own classroom. Paul's secret story was, in many ways, one of the most controversial stories that can be told during a teacher education program: he questioned his place in a public school system with a dominant culture positioning teachers as enforcers of rules and guardians of knowledge. Taken together, these secret stories likely resonate with the experiences of many teacher candidates in a variety of teacher education programs.

The sacred, cover, and secret stories offered during four rounds of interviews show that candidates' practicum experiences tended to reinforce many of the traditional assumptions and routines embedded in the culture of schools. The narratives of experience revealed that the candidates often struggled to situate themselves on the highly contextual professional knowledge landscapes of their host schools, particularly when such landscapes conflicted with the ideas they developed from the physics methods course and their personal beliefs about teaching. Although these stories provide insights into the challenges faced by candidates during practicum placements, they do not provide a clear understanding of how professional knowledge was constructed from experience.

Attending to Metaphors, Developing Knowledge-in-action

Considering the data in terms of Schön's (1983) concepts of reflection-in-action and knowledge-in-action sheds considerable light on the development of candidates' professional knowledge. Reflection-in-action names the process in which a professional frames a problematic situation, enacts a course of action, and reframes his or her understanding as the situation continues to unfold. As Schön noted, reflection-in-action is bounded by an "action present" (p. 62) that lasts as long as further action would make a difference to a particular situation. Knowledge-in-action names the inherent artistry of professional knowledge, acquired not through enacting propositions but through deliberate interactions with experiences, particularly those that are problematic and challenge existing assumptions. Throughout the interview process, participants used metaphors to describe and interpret their experiences in the physics methods course and the practicum. Careful attention to how these metaphors changed over the course of the B.Ed. year reveal the epistemological underpinnings of candidates' thinking about the nature of teaching and learning.

During the first round of interviews, the metaphors used by candidates reflected their initial assumptions about teaching and learning, formed largely in their apprenticeships of observation. For the most part, they equated teaching with *transmitting information*. This metaphor was implicit in phrases such as "repeat the textbook" (FG1, 10) and "you get up and talk to your students" (FG1, 3). Coming into the program, candidates expected to be told how to teach, although they were "pleasantly surprised" (FG1, 51) when some courses took different approaches. By the second round of interviews, the candidates began using more complicated metaphors that recognized the importance of students' involvement in the learning process. These metaphors reflect a *relational approach to teaching* because candidates recognized that their relationships with students made a difference to the effectiveness of their teaching. Max, for example, stated that exclusively focusing on his teaching made it difficult "to focus on how all the kids were learning" (FG2, 85). James built relationships with his students by "telling a personal story" (FG2, 38), while David did so by discussing "video games" (FG2, 39). Paul pushed the metaphor further, stating that the classroom "relationship is a specific part of the teaching" (Paul2, 29). The realization that teaching is more than conveying information in an entertaining way and that it depends at least in part on the relationship between teachers and their students was apparent in the second set of interviews.

The *relational approach to teaching* metaphor was extended in the third round of interviews. For the first time, Irene stated explicitly that a positive relationship between a teacher and their students was helpful, although she was quick to point out that relationships take time to develop. Max mentioned that he found it harder to develop a relational approach with students in his applied-level course who did not share his facility with mathematics. James felt that developing relationships with his students required a considerable amount of effort, particularly because it required him to "adjust" (James3, 9) his teaching strategies according to what he learned about students. David indicated that he continued to work hard to develop meaningful relationships with his students throughout his December practicum placement.

During the final round of interviews, however, participants changed the dominant metaphor from a *relational approach to teaching* to an *active-learning approach to teaching*. The metaphor of relationship did not disappear; it was joined by a new, more sophisticated metaphor for teaching. This change was significant because the candidates framed pedagogical approaches such as "learning by doing" (Irene4, 9) and "metacognition and students being responsible for their own learning" (David4, 1) as preferable to more traditional approaches such as lecturing and "explaining stuff really well" (Paul4, 37). *Active-learning approaches to teaching* put special emphasis on the nature of the relationship between students and teachers. Even though James and Irene were quick to point out that the lecture-based approaches to teaching were sometimes beneficial, the candidates tended to frame active-learning pedagogy in opposition to traditional approaches based on transmission. James stated explicitly that his future goal as a teacher was "to foster an active learning environment" (James4, 13). Irene, the biggest proponent of lecturing throughout the data collection, stated in her final interview that teaching was "not just telling somebody something" (Irene4, 29). David worried about his ability to go against the "norm" (David4, 27) of teaching-as-telling.

CHAPTER 8

Only Paul gave a clear indication of moving beyond this dichotomy. He articulated what might be termed a *pedagogy of engagement*, by recognizing that no particular teaching strategy, not even strategies such as POEs grounded in active-learning approaches, can guarantee students will learn effectively. Instead, Paul wanted to build his pedagogy around "keeping kids engaged and active and reflective and critical," recognizing that active-learning approaches are relatively ineffective if they are, for example, assessed in traditional ways. For Paul, a *pedagogy of engagement* meant thinking about teaching and learning in terms of the needs of the learner. It meant creating an environment where students could "take risks" and "learn how to learn" (Paul4, 32). Paul realized that being engaged—either during a lecture or a POE—is learning. He also recognized that relationships are a central part of teaching and that a teacher's role is to develop a "framework from which *we* [italics added] can share ideas without fear of being wrong" (Paul4, 32). He reframed the teacher's role as a co-learner in the classroom, thus interrupting the debate between student-centred and teaching-centred learning. In recognizing his participation as a learner in the classroom, Paul's final metaphor about the nature of teaching and learning brings to mind recent arguments by Davis and Sumara (2007), who suggest that teaching be framed as "a conscientious participation in expanding the space of the possible" (p. 65).

The second metaphor that evolved during the data collection period focused on the way that candidates described how they learned from Tom. From the first round of interviews, the candidates described an overall positive feeling toward Tom's teaching. The first metaphor might be named *trust the learner*, to borrow a phrase used by David during the first focus-group interview. Although candidates found it difficult to articulate precisely what they had learned from Tom at this stage, they named Tom's implicit trust in the class as a major feature of his teaching. Max stated that Tom "believed" (Max1, 8) in the candidates' abilities and went on to suggest that he was more motivated in the physics methods course because of the trust Tom showed toward the class. The praise for Tom's pedagogy continued into the second round of interviews, when candidates described several different ways in which they learned from Tom. James and Irene were impressed by the range of active-learning strategies that Tom used during the methods course, particularly when those strategies encouraged them to rethink how they learned. Max and Paul continued to use *trust the learner* as their guiding metaphor for thinking about Tom's course, albeit in different ways. Max continued to focus on his increased level of engagement with the physics course as a result of feeling trusted by Tom. Paul, on the other hand, perceived a problem with the trust Tom placed in the members of the physics course. He believed that some members of the class were not being as co-operative as they could be, resulting in the "class being too quiet" even though Paul could "see what he's trying to do and hoping for" (Paul2, 11). Although Paul was an early and vocal advocate of the way Tom taught the class, he was unable to articulate precisely the features of Tom's pedagogy that engaged him. Paul coined the term "*work-in-progress* [italics added]" (Paul2, 45) to describe how he learned from Tom.

The candidates devoted considerable time during the third focus group interview in January to interpreting Tom's pedagogy as a group. The metaphor of *trust the learner* seemed implicit in their discussion, but they struggled initially to name the content of the physics methods course. They realized that it was certainly not clarification of physics concepts, because Tom seemed more interested in discussing teaching and learning than in talking about physics. As Paul quipped, "Tom does everything so deliberately ... for some reason I can't figure out, [he] is really trying to never tell us anything about physics" (FG3, 53). Later in the same focus group interview, all five participants agreed that the *methods* that Tom used for teaching were, in fact, the content of the course. They realized that Tom did not believe that telling them how to teach would be as effective as teaching them in ways he hoped they would teach their students. Thus the metaphor of *trust the learner* was extended to *how we teach is the message*, which is also one of the phrases written on a poster at the front of Tom's classroom. The implicit assumption was that trust is a critical feature of how one should teach.

The metaphors of *work-in-progress* and *how we teach is the message* were extended during the final round of interviews in April. By the end of the B.Ed. program, the candidates had accepted that Tom's pedagogical approach was a *work-in-progress* throughout the year, with the messages behind his teaching becoming apparent at different times in the year for each participant. Irene said that eventually the message "just sunk in" (Irene4, 4); Max said that he learned from Tom through "osmosis" (Max4, 2); and James was encouraged by Tom's approach to "constantly reflect on the big picture" (FG4, 65). The candidates agreed during the final focus group that *how* Tom taught encouraged them to carefully analyze big picture issues in teaching and learning, as opposed to focusing on developing strategies for teaching specific physics concepts. David and Paul discussed the metaphor of *how we teach is the message* at considerable length. The way Tom taught the physics class encouraged David to try to enact similar approaches during his practicum experiences, even though he felt that he was "swimming against the current" (FG4, 16) of traditional school structures. Paul summed up the metaphor succinctly: "What I mostly learned from physics class was just the way Tom taught" (Paul4, 1).

The metaphors that candidates used to describe how they thought about teaching and how they learned from Tom changed considerably over the course of the 8-month preservice teacher education program. From an initial metaphor equating teaching with *transmitting information*, the candidates developed a richer and more complex view of teaching as they framed and reframed experiences during the practicum and in the physics methods course. Each of the three practicum experiences changed profoundly the candidates' views about teaching and learning. *Teaching-as-transmission* quickly gave way to a *relational approach to teaching*, characterized by an increased focus on the importance of understanding and valuing students' learning needs. By April, the metaphor changed to encompass *active-learning approaches to teaching*, characterized by the use of the student-centred pedagogies candidates experienced in the physics methods course. *Active-learning approaches* were seen by the candidates as more desirable than traditional, teacher-centred learning. Paul extended the metaphor further toward a *pedagogy of engagement* that positioned the teacher as one (particularly important) participant in the classroom learning environment. For Paul, specific teaching strategies were less important than the overall zeitgeist of

CHAPTER 8

his future classroom, which he hoped would be a safe environment for him to learn as his students learned.

Tom's initial impact on the participants is underscored by the first metaphor candidates used to describe how they learned in the physics course. The *trust the learner* metaphor features prominently throughout the data, although it developed into *how we teach is the message* during a poignant moment in the January focus group when candidates realized collectively that the content of the physics methods course was the way that Tom was teaching them. Paul first coined the metaphor *work-in-progress* to describe Tom's overall pedagogical direction, partly as a way to name his confusion about Tom's long-term plans for the course. The messages that Tom sent resonated at different times for different candidates, but each explicitly identified the way that Tom taught as an important source of their learning during the B.Ed. program.

REVISITING THE RESEARCH QUESTIONS

In answering the original research questions, it seems appropriate to offer *guiding principles* as broad conclusions to this study. Principles are dynamic, providing lenses that reveal assumptions, suggest future directions, and encourage debate (Kroll et al., 2004). These guiding principles are warranted assertions (Dewey, 1938), not objective truths. To that end, I offer a brief discussion of the data in light of each research question and conclude each section with a guiding principle of teacher education.

Constructing Professional Knowledge from Learning Experiences in a Physics Methods Course

The way that the physics methods course was taught provided experiences in which teacher candidates could identify, confront, and engage their prior assumptions about the nature of teaching and learning. Beginning with a POE in the first class sent a message that there are alternatives to the teaching and learning experiences with which candidates were most familiar from their long careers as students. Lesson study provided an opportunity for candidates to discover their personal potential to enact a reasonable impression of the teachers who had taught them.

Although the participants frequently stated that the course pedagogy had a positive effect on their learning, they tended to be unable to name specific features of the teaching that were productive until late in the course. One feature that had an early and ongoing impact was their teacher's focus on earning their trust by using pedagogies that helped to develop a safe environment. Each of the major themes for the course was introduced by the end of September, so that the same themes could be revisited in different ways later in the program. Guest speakers helped to underscore the importance of rethinking traditional approaches to teaching, particularly during the November on-campus weeks.

As the tensions that teacher candidates were feeling seemed to peak in January, they were provided with another novel experience: class time to direct their own professional learning, as a way of introducing them formally to self-directed learning (SDL). Teacher candidates thus had time to analyze their experiences as living contradictions and the implications of those experiences for how they would approach the remainder of the B.Ed. program. The participants realized that *how* they were being taught was more important than *what* they were being taught, and the self-directed learning experience became a touchstone for thinking about many of the unique pedagogical features of the physics class.

Learning experiences in the physics course in April served to remind candidates of each major theme in the course and to encourage them to live comfortably with the tensions of teaching and learning. It seemed fitting that the teacher candidates provided a learning experience for Tom during the final class, as he was invited to contribute to a class video. Throughout the year, he found ways to revisit the cognitive dissonance between candidates' expectations for teacher education and their experiences with active-learning pedagogies in the physics methods course. All five candidates who participated in the research stated explicitly that they learned from how the course was taught. A consideration of each participant's responses over the year reveals evidence that they reframed, to varying extents, their understanding of teaching and learning as a result of experiences in the physics methods course.

Guiding Principle 1: Providing a coherent set of pedagogically challenging learning experiences within a methods course can create opportunities for teacher candidates to confront and revise their assumptions about teaching and learning.

Constructing Professional Knowledge from Teaching Experiences during Practicum Placements

The participants in the study came to the teacher education program believing that coursework would provide them with theory that they could then practice in their host schools during their practicum placements. They were excited to begin the practicum in October, although a few admitted to some anxiety about potential negative effects their teaching might have on students' learning. While some seemed reluctant to return to the Faculty for the November on-campus classes, the participants soon recognized the value of having time at the Faculty to process their first practicum placement.

The candidates named several tensions they experienced as a result of their first practicum placement. These tensions arose because their practicum experiences did not match their prior assumptions about teaching and learning. Candidates were frustrated by their perceived inability to enact pedagogies in accord with their vision of the kinds of teachers they wished to be. The expectations candidates placed on themselves as a result of messages they took from the physics course coupled with the expectations of their associate teachers created tensions that caused some to experience themselves as living contradictions.

The intensity with which participants felt tensions from practicum experiences was partially revealed by the fact that participants spoke about their December practicum experiences only during their individual interviews in January, not in the

CHAPTER 8

focus group. Their narratives of practicum experiences tended to remain secret and private as they continued to struggle with the tensions that began in October. Some participants were frustrated by their perceived inability to enact active-learning pedagogies; others were implicitly or explicitly compelled to teach in more traditional ways by their associate teachers. One participant characterized the practicum as an artificial learning environment because, regardless of the level of freedom he had to plan his teaching, he could not ignore the fact that he was a guest in someone else's classroom. Two of the five participants were reluctant to return to their practicum placements. Another questioned his desire to remain in the teaching profession, due in large part to the culturally socialized, authoritarian traditions associated with teaching.

By April, the participants had found ways to live with the tensions they experienced on practicum. One of the biggest sources of relief for the tensions seemed to be the fact that they would soon have their own classrooms, and this reduced the stresses associated with being guests in their associate teachers' classrooms. Candidates had also realized that learning to teach is a lengthy process that would take years, not months, and so perhaps they were more forgiving of the disconnect between their intended and enacted pedagogies than at the beginning of the year. Four of the participants articulated a desire to move beyond the traditional, teacher-centred approaches to teaching and learning they had witnessed during their practicum experiences.

Guiding Principle 2: The practicum provides teacher candidates with an opportunity to confront the inevitable gap between their intended and enacted pedagogies, but the tensions that result from experiencing themselves as living contradictions do little to help candidates challenge the dominant culture of schooling.

Constructing Professional Knowledge from Collaborative Self-study

The familiar view of teacher education is that there is a significant gap between theory and practice, namely, that theory is learned in one place and taken to another place to be put into practice. This view is characterized by some as a sacred story of teacher education, sacred in the sense that most candidates and their teachers are unwilling to question the veracity of the story. Collaborative self-study proved to be a powerful way for two teacher educators to attend to what they see as a more productive way of framing the gap in teacher education, namely, as a gap between what candidates are taught and how they are taught.

Throughout the academic year, Tom and I met regularly to discuss our perceptions of the teaching and learning in the physics methods course. Specific attention was paid to the problems of practice that emerged over the course of the academic year and to the tensions those problems created. At the end of September, for example, we concluded that requiring candidates to plan lessons in groups might have been too demanding so early in the year. In November, we discussed the problem of keeping the course themes in candidates' minds during the short time they were on campus. In January, our shared sense of the tensions placed on candidates by the program encouraged us to analyze carefully the effects of the self-directed learning activity. Finally, we met before the candidates returned in April to discuss ways in which a teacher educator could provide learning experiences that connected to the big-picture issues of teaching and learning that had been developed earlier in the course.

The results of the collaborative self-study reveal not only how one teacher educator thought about teaching a methods course over a complete academic year, but also how two teacher educators came to understand teacher education in a more disciplined way. During each of the four blocks of classes, our discussion generated new understandings about how to teach teachers. Together, we were often able to name and interpret features of the teaching and learning in the physics methods course that had implications for how we will approach future methods courses. While we affirmed some of our long-held beliefs, such as the importance of building a productive relationship with teacher candidates and the power of Predict-Observe-Explain pedagogy to create a low-risk environment, we also reached new insight through careful analysis of practice. Specifically, we realized that Lesson Study has the potential to help teacher candidates discover their default teaching moves, although we would both approach Lesson Study differently in the future. We learned the value of stepping back and trusting candidates to make sense of the self-directed learning time. Finally, we came to understand in greater detail how difficult it can be for teacher candidates to talk openly about their learning experiences in a teacher education program, and how valuable it can be to find different ways to encourage them to engage in such discussions.

Guiding Principle 3: Collaborative self-study is a powerful way for teacher educators to analyze features of their practice with a view to helping candidates to identify, reframe, and extend their assumptions about teaching and learning.

REVISITING THE PERSPECTIVE OF THE TEACHER EDUCATOR

In the year following collection of the data for this research, Tom and I returned to our usual arrangement for the methods course during my doctorate program: Tom was the instructor of record and I was the teaching assistant for the physics methods course. We shared teaching responsibilities for the course; our usual practice was for each of us to take the lead for a portion of each 2½-hour class. We continued to meet regularly to discuss the teaching and learning issues of mutual interest. The main features of the course described in this book, such as POE, lesson study, and self-directed learning were again a part of our subsequent course, with some modifications based on what we learned in the previous year and the learning needs of a different group of teacher candidates. Tom elaborated on this point:

> We certainly learned from the Lesson Study and I think we did it better this year than last year. Part of that is the inevitable battle that every teacher has to have: When you hear an idea, you go and try it in what seems like the best possible way but you discover once you do it that there might be other ways to approach it that might be more productive. (Journal, February)

CHAPTER 8

Tom's comments reflect his underlying belief in the power of learning from experience. Lesson Study, for example, was a novel teaching approach for Tom during last year's physics course. Personal observations combined with data from this study helped us to understand that the most productive part of lesson study was the opportunity for teacher candidates to stand up in front of a room and begin to discover their default teaching behaviours. We also realized some of the limitations of the last year's Lesson Study, such as the repetitive nature of each lesson being taught twice and the expectation that candidates plan lessons in groups. To that end, we asked this year's group of teacher candidates to individually plan and teach lessons related to the Grades 9 and 10 science. Focusing on the intermediate science curriculum also encouraged candidates to focus on less familiar concepts from biology and chemistry. This change in approach, which occurred as a result of reflection-in-action in September of the previous year and reflection-on-action after considering data presented in this study, is an example of developing knowledge-in-action from the experience of teaching with Lesson Study.

One issue that became clear to me as a result of being a participant-observer in last year's physics class is that Tom's pedagogy of teacher education relies on candidates' willingness to engage deeply with metacognitive learning opportunities. The cultural traditions of school tend to provide few opportunities for students to monitor their own learning, so many of Tom's approaches feel unfamiliar and uncomfortable at the outset. Sometimes, this results in uncomfortable silences in the physics course. I asked Tom how he felt about learners who require more direction from their teacher's than he is willing to provide. Tom replied:

> I don't know how flippant it sounds, but I don't worry about the people who think they need someone else to be telling them, because I have no doubt they can find that somewhere else … I just have to believe that I need to keep sending a consistent message and then work at differentiating and adapting to the individuals as I get to know them. (Journal, February)

These comments made me think of the impulse I often feel to tell students about teaching in my own teacher education classroom, which led to the following exchange:

Shawn: When I get confused about a situation in a teacher education classroom, one of the things that I reach for is my relatively recent experiences as a physics teacher. Many times I have to fight really hard to avoid saying, "When I taught that, here is what I did." There is a tension between telling them what I know and letting them explore. Do you still feel a certain amount of tension around telling them about teaching?

Tom: We've talked this year about wanting candidates to shift away from thinking about their teaching toward thinking about their students' learning, as a way of judging what's going on in the classroom. It is interesting to see how hard it is to zero in on these issues. I wonder if there have been that many times this year when they were yearning to be told.

	I don't think there is anything in the data from last year that suggests that the students were struggling as a consequence of my not telling them how to teach.
Shawn:	I don't think so either.
Tom:	I think there is huge evidence that, regardless of consistencies or inconsistencies between participants, there was something happening here that was productive. We know that for the participant who had all the tensions [Irene], that's a healthy thing. That's what we are trying to create. That's "challenging their assumptions." (Journal, February)

Tom's metaphor for teaching the course might thus be thought of as *coherence*. He realizes that the learning experiences he provides are usually quite different than the types of learning experiences with which candidates are most familiar and comfortable. He brings out each of the course themes during the first few weeks of the program and provides a significant number of metacognitive opportunities throughout the course, even though many candidates may be reticent to talk about their own learning. By maintaining a coherent focus, Tom provides a range of experiences for candidates to think about learning to teach when they are ready. In the previous year, Paul and David took the opportunity earlier than the others, but by the end of the program each of the participants had engaged at some level with Tom's pedagogy of teacher education.

At the end of the interview, Tom and I spoke about the consequences of the fact I was moving to another institution to begin my academic career as an assistant professor:

Tom:	I am going to miss having someone to have all of these serious discussions with!
Shawn:	That was actually going to be my last point. Next year is going to be strange for both of us. It will be my first time teaching a physics methods course in my own right. We'll be at different universities. Do you have any thoughts about the impact that might have on both our pedagogies, because both of us have become accustomed to having the opportunity to immediately process what's happened in a class that we've co-taught?
Tom:	I've always wondered why it seems so much harder to write about teaching physics methods classes than it did to write about teaching physics, which I did after each class when I taught at a local high school. *When you are teaching a physics concept, you are teaching one concept at a time. When you are teaching about teaching, you're almost going after everything all the time* [italics added]. There is so much

CHAPTER 8

> and it is all knotted together. You can't talk about self-directed learning without talking about active learning, or meaningful learning, or metacognition. The package goes together. That may be one reason why it is hard to write about. Another factor is how long the classes are. The classes are twice as long as a high school class, so a lot more happens. One foil against that would be to start the year with two columns: A narrow column for the dates of the classes and a wide column for writing something in each box after class. That certainly would be useful. (Journal, February)

Tom and I plan to continue our critical friendship as I move into my role as a new academic. Writing seems a productive way for us to capture our assumptions and frame problems of practice for later discussion. One follow-up study would be to examine ways to listen to our students, perhaps by setting up small discussion groups with candidates in our methods courses. It will be particularly important for me to describe and interpret the ways in which my pedagogy of teacher education develops in a new institution, given that many of my prior assumptions about how to teach physics teachers were developed by the "reading positions" (Segall, 2002, p. 8) I developed as a part of this research. As Tom noted in the interview, it is one thing to hear about a good idea and quite another to experience it for oneself. I expect that a continuation of our collaborative self-study will help us continue to develop productive ways of thinking about teacher education.

Not surprisingly, the final interview generated a new idea that we are both keen to explore. The italicized portion of the interview transcript frames an important issue: teaching teachers is so complex because it is difficult to make one element of teaching the sole focus of a given class, and there is no obvious sequence for the many different elements of good teaching. For example, if I wanted to teach a group of physics teachers about assessment, I could not focus exclusively on assessment for any given class, because my pedagogy will still include many other elements such as my relationship with my students, how much time I choose to spend talking at the front of the class, the class readings I use, and so on. One of the things that this study makes clear is that candidates always take cues from *how* they are taught, regardless of the lesson's content focus. Although I might think that the content of my lesson is assessment, a particular teacher candidate who is paying attention to the nature of my relationship with the class during the lesson might take relationships, rather than assessment, as the content for that class. As Tom pointed out, teaching physics typically progresses one unit at a time; students are not asked to clarify their thinking about electricity during a unit on light. When the content of teaching is the act of teaching, every aspect of teaching and learning can be relevant at any time, including how the content is being taught.

DEVELOPING THE AUTHORITY OF EXPERIENCE

An underlying theme throughout the data analysis is the importance of finding ways to develop the "authority of experience" (Munby & Russell, 1994, p. 92) in teacher education classrooms. Simply having an experience in a practicum placement or in an education course does little to help teacher candidates construct professional knowledge unless they develop *authority* over those experiences. As Russell (1983) argued, schools are not set up so that the authority of position follows naturally from the authority of knowledge. It is entirely possible, and indeed likely in the cultural climate of schools, that the authority of position automatically granted to teachers can substitute for the authority of knowledge. Extending the argument to teacher education, we find that teacher educators may be granted a similar authority of position. A teacher educator for a methods course is presumed to be the locus of knowledge for teaching that subject matter, although associate teachers may be granted even greater authority of position.

Teacher candidates are put in a challenging position. On the one hand, it is important for them to develop authority over their experiences during the preservice teacher education program, yet they are "automatically placed under authority" (Munby & Russell, 1994, p. 92) of their course instructors. For example, Tom has an authority of experience for teaching physics because he has developed knowledge-in-action from his time as a physics teacher. Neither his authority of experience nor his knowledge-in-action are transferrable to teacher candidates. *He cannot tell them how to teach.*

This study presents considerable evidence that Tom successfully provides opportunities for candidates to develop authority over their own experiences in the physics methods course. The changing metaphors used by participants to describe the way they learned from Tom support the notion that *candidates are capable of developing knowledge-in-action from their learning experiences in a methods course.* With each subsequent round of interviews, the candidates developed more authority over how they learned from Tom. They also developed more authority over what they wanted to learn from the experiences in the methods course. By the end of the program, each candidate seemed to have a well-developed authority with respect to experiences in the physics methods course. They were able to articulate clearly the knowledge-in-action they constructed as learners in the course. The sequence of focus group and personal interviews helped to develop their authority of experience.

A major factor in candidates' abilities to develop authority over their learning experiences is Tom's ability to minimize his authority of position by focusing on active-learning pedagogies instead of lecturing candidates about teaching. His pedagogy of teacher education was confusing at times for many of the participants because they were unsure of the direction for the course. By stepping back and focusing on providing experiences for candidates to engage in a variety of autonomous learning activities, Tom encouraged members of the physics methods course to develop their abilities to regulate their learning. According to Zimmerman (2002, p. 65), self-regulated learners frame learning "as an activity that [they] do for themselves in a *proactive* way rather than as a covert event that happens to them in reaction to teaching." One of the unfortunate effects of the apprenticeship of observation is that students are unlikely to have had extended experiences learning how to regulate their own learning.

CHAPTER 8

Teaching students how to be self-regulated learners is a complicated task that requires more than knowledge of self-regulated learning strategies (Zimmerman, 1990). For example, the participants mentioned that they would have proceeded differently if given another opportunity to do a self-directed learning (SDL) activity. The candidates probably had propositional knowledge about how to productively use their SDL time, as they have likely heard maxims such as "Plan your time wisely" and "Set goals for yourself" from teachers throughout their time in schools.

Experience changes everything, however, and principled understanding of self-regulated learning strategies requires students to develop authority over their experiences. Zimmerman (2002, p. 68) reported that self-regulated learners engage in both "*self-judgment*" and "*self-reaction*" at the conclusion of a learning activity. The former heuristic refers to the degree to which a learner feels successful in an activity and the ways in which he or she attributes the causes of the success or failure. The latter heuristic refers to the degree to which a learner feels satisfied with the outcome of an activity and whether or not one feels motivated to continue learning. Many of the learning experiences during the physics course enabled teacher candidates to judge their relative success in an activity and to think about strategies they could use to improve their learning in subsequent activities.

According to Schunk (2005, p. 87), "good self-regulation requires that learners evaluate whether they will be able to accomplish the task, whether the environment is conducive to learning, and what changes are needed for better learning." While it is easy to agree to these goals for learning in principle, teaching someone how to become a self-regulated learner requires a sustained, committed effort to providing opportunities for learners to process their experiences, both individually and in groups. In their physics methods course, the participants thought not only about how to teach physics, but also about how they learned to teach from the practicum, the program, and the course itself. By encouraging candidates to take an active role in their learning, Tom was in fact teaching them how to be self-regulated learners. In so doing, Tom minimized the authority of his position as a teacher educator and provided a means for candidates to develop authority over their learning experiences in the physics course. *Opportunities for self-regulated learning can result in an increased authority over learning experiences.* For the participants in this study, one of the results of developing the authority of experience is the productive disruption of the effects of the apprenticeship of observation.

DISRUPTING THE APPRENTICESHIP OF OBSERVATION

The data presented in this book indicate that it is possible to disrupt the effects of the apprenticeship of observation by providing challenging learning experiences in a methods course. The data also call into question some of the value of practicum placements, which are typically held in high regard by teacher candidates, experienced teachers, and the general public. The practicum may reinforce, rather than challenge, the traditional routines of teaching and learning that are often criticized explicitly during calls for educational reform and implicitly in teacher education classes.

Coming into the teacher education program, the participants assumed that they would learn how to enact traditional pedagogies in a more efficient manner.

Several participants indicated that they believed they would be successful teachers because they understood their subject matter and had a clear idea of what a teacher is expected to do. Indeed, there were frequent references to favourite teachers and professors during the first round of interviews. Many participants seemed to eagerly await the tips and tricks that would make their practicum placements run more smoothly, on the assumption that propositional knowledge would serve them well. They made the familiar assumption that being told generates productive learning.

Teacher candidates' prior assumptions about teaching and learning, developed by their apprenticeships of observation, were disrupted by three distinct kinds of *experiences* in the physics methods course. First, the Lesson Study activity encouraged candidates to confront the fact that they enter a teacher education program with considerable knowledge about teaching that they do not realize they have. They can all, as Lortie (1975) suggests, do reasonable impressions of the teachers they have watched for many years. Approaches that deviated from traditional teaching strategies during the Lesson Study activity were rare. Candidates in the physics methods course spent most of their class time in September acting as an audience while their peers taught 20-minute lessons to the entire class. The potential monotony of listening to so many teacher-centred lessons may have contributed to the lack of peer interaction during the Lesson Study experience. Although this was a source of frustration for some of the participants, the passive experience of listening to a teacher talk, both during Lesson Study and in the program as a whole, may have encouraged some candidates to begin to question the value of assuming that listening is equivalent to learning.

Second, the active-learning pedagogies enacted throughout the year provided an opportunity for teacher candidates to have learning experiences that were quite different from what they expected. Predict-Observe-Explain activities showed candidates the value of shifting their focus away from right answers in physics. Rubbish Notes helped to call into question the well-established practice of requiring students to copy notes from the board. Self-directed learning invited teacher candidates to take greater ownership of their learning, including deciding whether or not to attend some of their classes during a period when they felt particularly overwhelmed with assignments and resumé-writing. They learned how to improve their abilities as self-regulated learners while developing authority over their learning experiences in the B.Ed. program.

Third, and perhaps most important, the effects of the apprenticeship of observation were disrupted by the nature of Tom's relationship with the teacher candidates in the physics methods course. From the outset they experienced opportunities to process how they were learning in the course and to suggest ways in which their learning could be improved. Tom spoke less than many teachers and teacher educators do, as was evident in many of the participants' comments, with the end result that the candidates in the methods class spent more time talking to one another than they did listening to their professor. Tom consistently demonstrated a desire for feedback from the teacher candidates on how to improve the quality of their learning in the physics class. Implicitly, and later explicitly, Tom shared intellectual control of the course with the candidates, a critical feature of a context of productive learning

(Sarason, 1996). Tom's commitment to sharing intellectual control with the candidates never wavered, even when he experienced frustrating teaching moments such as a Think-Aloud opportunity that was met with silence.

A lifetime of witnessing teaching rather than co-constructing teaching and learning experiences cannot be undone by one course in an 8-month teacher education program. Some of the cultural routines of teaching and learning socialized through the apprenticeship of observation may be useful and important for teacher candidates to continue, such as prior assumptions that teachers should care about their students or that experiments are an important part of learning science. The point of disturbing the apprenticeship of observation is to challenge and otherwise examine the traditional routines of teaching and learning in schools, not to invalidate them. There are times when a teacher needs to tell students something, but teacher candidates come with a clear understanding of how it feels to learn under those circumstances. More often than not, learning can be more powerful and productive when students take an active role in the construction of their knowledge. Teacher candidates have had extensive exposure to traditional teaching but school experiences with active learning have been relatively scarce. This research shows that active and independent learning experiences in teacher education classes can help teacher candidates understand and critique their prior knowledge of teaching and learning.

Although the socializing effects of school have been known for decades, there is little evidence that teacher educators have explored deeply the implications of this socialization for their own pedagogy. The sacred story of theory-into-practice tends to prevail in teacher education, as though the role of coursework is to provide propositions for candidates to enact during practicum placements. As Schön (1983) pointed out many years ago, knowledge-in-action is not transferrable, for it is grounded in personal experience. Teacher candidates arrive with considerable tacit knowledge-in-action as a result of their experiences as students. They can act in classrooms without knowing why they act as they do. Most associate teachers offer propositions to change actions they disagree with or seek to improve. Teacher candidates and associate teachers generally fail to question *why* candidates are inclined to act as they do during practicum placements.

This research has shown that teacher educators can play an important role in encouraging candidates to reframe their prior assumptions about teaching and learning. In order to disrupt these cultural assumptions, it is critical for teacher educators to focus on the teaching and learning that happens *within* their own classrooms. It is simplistic to assume that the only valuable conversations about teaching are those based on candidates' experiences during their practicum placements. While such conversations have an important place in teacher education, this study indicates that there can be even greater potential in encouraging teacher candidates to focus explicitly on the quality of their learning experiences in their teacher education courses. Practicum placements provide essential experience for teacher candidates, particularly when it comes to enacting the pragmatic routines they have only witnessed as students, but the kind of professional knowledge that candidates construct from practicum experiences may well be conservative rather than progressive. If teacher educators wish to improve how students learn in our elementary and secondary schools, then they must improve how teacher candidates learn in teacher education classrooms. Change comes from within a system and, as Sarason (1996) pointed out, teachers are likely to create a context of productive learning in their classrooms only if they themselves have learned in such a context. Methods courses, which may well be seen by the new teacher as the place where ideas and practice meet, appear to be particularly appropriate places to begin to disrupt prevailing cultural ideas about teaching and learning and to begin a movement toward active-learning pedagogies as a tradition, rather than an exception, in the culture of schools and teacher education. This study demonstrates that one way in which the acculturation effects of the apprenticeship of observation can be named, challenged, and disrupted with some degree of success in teacher education is by enacting principles of teaching and learning that are productive, research-based alternatives to the cultural tradition of teaching as telling.

DIRECTIONS FOR FUTURE RESEARCH

Several decades ago, Lortie (1975, p. 71) warned that "because of its casualness and narrow scope, the usual practice teaching arrangement does not offset the unreflective nature of prior socialization ... [and] there is little indication that it is a powerful force away from traditionalism and individualism." Most teacher education programs have little control over how an associate teacher works with a teacher candidate in the practicum. We can assume teacher education programs could have a greater measure of influence in their own education classrooms. This study shows clearly that a carefully planned and enacted pedagogy of teacher education can help teacher candidates develop productive new perspectives on teaching and learning in a methods course. In addition, this study highlights the potential value of providing teacher candidates with the opportunity to meet regularly in small groups to discuss their developing perspectives on teaching and learning.

The conclusions from this study suggest three avenues for further research, each with an increasingly broad scope. The first avenue would continue to develop the perspective of the teacher educator. I plan to continue my collaborative self-study with Tom as I move into an academic career. It will be particularly important for me to name and discuss how I negotiate the tensions around developing my authority of experience as a teacher educator and as an assistant professor in a new university context. Tom and I continue to be interested in exploring the challenges associated with using active-learning approaches in physics methods classrooms. Does enacting and modelling such an approach successfully require a teacher educator to understand his or her personal apprenticeship of observation? What are the most significant barriers to greater use of active-learning strategies by teacher educators?

A second avenue for research would focus on the perspective of teacher candidates in the methods classroom. What does it mean to enact a pedagogy of teacher education around naming and disrupting the deeply rooted cultural assumptions of schooling? Can structured experiences such as focus groups and individual interviews be provided in a course program to give candidates the opportunity to develop greater authority over their experiences? This study showed that it is possible to productively disrupt the effects of teacher candidates' apprenticeships of observation in a methods course. It would be important in future studies to follow teacher candidates into their early years of teaching. Extending the premise that the practicum tends to be a conservative force, it follows that the early years of a teaching career could also pull new teachers toward familiar patterns of schooling. Do the effects of experiencing and interpreting active-learning pedagogies in a preservice program persist beyond the program and influence the subsequent teaching of those who experienced them?

This study has analyzed one year in one teacher education methods course taught by an experienced teacher educator. Darling-Hammond (2006) and others have argued that coherence is an important factor in the overall success of a teacher education program. The third avenue for future research would move beyond an individual teacher educator in one classroom to consider the implications of this study for an entire teacher education program. To what extent are the individuals who teach in a preservice program aware of the significance of candidates' apprenticeships of observation and to what extent do those individuals agree that it is important for a program to challenge and disrupt the associated assumptions about teaching and learning? Will opportunities to participate in a series of focus groups and personal interviews help to develop coherence by helping candidates better understand the messages from various education courses and their interaction with practicum experiences? How can a preservice program of courses and practicum experiences be designed to systematically challenge candidates' apprenticeships of observation?

This book opened by suggesting that the challenge of learning to teach is primarily a cultural problem and that few, if any, of the changes that have occurred in teacher education in recent decades have attempted to address explicitly the acculturating effects of mass schooling. While teacher education programs have limited time to teach people how to teach, learning experiences in a methods classroom can encourage teacher candidates to think differently and deeply about issues of teaching. Are teacher educators ready to move beyond the rhetoric of theory-into-practice and tacit competition between coursework and the practicum? It would seem more productive for teacher educators to focus on developing and enacting pedagogies of teacher education that explicitly challenge the effects of the apprenticeship of observation.

APPENDIX A

RESEARCH DESIGN AND DATA ANALYSIS

Any study is always more than the sum of its methods. What gives it meaning and direction is not its methods but its methodology – the theories and pedagogies it assumes and utilizes for (and during) the process of conducting that research. (Segall, 2002, p. 28)

This appendix outlines the design of the study and justifies that design using a methodological framework composed of two traditions of qualitative research. The design of the research, including the central research questions, the methods of data collection, and the ethical dilemmas posed by the design are described. I conclude by outlining the methods of data analysis and describe how the results of the analysis are presented and interpreted throughout the book.

RESEARCH DESIGN

This research was an in-depth study of how teacher candidates and teacher educators construct professional knowledge from teaching and learning experiences during a preservice teacher education program. Specifically, the study focused on how teacher candidates learn to teach from both their experiences in a physics methods course and their practicum placements. The research also considered how teacher educators learn to teach teachers; the instructor for the physics methods course, an experienced teacher educator, is also a participant in the study. The perspectives of the teacher candidates, the teacher educator, and the researcher as participant-observer were combined to shed light on the role of experience in both learning to teach and learning to teach teachers.

Research Questions

The research questions that guide this study are:
1. How do teacher candidates construct professional knowledge from learning experiences in a physics methods course?
2. How do teacher candidates construct professional knowledge from teaching experiences during their practicum placements?
3. How do teacher educators construct their professional knowledge through collaborative self-study as they frame teaching as a discipline with teacher candidates in a physics methods course?

Data Collection

A primary source of data for this study was my personal research journal, which alternated between a bound paper notebook and electronic software such as MS Word

APPENDIX A

and MS OneNote. As a participant-observer in the physics methods course, I recorded field notes of the classes on my computer from the back of the classroom. The field notes for each class included descriptive notes about Tom's pedagogy, such as the types of teaching strategies that he used and the amount of time he allotted to each activity. The descriptive field notes were taken in such a way as to allow me to "return to an observation later during [data] analysis" (Patton, 2002, p. 303). The level of detail in the descriptions I wrote provided a useful basis of comparison with data obtained from other sources, as it allowed me to compare and contrast my recollections of events with those of the other participants in the study. I was also attentive to Patton's (2002, p. 303) reminder that "direct quotations, or as near as possible recall of direct quotations, should be captured during field work, recording what was said during observed activities." To that end, I often recorded what Tom said as he taught the physics methods class. Finally, I used my research journal to record personal reactions to teaching and learning events in the physics class, often drawing a comparison between my previous experiences as a teacher candidate, physics teacher, and teacher educator and my understanding of the developing culture in the physics methods course.

I did not record any of the interactions that occurred between the teacher candidates during the class, nor did I record quotations of what they said during class. Although I did not record my impressions of how individual candidates or groups of candidates engaged with the learning experiences that Tom provided in the class, my holistic observation of each class necessarily made an impression on how I described and interpreted the development of Tom's pedagogy of teacher education with the candidates in the course. Finally, I collected artifacts from Tom's teaching such as emails sent to the class list serve and course handouts. Although these artifacts did not figure prominently in my data analysis, they provided a useful set of "stimuli" for careful analysis of my data (Spindler & Hammond, 2000, p. 42).

The first two research questions seek to understand teacher candidates' perceptions of how professional knowledge is constructed from teaching and learning experiences. These questions were addressed in focus group interviews and semi-structured individual interviews. Focus group interviews allow a researcher to create "a social environment in which group members are stimulated by the perceptions and ideas of each other," and such interactions "can increase the quality and richness of data" (McMillan & Schumacher, 2001, p. 455). During the second class of the year, I introduced the teacher candidates enrolled in the 2007–2008 physics methods course to my research by outlining the purpose of my study, highlighting the time requirements, and distributing letters of information and consent forms. Five candidates, 4 male and 1 female, consented to participate in the study. Tom was not present during the participant selection process to ensure that he did not know the identities of those participating.

Focus group interviews were conducted with participating teacher candidates during each of the on-campus blocks (September, November, January, and April) of the preservice program. Each focus group lasted for approximately 90 minutes. In addition, the candidates participated in an individual, semi-structured, follow-up interview shortly after each of the focus group interviews. The follow-up interviews lasted between 20 and 60 minutes, depending on the nature and extent of the participants' responses. Each of the five teacher candidates participated in four focus group interviews and four individual follow-up interviews. Thus 24 interviews were conducted with teacher candidates over an 8-month period, and I was solely responsible for interviewing the participants. As the data analysis reveals, the process of participating in this series of interviews added a unique element to participants' experience of their preservice program.

The interviews were digitally recorded as MP3 files. During each interview, I used a bound paper notebook to take field notes that captured both direct quotations and my thoughts and ideas as the interviews unfolded. A paper notebook was used in lieu of a computer to encourage the participants to perceive the interviewer as directly engaging with them during the interview; a paper notebook seems much less intrusive than a computer screen during an interview (Patton, 2002; Quinn, 2005). Tom was not present during any of the focus groups or individual interviews. He did not have access to the data until after participants completed the teacher education program. The teacher candidates who participated in the research were instructed not to indicate to Tom that they were participating in the research, and to refrain from making identifying comments about courses and instructors, other than the physics methods course and Tom, throughout the interview process.

The third research question was addressed through a collaborative self-study between Tom and me. As Loughran (2005) notes, self-study can help teacher educators understand their practice through careful analysis of teaching and learning situations. My research journal served as a valuable catalyst for the conversations that Tom and I had about the physics methods course during the academic year. We spoke at length about the course at the beginning and end of each on-campus block, in addition to meetings that occurred spontaneously either after a class or in response to an issue that had arisen in class. Some of the lengthier meetings were digitally recorded as MP3 files; field notes were kept on all of our meetings. The focus of our discussions was to describe and interpret the ways in which Tom approached teaching the physics methods course. Throughout the self-study, we worked together to frame and reframe the teacher educator perspective of teaching the physics methods course. We built on our history of critical friendship founded on a shared commitment to understanding how preservice teachers learn to teach (Schuck & Russell, 2005). Perspectives developed by Bullough and Pinnegar (2001) guided the self-study component of the research. Data pertaining to the third research question allowed us to explicate pedagogies of teacher education and hence provide a basis of comparison between Tom's intended curriculum and the experienced curriculum of teacher candidates who participated in the study. Specific attention was paid to the problems of practice that emerged over the course of the academic year, the tensions these problems created, and our developing understanding of teaching as a discipline.

Ethical Dilemmas in the Research

This study received ethical clearance from the unit and the general research ethics boards. On the surface, the ethical dilemmas in this research may seem to pose

APPENDIX A

considerable challenges. There were multiple power issues to consider because my study was conducted in a class taught by my Ph.D. supervisor. First, there was a potential ethical risk to participating teacher candidates, whom Tom was required to grade based on their performances in the physics methods course, who were aware of the supervisor-student relationship between Tom and me, and who might perceive participation in my research as a factor in their final grades. Second, there was potential ethical risk to both Tom and me as participants in this research, which was inextricably linked to my academic progress in the Ph.D. program at Queen's University. These potential ethical dilemmas were addressed in three ways: Tom did not know who was participating in the research, data collection was limited to those who explicitly consented to participate in the study, and Tom and I agreed that the benefits of working together to understand teaching and learning far outweighed any personal or professional risks that might arise from collaborative self-study.

The ethical risk to the teacher candidates in the physics methods course was minimized because my research journal did not take note of their participation in the class. All teacher candidates were invited to participate in the research and were free to stop participating at any point in the year. The focus group and individual interviews took place outside of class time, on a different floor from the classroom and Tom's office. The identity of the participants was further protected by use of pseudonyms in the transcripts. Tom did not have access to the transcripts until after he had submitted marks for the course; the audio recordings of the interviews were not shared with him.

Although I was a participant-observer in the course, I did not have access to any form of course assessment; hence participation in the research was not linked to the honours/pass/fail assessment scheme in the course. I believe that participation in this study, with its emphasis on exploring the nature of teaching and learning both in a methods course and during teaching practicum experiences, provided participants with a useful opportunity to discuss their experiences during the preservice teacher education program. The research was not evaluative of the participants or the teacher education program at Queen's University. No names or descriptions that could be used to identify any course, instructor, or person other than those who gave consent to participate in the study were used during data analysis and reporting.

Given that Tom and I are not anonymous in the data, we are at a higher ethical risk in the study. Mitchell (2004, p. 1438) provides a comprehensive argument for regarding ethics in self-study as a "process of managing dilemmas," posing a series of questions (pp. 1439–1440) for self-study practitioners to consider regarding presentation and collection of data. Consideration of these questions, most of which involve the treatment of classroom artifacts created by students, helps to shed light on the fact that the ethical dilemmas associated with the self-study portion of this research are minimal. There is no pedagogical intervention being studied in this research. Tom taught the course according to his pedagogical judgment and we shared conversations about how to help candidates to learn in the physics class, as we had since 2005 when we co-taught the course. Neither of us was concerned about what might be revealed about our beliefs about teaching and learning as a result of this research. The reported data were unlikely to be damaging or harmful to either the teacher candidates in the physics methods course (both those who did and did not participate in the research), or to Tom and me.

Tom has significant experience with self-study research and is aware of both the risks and benefits of a critical analysis of his teaching practices (Russell, 2007; Schuck & Russell, 2005). I have made self-study of my development as a teacher educator an important feature of my doctoral studies (Bullock, 2007), because I too am convinced of the benefits of studying my own practice. In addition, there is a history of professional trust between Tom and me that began in 1997, when I was in Tom's physics methods course as a teacher candidate. Since that time, Tom has supervised my M.Ed. and Ph.D. programs and we have frequently collaborated in conference presentations and published articles. There were no tensions that arose between us as a result of this research. We are both committed to self-study as a way to improve our teaching practice and to name our professional knowledge as teacher educators.

DATA ANALYSIS

This section considers the methods used to analyze the data gathered in the study. Throughout this section I weave descriptions of how the data were organized and coded, a process which Patton (2002, p. 462) calls the "intellectual and mechanical work of analysis," together with a discussion of how the data were interpreted. The research journal that I kept throughout the process provided a valuable reference for understanding the process of data analysis and much of what is reported in this section comes from the notes I took as I organized and interpreted the data.

After completing an accurate transcription of the interviews that comprised the bulk of the data collected for this research, I took Quinn's (2005, p. 18) suggestion that data analysis begins with "scrutinizing one's transcriptions, and going back and forth among them." To that end, I began my analysis by reading and re-reading all the transcripts, first in chronological order, and then grouped according to participant. In this way I hoped to understand the data both in four distinct groups according to when it was collected (September, November, January, and April) and as progressions of individual participant's thoughts (i.e., reading all four individual interviews for each participant in a row). As I read, I noted recognizable issues and patterns in the data. These issues and patterns resulted from both inductive and deductive analysis: inductive in the sense that they arose from the data as I read, deductive in the sense that they were often named based on literature that I have reviewed in the past (Patton, 2002). A total of 248 single-spaced pages of transcripts were reviewed in this way.

The next step was to import all the interviews conducted with teacher candidates into ATLAS.ti (Muhr, 2004), a qualitative data analysis software program. Four hermeneutic units (HUs) were created, one for each month of data collection. Each hermeneutic unit contained one focus group transcript and five individual follow-up interview transcripts, one for each teacher candidate. Thus the first hermeneutic unit (HU1: September) contains six primary documents (PDs): FG1Transcript, David1, James1, Irene1, Max1, and Paul1. I began my formal data analysis by reading through the first primary document, highlighting text, and constructing codes based

APPENDIX A

on both my earlier read of the data and, to borrow a turn of phrase from Schön (1983), my analysis-in-action. The code tool was used to enter the list of codes and make comments about the characteristics of each code; 13 codes were created from the initial reading of the first focus group. I used the same codes for the remaining five primary documents, the individual interviews. Consideration of these primary documents prompted me to create four additional codes for the research. I then coded all six primary documents a second time with the full set of 17 codes.

The output feature of ATLAS.ti was used to generate a complete list of codes (including code frequency), comments, and quotations for the hermeneutic unit. I read through the quotation lists for all 17 codes so that I could determine their "substantive significance" (Patton, 2002, p. 467); quotations were compared to relevant literature with a view to providing a detailed, coherent picture of learning to teach from the physics methods course. Although I realized that the substance of the quotations mattered more than the quantity, I found the frequency table function of ATLAS.ti helpful for thinking about why certain codes appeared more often than others. Finally, I wrote a preliminary analysis of the codes in my research journal, where I noted themes and trends in the data.

The first step in analyzing the second hermeneutic unit was to export the codes used in HU1 as an XML (extensible mark-up language) file so that they could be directly imported, with comments, into the second hermeneutic unit. I analyzed the remaining three hermeneutic units in much the same way that I analyzed HU1, adding codes and comments as new issues arose in the data. One obvious difference between HU1 and the other hermeneutic units is that comments about practicum experiences are present. By the time I coded HU4, there were a total of 22 codes used to describe the data from the perspective of the teacher candidates who participated in the research.

With the hermeneutic units fully coded, I turned to the issue of naming themes in the data. I began by writing a short summary of the teaching and learning events that occurred in the physics course during each of the four on-campus blocks, based on observations I recorded in my journal. My research journal helped me to anchor many of the candidates' comments to my descriptions of events in the physics course. I used the co-occurrence explorer in ATLAS.ti to determine how the codes interacted with one another and thus to examine quotations that received multiple codes. At times, I used the super code feature of ATLAS.ti to rename the intersection of two codes and thus allow me to locate such intersections efficiently in the primary document. Finally, my research questions provided me with a filter through which to screen relevant codes. I created themes that addressed issues raised by the two research questions that pertained to the perspectives of the teacher candidates.

Once I had named the relevant themes, I used both the co-occurrence explorer and notes on the quotation outputs that I generated using ATLAS.ti to make decisions about where to place each code and super code within the given theme. An output for each theme was generated that included all the codes, super codes, and quotations associated with each theme. After reading and re-reading the output for each theme, I was satisfied that the data formed a coherent picture within each theme, thus satisfying Patton's (2002, p. 465) condition for "internal homogeneity." I also judged the themes to be representative of different phenomena, thus satisfying Patton's (p. 465) condition for "external heterogeneity." Finally, I used the co-occurrence explorer, the quotation outputs, and my research journal to, as Patton suggests, "move back and forth between the data and the classification system to verify the meaningfulness and accuracy of the categories and placement of data in categories" (pp. 465–466).

After I was satisfied with the placement of data within the themes, I began to write my analysis from the perspective of the teacher candidates. Throughout the writing process, I recognized that data analysis is a reflexive process and so I often worked back and forth between writing an analysis and re-visiting outputs that I had previously generated using features of ATLAS.ti such as the co-occurrence explorer, the quotation manager, and the code manager, as well as my research journal. The perspective of the teacher educator was analyzed and interpreted using a similar process to the one described for the teacher candidates. Finally, a set of conclusions for each analysis chapter was formed by reading the perspectives of the teacher candidates and the teacher educator with a view to interpreting the data relative to the issues raised by the research questions.

REFERENCES

Baird, J. R., & Northfield, J. R. (Eds.). (1992). *Learning from the PEEL experience*. Melbourne, Australia: Monash University Printery.

Barnett, J., & Hodson, D. (2001). Pedagogical context knowledge: Toward a fuller understanding of what good science teachers know. *Science Education, 84*, 426–453.

Beck, C., & Kosnik, C. (2006). *Innovations in teacher education: A social constructivist approach*. New York: State University of New York Press.

Ben-Peretz, M. (1995). *Learning from experience: Memory and the teacher's account of teaching*. New York: SUNY Press.

Bennett, K. P., & LeCompte, M. D. (1992). *The way schools work: A sociological analysis of education*. New York: Longman.

Berry, A., Loughran, J., & van Driel, J. H. (2008). Revisting the roots of pedagogical content knowledge. *International Journal of Science Education, 30*, 1271–1279.

Borko, H., & Putnam, R. T. (1996). Learning to teach. In D. C. Berliner & R. C. Calfee (Eds.), *Handbook of Educational Psychology* (pp. 673–708). New York: Simon & Schuster Macmillan.

Britzman, D. P. (1991/2003). *Practice makes practice: A critical study of learning to teach* (Rev. ed.). Albany, NY: State University of New York Press.

Bruner, J. (1986). *Actual minds, possible worlds*. Cambridge, MA: Harvard University Press.

Bullock, S. M. (2007). Finding my way from teacher to teacher educator: Valuing innovative pedagogy and inquiry into practice. In T. Russell & J. Loughran (Eds.), *Enacting a pedagogy of teacher education: Values, relationships and practices* (pp. 77–94). London: Routledge.

Bullough, R. V., Jr., & Pinnegar, S. (2001). Guidelines for quality in autobiographical forms of self-study research. *Educational Researcher, 30*(3), 13–21.

Calderhead, J. (1996). Teachers: Beliefs and knowledge. In D. C. Berliner & R. C. Calfee (Eds.), *Handbook of Educational Psychology* (pp. 709–725). New York: Simon & Schuster Macmillan.

Christensen, D. (1996). The professional knowledge-research base for teacher education. In J. Sikula, T. J. Buttery, & E. Guyton (Eds.), *Handbook of research on teacher education* (2nd ed., pp. 38–52). New York: Simon & Schuster Macmillan.

Clandinin, D. J., & Connelly, F. M. (Eds.). (1995). *Teachers' professional knowledge landscapes*. New York: Teachers College Press.

Clandinin, D. J., & Connelly, F. M. (1996). Teachers' professional knowledge landscapes: Teacher stories - stories of teachers - school stories - stories of schools. *Educational Researcher, 24*(3), 24–30.

Cochran-Smith, M. (2005). The new teacher education: For better or for worse? *Educational Researcher, 34*(7), 3–17.

Cochran-Smith, M., & Lytle, S. L. (1999). Relationships of knowledge and practice: Teacher learning in communities. *Review of Research in Education, 24*, 249–305.

Cohen, Y. A. (1971). The shaping of men's minds: Adaptations to imperatives of culture. In M. L. Wax, S. Diamond, & F. O. Gearing (Eds.), *Anthropological perspectives on education* (pp. 19–50). New York: Basic Books.

Cole, A. L. (2003). The denial of the personal, the preservation of the status quo in teacher education. *Journal of Teaching and Learning, 2*(2), 1–11.

Connelly, F. M., & Clandinin, D. J. (1995). Teachers' professional knowledge landscapes: Secret, sacred, and cover stories. In D. J. Clandinin & F. M. Connelly (Eds.), *Teachers' professional knowledge landscapes* (pp. 3–15). New York: Teachers College Press.

Craig, C. J. (1995). Knowledge communities: A way of making sense of how beginning teachers come to know in their professional knowledge contexts. *Curriculum Inquiry, 25*, 151–175.

Craig, C. J. (2004). Shifting boundaries on the professional knowledge landscape: When teacher communications become less safe. *Curriculum Inquiry, 34*, 395–424.

REFERENCES

Crocker, R., & Dibbon, D. (2008). *Teacher education in Canada*. Kelowna, BC: Society for the Advancement of Excellence in Education.
Cuban, L. (2008). *Frogs into princes: Writings on school reform*. New York: Teachers College Press.
Darling-Hammond, L. (2000). How teacher education matters. *Journal of Teacher Education, 51*, 166–173.
Darling-Hammond, L. (2006). *Powerful teacher education*. San Francisco: Jossey-Bass.
Darling-Hammond, L., & Bransford, J. (2005). *Preparing teachers for a changing world: What teachers should learn and be able to do*. San Francisco: Jossey-Bass.
Davis, B., & Sumara, D. (2007). Complexity science and education: Reconceptualizing the teacher's role in learning. *Interchange, 38*(1), 53–67.
Dewey, J. (1938). *Logic: The theory of inquiry*. New York: Holt, Rinehart and Winston.
Dufresne, R. J., & Gerace, W. J. (2004). Assessing-to-learn: Formative assessment in physics instruction. *The Physics Teacher, 42*, 428–433.
Einstein, A., & Infeld, L. (1966). *The evolution of physics*. New York: Simon & Schuster.
Ethell, R. G., & McMeniman, M. M. (2000). Unlocking the knowledge in action of an expert practitioner. *Journal of Teacher Education, 51*(2), 87–101.
Fenstermacher, G. D. (1994). The knower and the known: The nature of knowledge in research on teaching. *Review of Research in Education, 20*, 3–56.
Furlong, J., & Maynard, T. (1995). *Mentoring student teachers: The growth of professional knowledge*. London: Routledge.
Grimmett, P. P., & MacKinnon, A. M. (1992). Craft knowledge and the education of teachers. *Review of Research in Education, 18*, 385–456.
Grossman, P. L. (1990). *The making of a teacher: Teacher knowledge and teacher education*. New York: Teachers College Press.
Grossman, P. L. (1995). Teachers' knowledge. In L. W. Anderson (Ed.), *International encyclopedia of teaching and teacher education* (2nd ed., pp. 20–24). Kidlington, Oxford, UK: Elsevier Science Ltd.
Hewitt, P. (2006). *Conceptual physics* (10th ed.). San Francisco: Addison Wesley.
Hiebert, J., Gallimore, R., & Stigler, J. W. (2002). A knowledge base for the teaching profession: What would it look like and how can we get one? *Educational Researcher, 31*(5), 3–15.
Holland, D., & Quinn, N. (Eds.). (1987). *Cultural models in language and thought*. London: Cambridge University Press.
Hynes, D. (1987). Theory into practice. In J. Baird & I. Mitchell (Eds.), *Improving the quality of teaching and learning* (pp. 28–44). Melbourne, Australia: Monash University Printery.
Kagan, D. M. (1992). Professional growth among preservice and beginning teachers. *Review of Educational Research, 62*, 129–169.
Kane, R., Sandretto, S., & Heath, C. (2002). Telling half the story: A critical review of research on the teaching beliefs and practices of university academics. *Review of Educational Research, 72*(2), 177–229.
Kennedy, M. M. (2005). *Inside teaching: How classroom life undermines reform*. Cambridge, MA: Harvard University Press.
Knight, R. D. (2004). *Five easy lessons: Strategies for successful physics teaching*. San Francisco: Addison Wesley.
Knowles, J. G., Cole, A. L., & Presswood, C. S. (1994). *Through preservice teachers' eyes: Exploring field experiences through narrative and inquiry*. New York: Maxwell Macmillan International.
Kosminsky, L., Russell, T., Berry, A., & Kane, R. (2008). The boundaries of think-aloud as practiced by teacher educators. In M. L. Heston, D. L. Tidwell, K. K. East, & L. M. Fitzgerald (Eds.), *Pathways to change in teacher education: Dialogue, diversity, and self-study. Proceedings of the Seventh International Conference on Self-Study of Teacher Education Practices* (pp. 197–201). Cedar Falls, IA: University of Northern Iowa.
Kroll, L. R., Cossey, R., Donahue, D. M., Galguera, T., LaBoskey, V. K., Richert, A. E., et al. (2004). *Teaching as principled practice: Managing complexity for social justice*. Thousand Oaks, CA: Sage.
LeCornu, R., & Ewing, R. (2008). Reconceptualising professional experiences in preservice teacher education ... reconstructing the past to embrace the future. *Teaching and Teacher Education, 24*, 1799–1812.

REFERENCES

Lockhart, A. (1991). *Schoolteaching in Canada*. Toronto, Canada: University of Toronto Press.
Lortie, D. (1975). *Schoolteacher: A sociological study*. Chicago: University of Chicago Press.
Loughran, J. (2005). Researching teaching about teaching: Self-study of teacher education practices. *Studying Teacher Education*, 1(1), 5–16.
Loughran, J. (2006). *Developing a pedagogy of teacher education: Understanding teaching and learning about teaching*. London: Routledge.
Loughran, J. (2008). Seeking knowledge for teaching teaching: Moving beyond stories. In M. L. Heston, D. L. Tidwell, K. K. East, & L. M. Fitzgerald (Eds.), *Pathways to change in teacher education: Dialogue, diversity, and self-study. Proceedings of the Seventh International Conference on Self-Study of Teacher Education Practices* (pp. 218–221). Cedar Falls, IA: University of Northern Iowa.
Loughran, J., & Russell, T. (2007). Beginning to understand teaching as a discipline. *Studying Teacher Education*, 3, 217–227.
Loughran, J., Mitchell, I., & Mitchell, J. (2003). Attempting to document teachers' professional knowledge. *Qualitative Studies in Education*, 16, 853–873.
Loughran, J., Milroy, P., Berry, A., Gunstone, R., & Mulhall, P. (2001). Documenting science teachers' pedagogical content knowledge through PaP-eRs. *Research in Science Education*, 31, 289–307.
Martin, A. K., & Russell, T. (2006). Lost in teachers' college—deconstructing the teacher education façade: A case study of collegial self-study. In L. M. Fitzgerald, M. L. Heston, & D. L. Tidwell (Eds.), *Collaboration and community: Pushing boundaries through self-study. Proceedings of the sixth international conference on self-study of teacher education practices* (pp. 186–189). Cedar Falls, IA: University of Northern Iowa.
McMillan, J. H., & Schumacher, S. (2001). *Research in education: A conceptual introduction* (5th ed.). New York: Longman.
Mitchell, I. (2004). Identifying ethical issues in self-study proposals. In J. J. Loughran, M. L. Hamilton, V. K. LaBoskey & T. Russell (Eds.), *The international handbook of self-study of teaching and teacher education practices* (pp. 1393–1442). Dodrecht: Kluwer Academic Publishers.
Muhr, T. (2008). ATLAS.ti: The knowledge workbench (Version 5.5). [Computer Software]. Berlin, Germany: ATLAS.ti Scientific Software Development GmbH.
Munby, H., & Russell, T. (1990). Metaphor in the study of teachers' professional knowledge. *Theory into Practice*, 29(2), 116–121.
Munby, H., & Russell, T. (1992a). Frames of reflection: An introduction. In T. Russell & H. Munby (Eds.), *Teachers and teaching: From classroom to reflection* (pp. 1–8). London: The Falmer Press.
Munby, H., & Russell, T. (1992b). Transforming chemistry research into chemistry teaching: The complexities of adopting new frames for experience. In T. Russell & H. Munby (Eds.), *Teachers and teaching: From classroom to reflection* (pp. 90–108). London: The Falmer Press.
Munby, H., & Russell, T. (1994). The authority of experience in learning to teach: Messages from a physics methods class. *Journal of Teacher Education*, 4(2), 86–95.
Munby, H., Cunningham, M., & Lock, C. (2000). School science culture: A case study of barriers to developing professional knowledge. *Science Education*, 84, 193–211.
Munby, H., Russell, T., & Martin, A. K. (2001). Teachers' knowledge and how it develops. In V. Richardson (Ed.), *Handbook of research on teaching* (4th ed., pp. 877–904). Washington, DC: American Educational Research Association.
Nuthall, G. (2005). The cultural myths and realities of classroom teaching and learning: A personal journey. *Teachers College Record*, 107(5), 895–934.
Olson, M. R., & Craig, C. J. (2005). Uncovering cover stories: Tensions and entailments in the development of teacher knowledge. *Curriculum Inquiry*, 35, 161–182.
Patton, M. Q. (2002). *Qualitative research and evaluation methods* (3rd ed.). Thousand Oaks, CA: Sage.
Putnam, R. T., & Borko, H. (2000). What do new views of knowledge and thinking have to say about research on teacher learning? *Educational Researcher*, 29(1), 4–15.
Quinn, N. (Ed.), (2005). *Finding culture in talk: A collection of methods*. New York: Palgrave MacMillan.
Russell, T. (1983). Analyzing arguments in science classroom discourse: Can teachers' questions distort scientific authority? *Journal of Research in Science Teaching*, 20(1), 27–45.

REFERENCES

Russell, T. (1993). Teachers' professional knowledge and the future of teacher education. *International Analyses of Teacher Education.* Special issue of *Journal of Education for Teaching, 19*(4 & 5), 205–215.

Russell, T. (2005). Can reflective practice be taught? *Reflective Practice, 6*(2), 199–204.

Russell, T. (2007). How experience changed my values as a teacher educator. In T. Russell & J. Loughran (Eds.), *Enacting a pedagogy of teacher education: Values, relationships, and practices* (pp. 183–191). London: Routledge.

Russell, T. (2008, March). *Two principles for enacting a pedagogy of teacher education.* Paper presented at the meeting of the American Educational Research Association, New York.

Russell, T., & Bullock, S. (1999). Discovering our professional knowledge as teachers: Critical dialogues about learning from experience. In J. Loughran (Ed.), *Researching teaching: Methodologies and practices for understanding pedagogy* (pp. 132–151). London: The Falmer Press.

Sarason, S. B. (1990). *The predictable failure of educational reform: Can we change course before it's too late?* San Francisco: Jossey-Bass.

Sarason, S. B. (1996). *Revisiting "The culture of the school and the problem of change.* New York: Teachers College Press.

Sarason, S. B. (2002). *Educational reform: A self-scrutinizing memoir.* New York: Teachers College Press.

Sarason, S. B. (2004). *And what do you mean by learning?* Portsmouth, NH: Heinemann.

Schön, D. A. (1983). *The reflective practitioner: How professionals think in action.* New York: Basic Books.

Schön, D. A. (1987). *Educating the reflective practitioner: Toward a new design for teaching and learning in the professions.* San Francisco: Jossey-Bass Publishers.

Schuck, S., & Russell, T. (2005). Self-study, critical friendship, and the complexities of teacher education. *Studying Teacher Education, 1*(2), 107–121.

Schunk, D. H. (2005). Self-regulated learning: The educational legacy of Paul R. Pintrich. *Educational Psychologist, 40*(2), 85–94.

Segall, A. (2002). *Disturbing practice: Reading teacher education as text.* New York: Peter Lang.

Shulman, L. S. (1986). Those who understand: Knowledge growth in teaching. *Educational Researcher, 15*(2), 4–14.

Shulman, L. S. (1987). Knowledge and teaching: Foundations of the new reform. *Harvard Educational Review, 57,* 1–22.

Smith, K., & Lev-Ari, L. (2005). The place of the practicum in pre-service teacher education: The voice of the students. *Asia-Pacific Journal of Teacher Education, 33*(3), 289–302.

Spalding, W. B. (1959). Editor's foreword. In R. E. Schultz (Ed.), *Student teaching in the secondary schools: A guide to effective practice* (pp. v–vi). New York: Harcourt, Brace & World, Inc.

Spindler, G., & Hammond, H. (2000). The use of anthropological methods in educational research: Two perspectives. *Harvard Educational Review, 70,* 39–48.

Tavris, C., & Aronson, E. (2007). *Mistakes were made (but not by me): Why we justify foolish beliefs, bad decisions, and hurtful acts.* New York: Harcourt, Inc.

Tyack, D., & Tobin, W. (1994). The "grammar" of schooling: Why has it been so hard to change? *American Educational Research Journal, 31*(3), 453–479.

van Manen, M. (1991). *The tact of teaching: The meaning of pedagogical thoughtfulness.* London, Ontario, Canada: The Althouse Press.

Vick, M. (2006). "It's a difficult matter": Historical perspectives on the enduring problem of the practicum in teacher education. *Asia-Pacific Journal of Teacher Education, 34*(2), 181–198.

Waller, W. (1932/1961). *The sociology of teaching.* New York: Russell & Russell.

Wax, M. L., Diamond, S., & Gearing (Eds.), (1971). *Anthropological perspectives on education.* New York: Basic Books.

Wax, M. L., & Wax, R. (1971). Great tradition, little tradition, and formal education. In M. L. Wax, S. Diamond, & F. O. Gearing (Eds.), *Anthropological perspectives on education* (pp. 3–18). New York: Basic Books.

Whitehead, J. (1993). *The growth of educational knowledge: Creating your own living educational theories.* Dorset, UK: Hyde Publications.

Wolcott, H. F. (1967). Anthropology and education. *Review of Educational Research, 37*(1), 82–95.

REFERENCES

Zeichner, K. (2002). Beyond traditional structures of student teaching. *Teacher Education Quarterly, 29*(2), 59–64.
Zeichner, K. M., & Tabachnick, B. R. (1981). Are the effects of university teacher education 'washed out' by school experience? *Journal of Teacher Education, 32*(7), 7–11.
Zimmerman, B. J. (1990). Self-regulated learning and academic achievement: An overview. *Educational Psychologist, 25*(1), 3–17.
Zimmerman, B. J. (2002). Becoming a self-regulated learner: An overview. *Theory into Practice, 41*(2), 64–70.

p. 30

A3's course is based on an epistemology of experiential knowledge

*1's — ... of propositional kn.

p. 31

knowledge claims can be based made on an ⟨ epistemic basis / categorical basis